Ceramics
of the 20th Century

Tamara Préaud and Serge Gauthier

Ceramics
of the 20th Century

RIZZOLI
NEW YORK

Frontispiece

MIRÓ, Joan (Spain, 1893–) and ARTIGAS, José Llorens (Spain, 1892–1980). *An Important Person,* 1956. Ceramic. H. 104 cm. Fondation Maeght, Saint-Paul-de-Vence.
These two artists have worked together so closely that their names must remain linked. From 1944 to 1946 Miró devoted himself to ceramics and by 1945 his work had already been exhibited by Pierre Matisse in New York. Miró said: 'The glamour of ceramics attracted me like sparks.' From 1953 to 1956 Miró enthusiastically resumed his ceramic work and in 1956 the Maeght gallery exhibited 232 of his pieces. At that time he created sculptures as well as all kinds of other objects: pebbles, eggs, dishes and even 'anti-dishes'. In 1956 he began two large murals for the UNESCO building which were completed in 1958; these were followed by an important series of decorated walls in 1960 for Harvard, in 1968 for the Fondation Maeght which became Miró's counterpart to the Parque Güell, in 1970 for Osaka, in 1971 for Zurich, and in 1972 for the Paris Cinemathèque.

This book was printed in October 1982 by Polygraphische Gesellschaft, Laupen/BE
Filmsetting: Febel AG, Basle
Black-and-white lithography: Atesa Argraf S.A., Geneva
Colour lithography: Cooperativa lavoratori grafici, Verona
Binding: H. & J. Schumacher AG, Schmitten
Design and production: Marcel Berger

French language edition, La Céramique, art du XXᵉ siècle
© 1982 by Office du Livre

English translation © 1982 by Office du Livre
First published in the United States of America in 1982 by

*R*IZZOLI INTERNATIONAL PUBLICATIONS, INC.
712 Fifth Avenue/New York 10019

Library of Congress Cataloging in Publication Data
    Préaud, Tamara.
        Ceramics of the 20th century.
        Translation of: La céramique, art du XXᵉ siècle.
        Includes index.
        1. Pottery—20th century. 2. Ceramic sculpture—
History—20th century.   I. Gauthier, Serge.   II. Title.
III. Title: Ceramics of the twentieth century.
NK3930.P7313 1982   730'.09'04   82-50107
ISBN 0-8478-0436-4

Printed and bound in Switzerland

Table of Contents

1   **CHAPLET,** Ernest (France, 1835–1909). *'Mei-ping' Vase,* 1889. Porcelain. H. 53.5 cm. Musée des Arts décoratifs, Paris; 5695.

Chaplet was an early 'studio potter' and his pioneer role was far-ranging: he perfected slip decoration (1871–2), rediscovered stoneware on which he used matt glazes (1881) and carried out research into copper-red (from 1884). From 1882 to 1887 he directed the workshop opened by Charles Haviland to investigate decorative processes, where he worked together with numerous artists such as Paul Gauguin. Eventually he left for Choisy-le-Roi, where he concentrated on research into porcelain glazes. In 1900 he was awarded a gold medal in Paris. In 1905 blindness forced him to interrupt his work and he burned all his secrets.

Factories

The distinction between factories and independent potters is less obvious than might at first appear. It is difficult to distinguish the artist potter's studio, employing a few qualified craftsmen entrusted with executing the ideas of a designer, in which there is already a division of labour, from the true artisanal pottery, founded on the same production principles. When a factory allows an artist in its employ to sign his or her work, and he or she is active in an independent studio or some other enterprise, it might seem arbitrary not to consider him or her as a creative artist in his or her own right.

However, for the sake of clarity we shall discuss first those concerns with a large staff and output, and then examine the part played by the designers, whether they worked for a single factory or several. The industrialization of the means of production, a phenomenon that was still sporadic at the beginning of the twentieth century, did not progress with sufficient regularity for it to be a useful criterion.

The nineteenth century saw the survival of some of the great ceramic factories founded in the preceding century at Meissen, Sèvres, Berlin, Copenhagen and Nymphenburg, whereas others, such as the prestigious factory in Vienna, disappeared. On the other hand, from the middle of the nineteenth century the spirit of free enterprise gave an impetus to the setting up of many factories of varying size. At the same time certain economic factors and the development of new means of transport, in particular the railway, led to the reorganization of the industry. The rural areas provided cheap labour and an abundance of raw materials or fuels: we need but mention Staffordshire in England, the Limousin region and central France, Thuringia and Saxony in Germany, and Bohemia and Bavaria in the Austro-Hungarian empire. The same economic factors brought about the establishment of large groups whose products ranged from industrial or sanitary products to art ceramics. The companies of Doulton in England, Richard-Ginori in Italy and Kuznetsov in Russia are among such groups.

Finally, the need to find new outlets for their ceramic products induced entrepreneurs such as Alexandre Bigot or Emile Muller to investigate the use of ceramics as architectural ornament for interior and exterior surfaces. Architectural ceramic decoration achieved its first success at the time of the Universal Exhibition of 1889. Stoneware in particular won favour among many architects who wished to integrate new materials into their work: Hector Guimard's Castel Béranger in Paris in 1897, Otto Wag-

ner's Majolika-Haus in Vienna in 1898 and Antonio Gaudí's Parque Güell in Barcelona in 1900.

Looking back on the production and evolution of these factories from the vantage-point of the present day, one has to relate them to progress in the arts in general—in so far as this can be followed from formal statements of new attitudes, or at least from historical descriptions of them. Together with capitalism came 'the triumph of the middle class'. The new bourgeois wanted to mark their social ascent and, like the aristocrats they sought to replace, were conscious of the need to create an environment which reflected their wealth and also their appreciation of beauty and refinement. Since their taste was unformed and they lacked the courage to innovate, they encouraged a retrospectively oriented art, which one might call 'historicist'. Works from the past were taken as models. In addition, the less well-to-do sections of the middle class developed an ambition to share in this patronage of the arts. The increasing mediocrity of imitative works was further encouraged by the invention of cheaper methods of reproduction. In this way electro-plated ware took the place of silver, and pewter that of bronze. The Universal Exhibitions which followed in regular succession the one held in London in 1851 gave rise to imitative works as well as pieces conceived in a spirit of competition, and this made the trend more prevalent throughout Europe. Nostalgic and pretentious references to the past were reinforced by the establishment and opening of public museums, which made the collections of connoisseurs available. Nevertheless the increase in great private collections led to a rapid turnover and helped to form taste. Their role in training craftsmen was considerable, as can be seen from the fact that Charles-Jean Avisseau and Ulysse de Blois, for example, started out as restorers of Renaissance pottery. Moreover, techniques of reproduction were making great progress at that time. The publication in large editions of illustrated works communicated knowledge of early art works to a vast public.

The historicist trend did not, however, play a purely negative role since it inspired a renaissance of old techniques. 'Aesthetic historicism', permeated by a degenerate form of the rococo style, contributed to the rediscovery of techniques of glass-making and enamelling on metal. In the field of ceramics it resulted in the revival of both faïence and lead-glazed earthenware. This began in France with the work of Avisseau, who worked in the style of

(continued on p. 16)

2

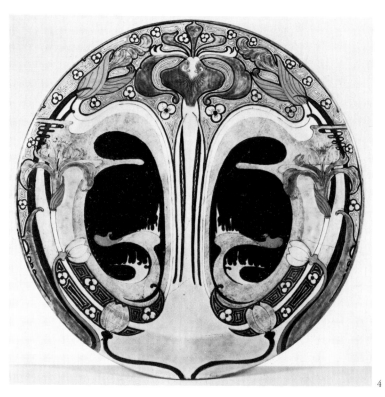

4

2 BERLIN (Germany, Königliche Porzellan-Manufaktur). *Coffee-cup and Saucer*, 1902–3. Porcelain. H. 4.5 cm. Märkisches Museum, Berlin; II, 64.107 B (a,b).
It was not until the arrival in 1902 of Theodor Schmuz-Baudiss that *Jugendstil* truly made itself felt in the tradition-bound Berlin factory (see Pl. 58). He encouraged a complete change of outlook. The new forms were either very simple or were embellished with exuberant, sometimes naturalistic, relief decoration. The pieces made comprised plaques, plates and vases, mostly decorated in underglaze colours, which were frequently sprayed on. This example is the work of Max Schröder.

4 PURMEREND (Netherlands, Haga, factory of Wed. N. Brantjes). *Dish, c.* 1900. Stoneware. D. 44.7 cm. Bethnal Green Museum, London; C. 100-1967.
This pottery was established in 1894 in a former cement factory. From 1897 it was directed by the Brantjes, whose partner had taken over the Zuid Holland factory at Gouda. In 1906–7, when the concern was taken over by the Amstelhoek factory of Amsterdam, the artistic director was C. J. Lanooy, who also worked as an independent ceramist. The wares produced were often boldly conceived, with stylized and strongly coloured decoration reminiscent of the earliest pieces made at Rozenburg.

3

3 HÜTTENSTEINACH (Germany, Swaine & Co.). *Butter-dish*, 1900–2. Porcelain. H. 9.5 cm. Kunstgewerbemuseum, Cologne; E 4879 a, b.
This factory, founded in 1854, initially produced vessels with traditional decoration. Theodor Schmuz-Baudiss (cf. Pl. 58), co-founder in 1897 of the Munich Vereinigte Werkstätte, was the designer from 1900 to 1902. He was responsible for several sets, including the 'Pansy' service, for the combined studios. The factory eventually merged with that of the Schoenau brothers, also at Hüttensteinach.

5 COPENHAGEN (Denmark, Royal Danish Porcelain Factory). *Vase*, 1908. Porcelain. H. 44 cm. Bröhan Collection, Berlin.
The Scandinavian pieces sent to the *Exposition Universelle* in Paris in 1889 were a revelation and enjoyed considerable success. The Royal Factory was distinguished by its simple forms, stylized decoration based on themes taken from nature and its use of underglaze colours in muted tones or with crystalline effects. It all seemed very new and was widely copied immediately. This vase, designed and made by Jenny Meyer, is entirely typical of this new spirit, which lasted until the outbreak of the First World War.

6 SÈVRES (France, Manufacture nationale de porcelaine). *Jardinière on Stand*, 1903. Soft-paste porcelain. H. 131 cm. Archives, Manufacture nationale de Sèvres.
During his all too brief period as head of the factory, Théodore Deck rediscovered the formula for soft-paste porcelain, a more malleable body, to encourage artists untrained in ceramics to work in association with the Sèvres factory. In addition to two vases with high relief decoration by Jules Dalou, Hector Guimard created three shapes for manufacture in soft-paste. They demonstrate his taste for the flowing line allied to a solid structure, features that characterize his work.

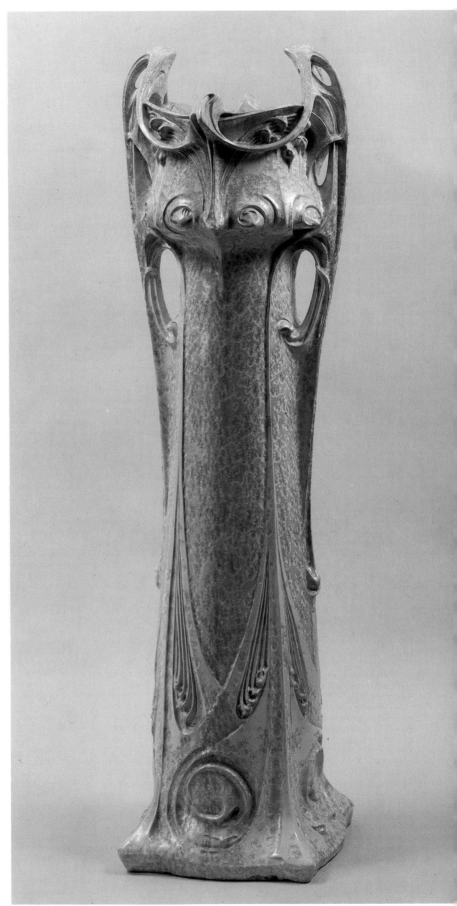

5

6

7

8

9

7 **FLORENCE** (Italy, Arte della Ceramica). *Vase, c.* 1900. Maiolica. H. 36.5 cm. Musée Ariana, Geneva; C 280.

This factory was founded in 1896/7 by Galileo Chini, its artistic director for many years, and his friend Vittoria Giunti; they were soon joined by Galileo's cousins, Guido and Chino. In 1902 the factory moved to more spacious premises in the suburb of Fontebuoni. Galileo and Chino Chini left the company in 1904 and in 1906 founded the Chini & Co. Manifattura Fornaci S. Lorenzo at Mugello, which was destroyed by bombing in 1944. They produced tin-glazed earthenware and stoneware, pots, tiles and panels, decorated with lustres and traditional Italian motifs, along with works in the so-called 'Liberty style'.

8 **FLORENCE** (Italy, Figli di G. Cantagalli S.A.I.). *Vase, c.* 1900. Stoneware. H. 31 cm. Bethnal Green Museum, London; 1585–1900.

The Cantagalli dynasty of potters can be traced from its famous 15th-century founder Bartolomeo Antonio to the point when Ulisse took over the family concern in 1878. He continued to make good replicas of early maiolica, winning a gold medal in Milan in 1883 for copies of Della Robbia's work, but was equally interested in creating pieces in the 'Liberty style', distinguished by floral and zoomorphic decoration.

9 **CINCINNATI** (U.S.A., Rookwood Pottery). *Vase,* 1900. Earthenware. H. 26 cm. Bethnal Green Museum, London; 1686–1900.

The revival of American ceramics was brought about by two women from Cincinnati who both began by decorating porcelain. Whereas Mary Louise McLaughlin always worked alone, Maria Longworth Nichols opened a pottery in 1880 which gained immediate success. In 1889 she won a gold medal at the *Exposition Universelle* in Paris. *Barbotine* decoration was then extremely popular, but was used by Nichols for more sober and stylized compositions, unlike the products of the Haviland Auteuil studio, where the style was closer to that of Impressionist painting. The decoration on this example is the work of Harriet E. Willcox.

10

11

10 **MOORE,** Bernard (England, 1850–1935) *Vase, c.* 1905. Earthenware. H. 24 cm. Victoria and Albert Museum, London; C. 16-1948.
Bernard Moore was first and foremost a chemist interested in research into glazes. He attempted to reproduce the effects obtained by oriental potters, such as *flambé* reds, turquoises and lustres. From 1905 to 1915 he had his own studio, at which several young artists worked. As a technical adviser, he helped a number of factories to resolve their problems, for example, assisting Doulton's in finding a formula for copper-red.

11 **MOORCROFT,** William (England, 1872–1945). *Vase, c.* 1902. Stoneware. H. 23.7 cm. Victoria and Albert Museum, London; Circ. 318-1976.
In 1898 William Moorcroft was appointed to direct the art pottery section of the James McIntyre Company at Burslem. He produced wares decorated by the process of underglaze transfer-printing. Among them was the enormously popular 'Florian Ware', which had a white ground and underglaze decoration of stylized plant forms outlined with a trail of white slip, applied in a great variety of ways. In 1913, on the closing of this studio, he founded his own, taking his decorators with him. While continuing to issue variations on this theme and updated versions of his early patterns in the taste of the day, he devoted himself principally to work on *flambé* ground colours.

12

13

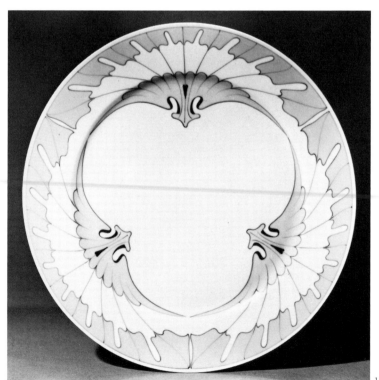

14

15

16

12 **DUFRÊNE**, Maurice (France, 1876–1955). *Tea Service, c.* 1900. Porcelain. H. of tea-pot 13 cm. Professor H. Hentrich Collection, Düsseldorf.
Maurice Dufrêne was one of the comparatively few French designers to display versatility. On graduating from the École des Arts décoratifs in 1900 he was engaged by Julius Meier-Graefe, with whom he had worked since 1898 when the latter had opened the *Maison Moderne;* this was the second shop designed to promote the decorative arts, after Samuel Bing's *Galeries de l'Art Nouveau,* which opened in 1895. For *La Maison Moderne* Dufrêne created jewellery, glass and ceramics, sometimes made by Dalpayrat, and for *L'Art Nouveau* fancy leather goods. This service was also produced in a version decorated with stylized roses.

13 **NYMPHENBURG** (Germany, Nymphenburger Porzellan-Manufaktur). *Fish Plate, c.* 1904–5. Porcelain. D. 23.5 cm. Bethnal Green Museum, London; C. 18a-1970.
In 1757, ten years after its foundation, this factory was bought by Maximilian III Joseph of Bavaria. At first its reputation rested on sculptural pieces by Franz-Anton Bustelli, Dominicus Auliczek and Johann-Peter Melchior. In 1862 it was leased to a private company, and in 1888 revived by Albert Bäuml, who decided to restore it to its early splendour by re-issuing the models which had been responsible for its success. He also commissioned artists to create new models. The 'Moderna' service was designed before 1900 by the painter and engraver Hermann Gradl, and is one of the earliest and purest examples of *Jugendstil* in Germany.

14 **MEISSEN** (Germany, Staatliche Porzellan-Manufaktur). *Plate, c.* 1901/2–2/5. Porcelain. D. 26.8 cm. Kunstgewerbemuseum, Cologne; E 4744.
The first European manufacturer of hard-paste porcelain, state-controlled since 1831, carried on producing pieces in an earlier style to satisfy the taste of its clientèle. Its *Jugendstil* creations were a result of the employment of artists from outside, such as Henry van de Velde or Peter Behrens, and were the result of the gradual disappearance of the old personnel rather than of deliberate policy. Along with the 'Crocus' service, designed in 1896, this 'Wing' design, created by Konrad and Rudolf Hentschel in 1901–2, is one of the earliest examples of the new style at Meissen.

15 **DE MORGAN,** William Frend (England, 1835–1917). *Vase,* 1898–1907. Earthenware. H. 22.5 cm. Victoria and Albert Museum, London; 861-1905.
A friend of the Pre-Raphaelite painters and of William Morris, de Morgan designed glassware and became interested in ceramics through his concern with the chemistry of glazes. He discovered the secret of lustre and throughout his active period at Chelsea (1872–81), Merton Abbey (1882–8), and Fulham Road (from 1888 to 1898 in association with the architect Halsey Ralph Ricardo, then from 1898 to 1907 with the Passenger brothers), he produced pots and tiles with decoration strongly influenced by the Middle East. He cut short his career in order to concentrate on literature, leaving his associates to carry on producing the designs until about 1911.

16 **PÉCS,** (Hungary, Vilmós Zsolnay). *Vase, c.* 1900. Stoneware. H. 39 cm. Bethnal Green Museum, London; 1350–1900.
In 1865 Vilmós Zsolnay took over his brother's studio which he soon made famous. On his death in 1900 his son Miklós continued to direct the enterprise, which was nationalized in 1949. Father and son became well known for their work on porcelain and glazes, producing crystalline effects, especially lustres of varied tones, the best known being the fiery red Eosin glaze.

Bernard Palissy, and that of Ulysse de Blois, who adopted the style of Rouen and Nevers pieces made in the seventeenth century. These two men anticipated the research into Oriental art carried out by Théodore Deck and Eugène-Victor Collinot and by William Frend de Morgan in England, where an analogous country-wide movement favouring a return to the past led to the revival of incised slip decoration. The effect of the movement can also be seen in Germany, while in Italy historicism led to the copying of Della Robbia pieces and to the type of decoration practised by Joseph Devers of Turin on crude stanniferous glazes. The second renaissance was that of stoneware, which was restored to credit by Jules-Claude Ziegler and likewise was rediscovered in England and Germany as well.

In this way Europe not only discovered its own archaeological past but also the cultures of the world beyond its shores. The development of means of communication, the great voyages of exploration with their harvests of exotic objects and their publications, the expeditions and colonial occupations led to an appreciation of the arts of far-off lands: the ancient Orient, then the Far East and North Africa. The Japanese entry submitted to the exhibition of 1867 was a true revelation and aroused immediate admiration; it led to the birth of a new type of art collecting. It also greatly encouraged the popularity of stoneware, of which models could be seen, for example, in the collections formed by the Goncourt brothers or by Justus Brinckmann for the Hamburg Museum. This appreciation was further stimulated by the research of Jean Carriès. A short time later Chinese works of art were to be similarly influential.

Even more fundamental was the question that the nineteenth century asked itself regarding the actual status of the decorative arts. On a more theoretical level this concerned the divergent notions of 'art' and 'technique'. The problem involved several categories of fundamental ideas. Various solutions were sought and found, some social, others economic and yet others aesthetic. On one hand, we can see the progressive integration of arts previously considered 'minor' into the field of fine arts until the differences between these two forms of creative activity were eliminated, as Ruskin had advocated. The first sign of recognition was that museums were established to collect these previously scorned 'minor' works and societies were formed to promote them. In 1851 the National Collection of Decorative Art appeared in London, the ancestor of the present-day Victoria and Albert Museum, and in 1888 the Arts and Crafts Exhibition Society organized its first exhibition in the same city. In Paris the Union centrale des arts décoratifs was born in 1862 and founded its own museum in 1878. The outcome of all this was that potters gained the right to show their work in the same salons as painters and sculptors. From 1891 onwards the Société nationale des Beaux-Arts admitted works of 'industrial art' to the Salon du Champ de Mars, an example followed by the Société des artistes français in 1895, and then by artists in Munich two years later. This revival of craftsmanship was championed in France by Eugène-Emmanuel Viollet-le-Duc, who shared with the English a love of the Gothic. In reviving an awareness of the decorative possibilities offered by Nature he contributed greatly to the establishment of a new style.

Another aspect of this question of the status of the decorative arts was economic and more complex. It pertained to their relations with industry. The development of mechanization and the massive production of objects that were often ugly or badly designed soon provoked a vigorous reaction. Logically enough this came from England where industrialization had first made itself felt. From 1850 onwards the theorist John Ruskin denounced mechanization as the enemy and extolled the return of the craftsman, who alone respected the human dimension and guaranteed beauty. But the position of Ruskin and his friend William Morris, founder of the Arts and Crafts movement, rested on a contradiction. On one hand they declared that art had a social function and was intended to improve the people's environment—views shared in France by Pierre-Joseph Proudhon, who in 1865 published his 'Principles of Art and its Social Purpose', and by the painter Gustave Courbet, and in Russia by the followers of Chernyshevsky. On the other hand they denied all association between art and industry in order to promote the craftsman. For industry alone was in a position to produce at prices accessible to all, while the craftsman's method of production made his work too costly. In contrast, the Columbian Exhibition in Chicago in 1893 insisted on the essential relationship between mechanization and artistic output.

One other important aspect of nineteenth-century thinking on the decorative arts relates to the very notion of decoration. The juries of the great exhibitions declared again and again that regrettably this did not seem to be carried out according to any principle. Standing for a new aesthetic order, these juries demanded that decoration become accepted for what it was, and that in particular it should give up its attempts to create an illusion of depth quite beyond its capabilities. Moreover, they stipulated that manufacturers should take steps to adapt properly conceived patterns not only to the shapes but also to the materials they were using, and accordingly preached that it was necessary to study the history of ornamentation. So it was that in German universities art appreciation and history were elevated to the rank of autonomous disciplines. In 1879 Gottfried Semper published in Munich the second volume, entitled *Ceramics*, of his treatise *Style in the Technical and Tectonic Arts, or Practical Aesthetics*. Works on the applied arts proliferated, offering designers descriptive catalogues of early patterns or modern decorative forms, and schools of design were founded. A new profession appeared, that of designer, whose function was to conceive decorative schemes which could be adapted to different materials. Among the pioneers of this new profession were the Englishmen Walter Crane and Christopher Dresser and the Swiss Eugène Grasset.

Nineteenth-century art evolved in the context of these changing ideas and practices, and all these developments affected ceramics. After the triumph of historicism and then exoticism, a reaction set in which was to affect practically the whole of Europe.

(continued on p. 19)

17

18

17 **LONDON** (England, R.W. Martin & Bros.). *Vase,* 1903. Stoneware. H. 25.4 cm. Victoria and Albert Museum, London; Circ. 417–1919.
In 1873 Robert Wallace Martin, who had been trained as a sculptor, established a studio in Fulham with his three brothers: Charles was in charge of administration, Walter of throwing, firing and perfecting of colours, and Edwin of decoration. In 1877 they built their own kilns at Southall, opening a shop in London two years later. Their best-known pieces are the masks and grotesque animals modelled by Robert Wallace, but they also made pots with incised decoration and works in Japanese taste, which reflected their interest in the surfaces of their pieces.

18 **STOKE-ON-TRENT** (England, Minton's). *Vase, c.* 1906. Earthenware. H. 13.4 cm. Victoria and Albert Museum, London; Circ. 608–1966.
Despite the rapid failure of the art pottery studio which they opened in London in 1871 and entrusted to W. S. Coleman, Minton's did not give up their attempts to adapt their products to the new taste; they were more strongly influenced by the developments in the field of design taking place in Scotland (Glasgow) and Germany than by the langorous charms of Art Nouveau. This decoration is the work of Léon F. Solon and J. W. Wadsworth.

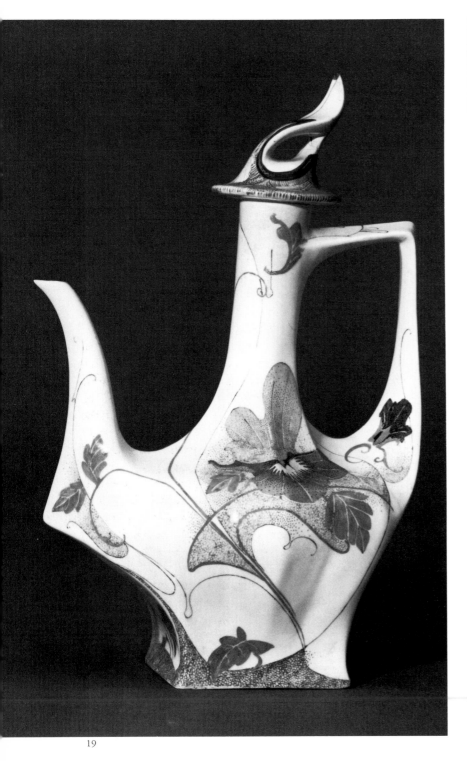

19

20

19 **ROZENBURG** (The Hague, Netherlands, Haagsche Plateelbakkerij). *Tea-pot,* 1904. Porcelain. H. 23.5 cm. Bröhan Collection, Berlin.
After the departure of Gudenberg and Colenbrander, it was Juriaan Kok, artistic consultant in 1893 and director in 1894, to whom the Rozenburg factory owed its revival. This second period of expansion, resulting from the perfecting in 1899 by the chemist M. N. Engelden of an extremely fine 'eggshell' body saw the production of a large number of remarkably original objects of angular and attenuated form with asymmetrical decoration in acid colours. This pattern was designed by W. P. Hartgring and executed by him in association with Madame C. W. J. Hart. The concern closed in 1914, one year after Kok's departure.

20 **FEURE,** Georges de (France, 1868–1928). *Chocolate-cup,* before 1908. Porcelain. H. 27.5 cm. Musée des Arts décoratifs, Paris; 15,246.
Georges de Feure was a painter and litographic artist who illustrated many periodicals and monographic works. He also worked for Bing, for whom he designed the Dressing and Drawing Rooms, and their furniture, hangings and stained glass, for Bing's pavilion at the *Exposition Universelle* of 1900. In addition Feure created designs for useful wares and porcelain figures for the *Galeries de l'Art Nouveau.*

Artists refrained from leaning on the past while welcoming the most varied new influences. For instance the influence of Japonism (*japonaiserie*) is evident in the stylization of finely observed naturalistic motifs and in composition. Symbolism, in its use of the female figure and the fluid line, and Impressionism, in its fondness for colour, both reflected Japanese taste. Everywhere associations of artists sprang up in opposition to official schools in order to encourage the birth of a new art concerned with the whole environment: buildings and schemes for interiors, furniture and functional and decorative objects. The promoters of this movement were almost always architects: the 'Groupe des Vingt' was born in Brussels in 1884 around Victor Horta and Henry van de Velde; in 1897 the Vienna Secession group brought together the architects Josef Hoffmann and Joseph Maria Olbrich and the painter Gustav Klimt; and in the same year the Vereinigte Werkstätte group was established in Munich.

The new style was to spread very rapidly. The Universal Exhibition of 1900 in Paris marked simultaneously its triumph and the beginning of its decline. The speed of its diffusion can be explained both by the general conditions already described and by the influence of the various publications allied to the cause which rapidly appeared: for example, illustrated journals such as *L'Art moderne,* published from 1881 in Brussels, *The Studio* in England from 1893, *Jugend* in Munich in 1896 and *L'Art décoratif* in France. Another factor was the galleries or groups of artists dealing in works of art. In 1874 Arthur L. Liberty opened his 'East India House', for which William Morris, Arthur H. Mackmurdo and Charles A. Voysey were soon to work. The Hohenzollern Kunstgewerbehaus in Berlin, established in 1879, was the first in Europe to sell furniture in the Arts and Crafts style; and in 1895 Samuel Bing opened the Bazaar *l'Art nouveau* in Paris, which broke new ground when it abandoned the practice of showing objects in the shop windows and instead put them into a setting. This was soon followed by Julius Meier-Graefe's *La Maison française*, which sold and exhibited works by foreign as well as French artists. Part of the same movement was Hendrikus P. Berlage, who founded Het Binnenhuis in Amsterdam in 1900. Various associations of artists in Germany and Austria-Hungary performed a similar function as patron and promoter, although this role was sometimes played by a single individual; for instance, the Grand Duke Ernst Ludwig of Hesse brought Joseph Maria Olbrich to Darmstadt to build the Mathildenhöhe. Only the Swiss entrusted this role to a museum, the Kunstgewerbemuseum in Zurich.

In order to survive, ceramic factories were naturally obliged to adapt to changes in taste. This evolution began at different times and was carried out more consciously and completely in some regions and factories than others. The smaller enterprises were of course much better placed to adapt quickly than the old ones, which were hampered by the burden of their traditions.

From the nineteenth century onward technological progress and artistic innovations made possible the transition to a new style. On the technological level, productivity was improved by the adoption of the two-chamber kiln, heated at first by coal and charcoal and then by gas. Before the first trials of tunnel-ovens or continuous kilns, certain processes had been thoroughly mechanized, mainly the preparation of the body and the manufacturing of mass-produced pieces such as bricks, tiles or electrical insulators. The development of the thermo-electrical pyrometer, Seger cones and instruments to control the atmosphere in the kilns, research into coefficients of expansion, and progress in the analysis of materials and the chemical reactions to which they were subject permitted the development of new glazes better suited to modern taste.

In the field of decoration the dominant trend was the reproduction of earlier pieces which had by now become traditional, such as the Meissen 'onion pattern'. The establishments which were fastidious in their search for refinement and more aware of important artistic trends progressed from the neo-classical style popular in the first quarter of the century to an eclecticism tending towards the exotic. On the whole the most popular type of decoration was miniature paintings within cartouches. In Germany and in France well-known pictures were scrupulously copied on to plaques, vases and plates. Unfortunately these scenes were often ill suited to the forms which they decorated. It appears that the Sèvres factory was the first to become aware of the need to rethink decorative schemes and processes. A committee formed in 1848 dictated the principles of the new aesthetics, and a first step was taken with the perfecting of the process of painting in *pâte-sur-pâte*. To start with, this process was used to imitate Chinese wares decorated in relief in white on a celadon ground. The first trials took place at Sèvres in 1848. This type of decoration was soon used, with variations in ground colour and materials, throughout Europe. It is to be found on wares from Berlin and on those by Boch or Minton, but pieces with decoration of this type, although in a new technique, could scarcely be considered to represent real progress. On the other hand, coloured bodies, while they derive from the same principle, were used in a much freer and more original fashion and were the first products to display Japanese inspiration. These coloured bodies allowed some effects very similar to those obtained, with their *barbotine* technique (painting in coloured slip), by Ernest Chaplet and the artists associated with him in the workshops for artistic research opened by the Haviland brothers at Auteuil in 1872. During this period several large factories reacted against automation by opening similar workshops. This was the case with Henry Doulton, who from 1871 co-operated with the director of the Lambeth School of Art and invited his pupils to work in a studio to produce decorative work, and eventually set up a firm making art ware at Burslem in 1877. In a similar fashion Minton operated a short-lived studio in London, which lasted only from 1871 to 1872.

In the 1870s the two most important artistic factories, Sèvres and Berlin, began far-reaching programmes of reform. Shapes had to be simplified by eliminating complicated methods of production involving the joining together of separate parts of a piece. Both factories especially wanted to formulate a body that could

(continued on p. 28)

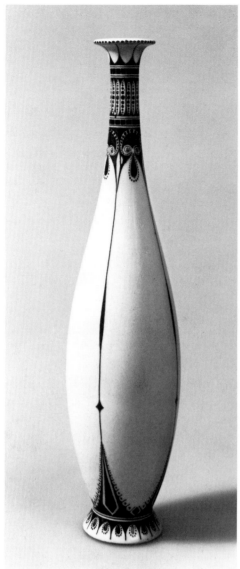

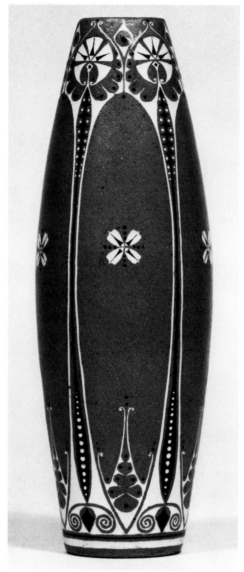

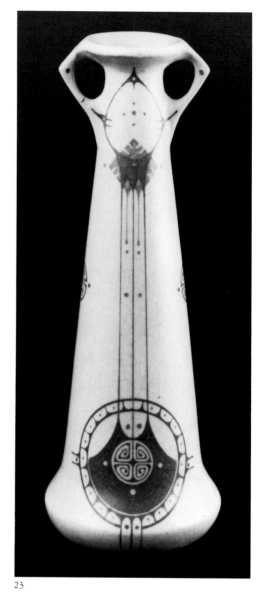

21

22

23

21 **OEGSTGEEST-LEZ-LEIDEN** (Netherlands, Amphora Factory). *Vase,* date unknown. Stoneware. H. 26 cm. Museum Bellerive, Zurich; 1974–29.
The designer Christian Johannes van der Hoef, artistic director of the Amstelhoek factory in Amsterdam from 1894 to 1910 (cf. Pl. 22), also designed for many other concerns. His works are distinguished by restrained, attenuated forms and highly stylized geometrical decoration, which undoubtedly owes much to Javanese batiks, as does all contemporary Dutch decorative art.

22 **AMSTERDAM,** (Netherlands, Amstelhoek Factory). *Vase,* 1900–2. Stoneware. H. 21.8 cm. Museum für Kunsthandwerk, Frankfurt; 5564.
This factory was founded in 1894–5 by W. Hoeker. From 1894 to 1910 its artistic director was the designer Christian Johannes van der Hoef, who worked for a number of other Dutch factories at that time. His pieces are characterized by restrained, attenuated forms; the decoration, in a limited palette, is geometric in style and is carved through a layer of slip or else makes use of a niello-type technique. The factory was taken over in 1907 by the Haga factory at Purmerend and in 1910 by the de Distel concern.

23 **AMSTERDAM,** (Netherlands, Plateelbakkerij de Distel). *Vase, c.* 1900–5. Stoneware. H. 21.1 cm. Gemeentemuseum, The Hague; MC 82–1973.
The de Distel factory was founded in 1895 by J. M. Lob; until 1911 the principal designer responsible for decoration was Lambertus (Bert) Nienhuis, who made

this example. Following its take-over of the Amstelhoek Company in 1910, the de Distel concern merged in 1923 with a ceramics group at Gouda, which led to the closure of its Amsterdam studios. Its output consisted of pots and ornamental tiles. Bert Nienhuis also worked for other factories, while continuing to produce highly original pieces in his own studio.

24 **ROZENBURG,** (Netherlands, The Hague, Haagsche Plateelbakkerij). *Vase,* 1903. Earthenware. H. 32 cm. Bröhan Collection, Berlin.
This factory was founded in 1885 by Wilhelm Wolff von Gudenberg who was himself responsible for the models before Theodorus Colenbrander was engaged as artistic director. In 1889 they both left the factory, which as a result of their influence went through an initial phase of ostentation, characterized by the use of astonishingly stylized forms and the adoption of naturalistic decoration in brilliant colours, which contrasted sharply with the pastel tones of contemporary *Jugendstil.* Despite its later date, this vase, from the hand of one of their more productive collaborators, W. P. Hartgring, is still totally impregnated with their influence.

25

26

27

25 **MASSIER,** Pierre-Clément (France, 1845–1917). *Vase,* before 1909. Earthenware. H. 30.5 cm. Musée nationale de céramique, Sèvres; MNCS 15,036. The two brothers Delphin and Clément Massier, sons of a traditional potter at Vallauris, and their cousin Jérôme, each owned their own workshop. Clément's studio was to become the most celebrated, because of his association with such artists as the Symbolist painter Lucien Lévy-Dhurmer and the sculptor Alexander Munro. Clément Massier was also famous for the lustres he perfected, inspired by Hispano-Moresque maiolica, but used by him in a totally original palette.

26 **ALTONA** (Germany, factory of Hermann and Richard Mutz). *Vase,* 1903. Stoneware. H. 49.4 cm. Altonaer Museum, Hamburg; 1909/36.
In 1893 Richard Mutz became a director of a factory mainly producing kitchenware, which had been bought by his grandfather in 1845 and modernized by his father. Influenced by Japanese ceramics which he had seen in Hamburg, Richard Mutz made decorative and useful wares, decorated with drip-, matt and iridescent glazes, and went into temporary partnership with the sculptor Ernst Barlach, who designed this piece. In 1903 he left Altona to set up his own workshop in Berlin, where he specialized in architectural ceramics and tiles.

27 **KÄHLER,** Hermann August (Denmark, 1846–1917). *Vase, c.* 1915. Earthenware. H. 31 cm. Kunstindustimuseet, Copenhagen; B 17/1916.
In 1872 Hermann August Kähler took over the firm founded by his father in 1839, which up to then had been making kitchenware. His ceramic researches, which centred particularly on earthenwares, neglected by his compatriots, led to discovery of a copper-based red suited to this material. He designed many shapes and worked with several artists, including Svend Hammerschøi, who designed this piece. Since H. A. Kähler's death the factory has been run by his son Hermann.

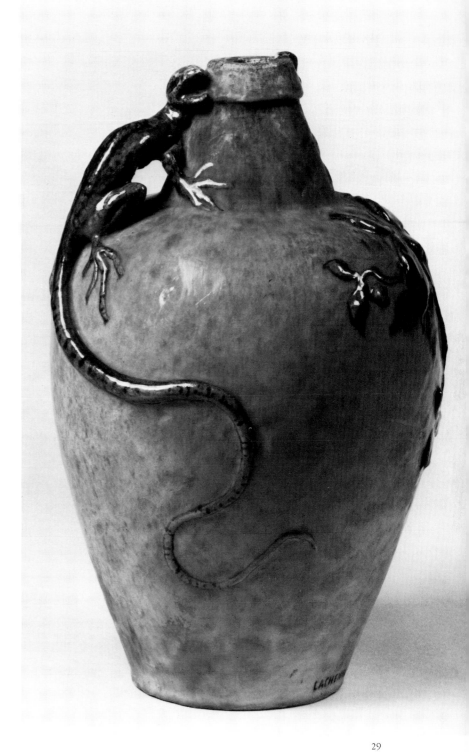

28 WOODVILLE (England, Bretby Art Pottery). *Vase, c.* 1905. Stoneware. H. 37.9 cm. Victoria and Albert Museum, London; Circ. 98–1970.
This factory was opened in 1883 by William Ault and Henry Tooth, former director of the Linthorpe Pottery. Initially the wares were conventional and had simple glazes, but, following Ault's departure, the production became more varied and daring. In addition to painted decoration, *trompe-l'œil* effects were introduced imitating fruits, wood, and metal as well as relief motifs that showed Japanese influence.

29 LACHENAL, Edmond (France, 1855–1930). *Vase,* 1894. Earthenware. H. 31 cm. Musée nationale de céramique, Sèvres; MNCS 9880.
After initial training from the age of fifteen in Théodore Deck's studio, Lachenal opened one of his own in 1884 in the Malakoff district. In 1887 he moved to Châtillon-sous-Bagneux. In addition to his well-known sculptural works (cf. Pl. 133), and his schemes for such factories as Keller and Guerin at Lunéville, he produced work in faïence and stoneware, decorated in the main with naturalistic reliefs which on occasion formed the handles or overran the entire body of the pot, as on his vases in the form of a flock of ducks or an arrangement of foliage.

30 **LAMBETH** (England, Doulton & Co.). *Vase, c.* 1905. Stoneware. H. 15.5 cm. Victoria and Albert Museum, London; Circ. 135–1952.
Henry Doulton was one of the first industrial manufacturers to open an art department at his Lambeth firm, and maintained close links with the director of the local art school, whose pupils were made welcome. This studio soon adopted the Art Nouveau style, which led to the production of 'art stoneware' alongside traditional domestic wares. The success of this venture played an important part in the development of English ceramics.

31 **DECŒUR,** Emile (France, 1876–1953). *Pitcher, c.* 1903. Stoneware. H. 32 cm. Professor Dr. H. Hentrich Collection, Düsseldorf.
Emile Decœur's early work is not widely known, perhaps because the potter himself disowned his 'youthful mistakes'. A pupil of Edmond Lachenal from 1890, after 1901 he exhibited naturalistic stoneware and porcelain pieces with lustrous, matt or *flambé* glazes. After a brief association with Fernand Rumèbe, he left to set up on his own at Fontenay-les-Roses in 1907.

32 **LAEUGER,** Max (Germany, 1864–1952). *Vases,* 1898 and 1900. Glazed earthenware. H. 14, 25.5 cm. Bethnal Green Museum, London; 225–1899, 1956–1900.
After his studies as a painter and decorator, Max Laeuger developed into a versatile designer, working in many media. He was a co-founder in 1907 of the Deutscher Werkbund. His contribution to ceramics was considerable, for in addition to his activity as a teacher and theorist, he manufactured and decorated pots, mainly at Kandern in the Black Forest, and was one of those mainly responsible for the stoneware revival and the renaissance of traditional decorative techniques. He also worked with glazed earthenware which he decorated with slip, using a technique quite different from that practised in France at the same period.

33

34

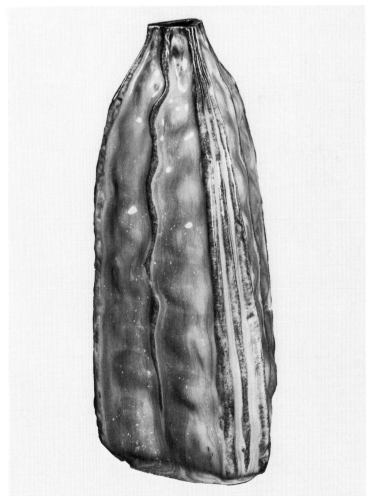

35

33 **BINDESBØLL**, Thorvald (Denmark, 1846–1908). *Dish,* 1901. Glazed earthenware. D. 46.7 cm. Kunstindustrimuseet, Copenhagen; 1175.
The architect Thorvald Bindesbøll became involved with the decorative arts very early in his career. He is well known not only for his designs for furniture, silver and book-bindings, but also for ceramic works which were usually of plain earthenware with a lead glaze. His vivid colours are in strong contrast to the dull, bluish palette used at the time by the Royal Copenhagen Factory, just as his carved abstract decoration is markedly original for its time.

34 **BIGOT**, Alexandre (France, 1862–1927). *Plate,* 1908. Stoneware. D. 27.5 cm. Musée des Beaux-Arts, Tours; 911–601–7.
Alexandre Bigot, a teacher of physics and chemistry, decided to devote himself to ceramics after admiring stoneware from the Far East shown at the *Exposition Universelle* of 1889. Initially he made pieces with simple shapes, decorated with matt glazes, for which he was awarded a grand prix in 1900. He was one of the main exponents of the use of stoneware in architecture, for interior and exterior surfaces, and produced a lavish series of decorative elements to be incorporated into buildings, as well as some purely decorative pieces. He also produced ceramic versions of the work of contemporary sculptors.

35 **CARRIÈRE**, Ernest (France, 1858–1908). *Seed-jar,* date unknown. Stoneware. H. 21.7 cm. Musée du Petit Palais, Paris; 127 Galliéra.
Brother of the artist Eugène Carrière, Ernest was a painter as well as a sculptor. From 1890 he occasionally worked together with Théodore Deck. He seems to have had an independent studio and some months before his death was appointed artistic director of the Manufacture national de Sèvres. His work is often embellished with naturalistic reliefs.

36

37

36 **DALPAYRAT,** Pierre-Adrien (France, 1844–1910). *Vase, c.* 1900. Stoneware. H. 37 cm. Bethnal Green Museum, London; 952–1901.
After spending time in several factories, in 1889 Dalpayrat established his own stoneware workshop at Bourg-la-Reine with the sculptor Alphonse Voisin-Delacroix; on the latter's death in 1893 he went into partnership with Adèle Lesbros until about 1905. He made stoneware and earthenware, but after 1902 became more particularly interested in porcelain. He produced ceramic versions of the work of such contemporary sculptors and decorators as Constantin Meunier, Ferdinand Faivre and Maurice Dufrêne and created some pieces with high-relief anthropomorphic and zoomorphic themes or naturalistic forms; he also became known for his 'rouge Dalpayrat' and *flambé* glazes.

37 **DAMMOUSE,** Albert-Louis (France, 1848–1926). *Vase, c.* 1900. Stoneware. H. 19.5 cm. Bethnal Green Museum, London; C. 837–1917.
Dammouse studied sculpture and painting, then learned ceramics with Marc-Louis Solon and went on to open a studio at Sèvres in 1871. Apart from his own creations, he designed models for several factories in the Limoges region. From 1882 he was associated with the Haviland studio at Auteuil and won a gold medal in 1889. He produced earthenware, stoneware and porcelain before turning eventually to *pâte-de-verre*.

38 **HOENTSCHEL,** Georges (France, 1855–1915). *Two Pears, c.* 1902. Stoneware. H. 15.5, 12.5 cm. Musée des Arts décoratifs, Paris; 10,184, 10,186.
Hoentschel is particularly well known as a collector of French 17th- and 18th-century art (his collection is now in the Metropolitan Museum, New York) and as an interior decorator. He was a great friend of Carriès, a fine collection of whose works he bequeathed to the city of Paris. Under Carriès's influence he created stonewares in the Japanese taste. Fruit, apples, pears and especially gourds, naturalistic in form but imaginative in colouring, very often appear as subject-matter in ceramics around 1900.

38

39

40

39 **LIMOGES** (France, Gérard Duffraisseix and Abbot). *Vase, c.* 1901. Porcelain. H. 30 cm. Musée des Arts décoratifs, Paris; 15,233.
Profiting from the Haviland name, which David Haviland had made famous, Charles-Field Haviland arrived in Limoges in 1852. In 1859 he set up a company there and exported wares which he had decorated to the United States. He eventually bought the kilns at Vierzon to make his own products, before taking over the Alluaud factory in 1876. In 1881 he retired, leaving control in the hands of the Gérard Duffraisseix and Morel company. Until 1903 the factory operated in association with Samuel Bing, who commissioned them to make wares such as this piece, designed by E. Colonna.

40 **COLORADO SPRINGS**, (U.S.A., Van Briggle Pottery Company). *Vase, c.* 1901. Earthenware. H. 24 cm. Bethnal Green Museum, London; C. 60–1973.
A decorator for the Rookwood Pottery from 1887, Artus van Briggle was sent by the factory to Paris to study painting and modelling. On his return in 1896 he conducted investigations into matt glazes, eventually leaving for Colorado, where he experimented with local clays. In 1901 he opened his own pottery. After his death in 1904 his wife continued to run the firm until 1913; in 1920 it was relaunched and reissued the original works, but the reproductions lacked the quality of the originals.

41 **JEANNENEY**, Paul (France, 1861–1920). *Vase,* 1903. Stoneware. H. 25.5 cm. Alain Cical Collection, Houilles.
Jeanneney's collections of Far Eastern ceramics considerably influenced his own work as well as that of his friend Carriès. After Carriès's death Jeanneney bought the Château de Montriveau, where he made some stonewares that were very similar to their Japanese and Chinese models, and were decorated with matt or lustrous glazes, usually muted in tone. At the same time he continued to produce sculpture.

41

be fired at a much lower temperature than that used for hard-paste porcelain. This would allow a greater range of high-temperature colours, which would be much more attractive to the eye since they blended better with the glaze. Various factors played a part in arousing this awareness: the Persian and Isnik-inspired faïence shown by Théodore Deck as early as 1861 in Paris had created a stir; reds deriving from copper and imitating Chinese *sang-de-bœuf*, which potters had sought since the middle of the century, were achieved experimentally on hard-paste porcelain as early as 1848 at Sèvres, then on earthenware by Hippolyte Boulenger at Choisy-le-Roi in 1877 and by Théodore Deck on porcelain from as early as 1880. Hermann Seger in Berlin and Georges Vogt at Sèvres succeeded at practically the same time in finding a new body fired at roughly 1280°, decorated with *flambé* glazes obtained from copper. Georges Vogt very quickly published his results, remarking on the appearance of crystals in the presence of zinc oxide. The information was picked up and systematically exploited in Copenhagen, and crystalline glazes were among the successful products shown by Danish manufacturers in Paris at the 1889 exhibition; they were then used in a great number of establishments.

Metallic lustre decoration inspired by Hispano-Moresque ware was another type of glaze effect rediscovered during the century. As early as 1862 lustre glazes were shown in London by the Italian Carocci of Gubbio and Théodore Deck. They were subsequently adopted in England by William Frend de Morgan from 1872, as well as by the Pilkington Company for designs after Walter Crane and Gordon M. Forsyth, and also in France, with a most unusual feeling and range of colours, by Clément Massier at Golfe-Juan from 1888. In Denmark they were used by the potter Hermann A. Kähler, originator of copper-red glazes on faïence, and in Hungary by Vilmós Zsolnay, well known from 1892 for a brilliant red lustre called Eosin.

In the actual composition of painted decoration the first sign of novelty was the appearance of Japonism, that is to say ceramics heavily influenced by Japanese prints. The first example is the service designed by the engraver Félix-Joseph-Auguste Bracquemond for the dealer François-Eugène Rousseau and made by Lebeuf, Milliet and Company of Creil and Montereau. The service exhibits all the characteristic features, including motifs inspired by nature, which manage to be realistic yet at the same time stylized; they are asymmetrically placed. This new type of decoration was soon adopted by Théodore Deck and at Sèvres. Both produced floral vases and other wares with decoration spreading freely over their entire surface. This was one of the essential components of Art Nouveau which was now launched on its career.

The Scandinavian factories were the first to break completely with the patterns hitherto used in ceramics. In 1885 Arnold Krog became artistic director of the Royal Porcelain Factory of Copenhagen and Pietro Krøhn that of the newer factory of Bing and Grøndahl. Both scored a huge success in Paris in 1889. Krog triumphed with his patterns inspired by Japanese stencils, painted under the glaze in a very restrained gentle bluish colour scheme, and with his similarly coloured animal sculptures, which imposed

a simplification that was soon widely imitated in Germany. Krøhn was more important as a modeller, as can be seen in his 'Heron' service, still overloaded with gilding, but exhibiting originality in its use of arabesques and in its inclusion of sculptural elements. In Sweden the Rörstrand factory, under the artistic direction of Alf Wallander (1895–1914), was soon converted to the new style. This was expressed in wares with naturalistic motifs, modelled in low relief and decorated with soft underglaze colours. At Gustavsberg Gunnar Wennerberg and then Josef Ekberg were to devise patterns and shapes in the same spirit.

New ground was also broken very quickly in Holland. In 1884 Theodorus A.C. Colenbrander became artistic director of the Plateelbakkerij Den Haag, founded in 1883 by Wilhelm von Gudenberg. Until his departure in 1889 Colenbrander created designs that were novel in their use of baroque motifs on restrained shapes, and completely original in the solidity of their motifs and strong colour schemes.

During the 1880s art pottery was born in the United States. The Rookwood Pottery in Cincinnati was founded by Maria Longworth Nichols, who was skilled in the decoration of pots after the style of European pieces in the Japanese style. The output of the new firm was essentially Art Nouveau in spirit.

The last decade of the century saw the style firmly established. All the characteristics of works produced at the beginning of the twentieth century actually made their appearance before 1900. This justifies our discussion of the formative years of a period in the decorative arts that was as brilliant as it was ephemeral.

In 1893 William Grueby opened a factory in Boston which produced pieces delicately moulded in relief and covered with characteristic matt glazes. The following year Juriaan Kok became the new director of the Plateelbakkerij Den Haag, which in 1900 took the title Royal Porcelain and Faïence Factory of Rozenburg by which it is known today. In 1899 its chemist, M.N. Engelden, perfected an extremely fine 'egg-shell' porcelain body. This body made possible the realization of tortuous shapes of which the stylized motifs and asymmetrical compositions are typical of Art Nouveau, unlike their acid colours which are invariably set in very fine parallel trails rather than flat lines. The factory closed in 1917, after the departure of Kok in 1913, without having altered the vocabulary of motifs and shapes established in the first years of the century. *(continued on p. 34)*

42 **CARRIÈS**, Jean-Joseph-Marie. (France, 1855–94). *Vase*, date unknown. Stoneware. H. 23.5 cm. Musée du Petit Palais, Paris; 522.
After studying at the Lyons and Paris Fine Arts schools, Carriès worked in wax, plaster and bronze before turning to stoneware in or about 1888. Strongly influenced by Japanese pottery exhibited in 1878, he set up at St-Amand-en-Puisaye, a traditional pottery centre, and gathered around him a large number of followers. Besides Japanese-influenced wares of restrained form and subtle glazes, occasionally enhanced with gilding, his work included busts of theatrical or historical characters, masks and fabulous beasts intended for a monumental doorway—which, however, he was unable to complete.

43   44

43 **BARNSTAPLE** (England, C. H. Brannam Ltd.). *Vase,* beginning of 20th century. Earthenware. H. 21.6 cm. Victoria and Albert Museum, London; Circ. 339–1965.

In 1879 Charles Hubert Brannam inherited the family pottery. He had studied the decorative arts and set about producing art pottery, using traditional decorative procedures: *sgraffito* decoration through one or more layers of coloured glaze, with naturalistic themes sometimes picked out in coloured slip. His 'Barum Wares' were soon well known, and were sold at Liberty's store. During the first decade of the 20th century he also produced monochrome pieces, mostly glazed in blue and green tones.

44 **TIFFANY,** Louis Comfort (U.S.A., 1848–1933). *Artichoke-flower Vase,* 1905–19. Porcelain. H. 26.5 cm. Philadelphia Museum of Art, Philadelphia, Pa. (gift of Mr. and Mrs. Thomas E. Shipley Jr.); '66–19–24.

L. C. Tiffany was a major figure of the Arts and Crafts movement in the United States. He is particularly well known for his creations in glass, and for his large shop, 'Tiffany Studios', but he was also very closely involved with ceramics. He displayed the work of American and French potters, and exhibited for the first time at St. Louis in 1904 pieces which he manufactured until 1919. It is not quite clear to what extent he was personally responsible for the creation of these objects, whose predominantly floral motifs had much in common with Art Nouveau.

45 **BOSTON** (U.S.A., Grueby Faïence Company). *Vase,* 1898–1911. Earthenware. H. 30.5 cm. Philadelphia Museum of Art, Philadelphia, Pa.; '75–95–1.

After seeing the work of Delaherche at Chicago, William Grueby set out in 1893 to find a matt glaze that would enhance his restrained, undecorated forms. By about 1897–8 he had succeeded in perfecting several ranges in yellow, brown and especially green glazes. His first forms were designed, as is this example, by George Prentiss Kendrick; although some were reproduced on a number of occasions, they were always thrown, the relief decoration being applied later, and never moulded.

46 **McLAUGHLIN,** Mary Louise (U.S.A., 1847–1939). *Vase,* 1905. Porcelain. H. 10.2 cm. Cincinnati Art Museum, Cincinnati, Ohio (gift of Porcelain League of Cincinnati); 1914.5

Along with Maria Longworth Nichols, Mary Louise McLaughlin was responsible for the American ceramic movement which originated in Cincinnati in the 1870s. Trained initially as a painter, and then as a porcelain decorator, she subsequently became concerned with perfecting technical processes such as the rediscovery of the *barbotine* technique, as shown by the Haviland Auteuil studio in some examples exhibited in the United States as early as 1876, and lustres for which she was awarded a silver medal at the *Exposition Universelle* in Paris in 1889. She eventually concentrated entirely on porcelain, which she produced from 1899 to 1906 under the name of Losanti ware.

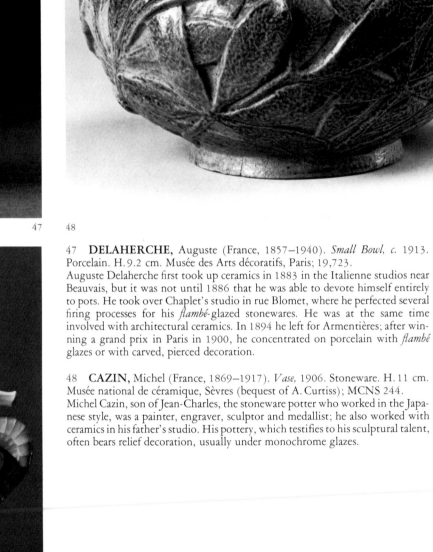

47　48

47 **DELAHERCHE,** Auguste (France, 1857–1940). *Small Bowl, c.* 1913. Porcelain. H. 9.2 cm. Musée des Arts décoratifs, Paris; 19,723.
Auguste Delaherche first took up ceramics in 1883 in the Italienne studios near Beauvais, but it was not until 1886 that he was able to devote himself entirely to pots. He took over Chaplet's studio in rue Blomet, where he perfected several firing processes for his *flambé*-glazed stonewares. He was at the same time involved with architectural ceramics. In 1894 he left for Armentières; after winning a grand prix in Paris in 1900, he concentrated on porcelain with *flambé* glazes or with carved, pierced decoration.

48 **CAZIN,** Michel (France, 1869–1917). *Vase,* 1906. Stoneware. H. 11 cm. Musée national de céramique, Sèvres (bequest of A. Curtiss); MCNS 244.
Michel Cazin, son of Jean-Charles, the stoneware potter who worked in the Japanese style, was a painter, engraver, sculptor and medallist; he also worked with ceramics in his father's studio. His pottery, which testifies to his sculptural talent, often bears relief decoration, usually under monochrome glazes.

49 **RÖRSTRAND** (Sweden). *Soup-tureen, c.* 1900. Porcelain. H. 35 cm. Bröhan Collection, Berlin.
Of the Scandinavian factories which adopted the Art Nouveau style, Rörstrand of Sweden is distinguished from its Danish competitors by the use of a brighter underglaze palette, and particularly by the use of free modelling on forms that are usually thrown. This piece is the work of the painter and modeller Alf Wallander, artistic director of the factory from 1895 to 1914. A designer capable of working in various media, he was responsible, with his colleague Waldemar Lindström, for many designs for ceramics.

49

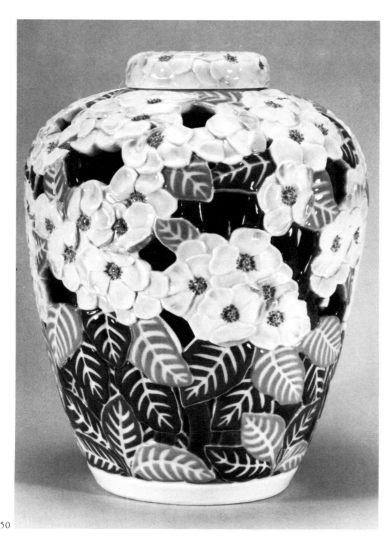

50

50 **COPENHAGEN** (Denmark, Bing & Grøndahl Actiebolag). *Vase and Cover,* 1900. Porcelain. H. 30.2 cm. Museum für Kunsthandwerk, Frankfurt; St. 187.

The first private Danish factory was founded by a former employee of the Royal Danish Factory, Frederik Grøndahl, in partnership with the Bing brothers, whose heirs took over control of the firm around 1883. Pietro Krøhn, who was engaged as artistic director (1886–97), introduced underglaze painting and naturalistic motifs. His 'Heron' service, exhibited in 1889, marked the commencement of one of the principal trends of Art Nouveau in ceramics. In 1897 he was succeeded by J. F. Willumsen, whose naturalistic reliefs and animal sculptures were responsible for the success of the factory in 1900. This vase was designed by Fanny Garde.

51 **ROBINEAU,** Adelaide Alsop (U.S.A., 1865–1929). *Scarab Vase,* 1910. Porcelain with carved and pierced decoration. H. 41.6 cm. Everson Museum of Art, Syracuse, N.Y.; P.C. 30.4.78.

A founder-figure of American pottery, Adelaide Robineau was originally a porcelain-painter. From 1899 she edited the important review *Keramik Studio.* Rejecting the stereotyped forms of industrial ceramics, and influenced by Taxile Doat whose *Grand-feu Ceramics* she published, first in serialized form and then as a handbook, she became a potter in 1905. She produced robust shapes in porcelain, decorated with detailed carved and pierced decoration on the unfired body, and was the first American potter to gain recognition in Europe. This vase won her the grand prix at Turin in 1911.

51

In Italy Giulio Richard merged the old porcelain manufacture established at Doccia by the Marquis Carlo Ginori with his own faïence factory in Milan to form the Società Ceramica Richard-Ginori in 1896/7. The following year Galileo Chini founded 'Arte della Ceramica' in Florence. Unlike the majority of Italian concerns, where pieces in Renaissance style continued to be made, the two establishments sought to modernize their production. A few short-lived attempts at modernism took place elsewhere in Italy. The arrival in Albissola of Luigo Quaglino, a native of Turin, who was in partnership with the ceramist Niccoló Poggi in the very last years of the nineteenth century, resulted in the production of pieces strongly marked by Symbolist and pre-Raphaelite influence. The dissolution of the partnership in 1902 put an end to these creative efforts. At the end of the decade Art Nouveau came in at Sèvres. In 1897 Alexandre Sandier took over the artistic side and a generation of young painters changed the decorative style completely. Vessels now bore naturalistic motifs modelled in relief or vast smooth surfaces; some compositions featured stylized flora and fauna. The only reminder of the past was the characteristic Sèvres statuette in biscuit porcelain, small-scale versions of works purchased by the State at the salons or else specially devised works such as the centrepiece known as 'The Game of the Scarf' by Agathon Léonard, composed of fifteen figures, which achieved a huge success at the 1900 exhibition.

A number of small factories here and there adopted the new style. The stylistic revolution was complete in Holland where two types of production can be recognized. On one hand there were several factories in and around Gouda producing wares of simple shape, ornamented with stylized naturalistic motifs in a strong and sometimes sombre range of colours, similar to the creations of Th. Colenbrander. On the other hand there were the 'Amphora' and 'Distel' factories in Amsterdam, the 'Holland' in Utrecht and the 'Haga' at Purmerend which all worked in a similar idiom, since they shared a designer, Christian Johannes van der Hoef. Their pieces had slender restrained shapes, delicate linear geometricized patterns, most often obtained by a technique similar to that used for niello work.

Elsewhere the changeover was both less decisive and less homogeneous. In England Art Nouveau pieces were made by several factories, notably by Doulton's and at Pilkington's Lancastrian Pottery, but their production as a whole was not adapted to the new style. In Italy some concerns did join in the trend and architectural ceramics soon began to appear, the best being produced by Richard-Ginori and the 'Arte della Ceramica' factory. Richard-Ginori also produced services and vases decorated with female figures and other sculptural elements in biscuit porcelain. The 'Arte della Ceramica' concern displayed great imagination in its pre-Raphaelite patterns, which at first were floral but soon began to show the influence of the Vienna Secession movement. In France some factories working on their own or for Paris dealers created shapes and decorations characterized by their fluidity, their subdued tones, and their plant or animal motifs, such as the 'Water Lily' table service exhibited by Haviland in 1900.

In Germany the large long-established factories were slow to adopt the 'Jugendstil', unlike a number of small factories, where it was soon taken over, but in 1896 the designer Konrad Hentschel created for Meissen the 'Crocus' service, its shapes and decoration directly inspired by floral forms; however, the great majority of customers still preferred reproductions of earlier pieces. This adherence to the past aroused vigorous criticism, but it was only after the death of the senior designer, Emmerich Andresen, in 1902 and the retirement of the senior painter, Ludwig Sturm, in 1904 that a change could be brought about. Once again, this change emanated from outside designers, and took place in an episodic manner: Konrad and Rudolf Hentschel created several patterns between 1901 and 1904, one with a motif of wings and another with cyclamen flowers; around 1903-4 Henry van de Velde imbued several linear compositions with an elegance which corresponded perfectly with the nature of the porcelain body. He designed a tea service (1903) whose geometric forms were too original to gain general acceptance; and simultaneously Richard Riemerschmid also produced geometric patterns for Meissen.

The factory which adopted the 'Jugendstil' whole-heartedly was that of Berlin. Like Sèvres, it used a low temperature body and a range of ornamental coloured grounds, with *flambé* and crystalline glazes, the latter perfected about 1888 by Albert Heinecke. As at Sèvres, from the last years of the nineteenth century onward trinkets and small decorative objects had been produced here in great quantities. Their plain forms sometimes had large areas which could be embellished by decorators. Their rims or borders were occasionally enriched with relief ornamentation; and at other times they were overloaded with naturalistic motifs in relief, with the occasional human figure. Theodor Schmuz-Baudiss, who did not become artistic director until the departure of Alexander Kips in 1908, joined the establishment from 1902 and immediately introduced new fluid forms suited to the underglaze decoration that he favoured. These pieces are distinguished from Danish products by the intensity of their colouring, the severity of their composition and their technique, for the design was first incised and then the colours were sprayed on.

Finally, at Nymphenburg Hermann Gradl created (before 1900) the 'Modern' service, with seaweed and fish motifs, and in 1905 Adelbert Niemeyer came up with his delicate linear compositions. But the factory's main output was still coloured figures, either Joseph Wackerle's ladies in crinolines or Theodor Karner's stylized animals.

Some of the small factories which adopted the new style occasionally specialized in this sort of animal sculpture, as did the Heubach brothers at Lichte; others, such as Carl Thieme at Pottschappel, carried out research into *flambé* and crystalline glazes. At Selb Philip Rosenthal began to produce pieces in the modern style with underglaze decoration and in 1902 attempted to design pieces left 'in the white'. But most factories did not follow any well-defined policy, allowing this to develop according to the taste of whomever they currently employed. The production of the earliest pieces by Th. Schmuz-Baudiss resulted in an hour of glory for the factory of Swaine and Company of Hüttensteinach.

One may add that in Russia some examples from the Imperial Factory at St. Petersburg evince an interest in this style, which originated in the West.

Art Nouveau had thus spread rapidly throughout Europe and even reached the United States. But this momentum seems to have outrun all its strength and within a few years the movement became stricken with total paralysis. The first decade of the century saw both its triumph and its downfall. The speed of its decline derives perhaps from the fact that its greatest novelty had been its strong opposition to a past of which it was nevertheless the heir, however unwilling. Like other styles before it, its advocates had limited their thinking to the nature of the decorative motifs chosen and their relationship to the forms they were to go with. This is perhaps what Hermann Muthesius implied when he wrote in 1906: 'The contribution of the Latin people to the renewal of modern art is nothing more than a superficial game... They want gaiety in art and... when they create something new, think only of combinations of amusing lines'.

Genuine rupture with the past resulted in an awareness of the fundamental problems of the potter's art. Curiously enough, this break occurred in Vienna, where historicism had reigned supreme until the very last years of the century. The 'Jugendstil' was nothing more than a brief interlude, exemplified in ceramics by the vases and figures decorated in pale colours by the firms of Friedrich Goldscheider, Alexander Förster and Josef Böck. In contrast, the Vienna Secession, formed in 1899 around the painter Gustav Klimt, set about combating the 'Jugendstil' movement.

In the same year two members of the group, Josef Hoffmann and Koloman Moser, became teachers at the Kunstgewerbeschule where they ran a course covering many aspects of the arts. Its main emphasis followed the work of the 'Group of Four' formed in Glasgow around Charles Rennie Mackintosh: the structure of the design must be clearly discernible. In addition, according to Hoffmann, the students had to make it their aim to 'give to objects the most practical and functional form, while rendering it precious and original by good proportion and pleasing shapes, well suited to the medium'. The two major problems of art, the functional aspect of form and the necessity of adaptation to the material, were laid down at this time. Thirdly, Hoffmann's statement implies concern for qualitative norms: 'good proportions', 'attractiveness', 'originality'. The solution of the problem of choice between function and truth called for a pragmatic approach to ornamentation. As early as 1892 Louis Sullivan declared: 'Ornament is a luxury, not a necessity'. In 1899 Hoffmann and Moser had drawn up for Josef Böck designs of shapes which were to be left devoid of decoration; at the same time they were designing glass, metalwork and furniture. Some of their projects are elaborate and profusely ornamented; others are very simple, leaving the material in its natural state. In 1903 they founded the Wiener Werkstätte with themselves as artistic directors, and

Adam, Linke and Macht as technical directors. The purpose of this association was to produce and sell their pieces or those of their pupils. Until then this role had been played by Josef Böck who [104] had contacts with factories in Bohemia and Germany. We have seen that around 1902 Philip Rosenthal had attempted to make [57] and sell undecorated pieces, but economic necessity had forced him to give this up. The chaste patterns conceived approximately at this time by Joseph Maria Olbrich for the firm of Boch are a [61] perfect example of what one would today call 'minimal design'. Adolf Loos, another Secessionist, published his article 'Ornament and Crime' in 1908.

The quest for a new style found an echo in the products of Hugo Kirsch. His firm was founded in 1905 and made figures and vases whose geometric ornamentation emphasized their structure. It was even more strongly echoed by the Wiener Keramik workshop founded in 1905 by Michael Powolny, Berthold Löffler and [55] the sculptor Lang. They produced vases with linear patterns, animal sculptures and putti modelled by Powolny which were strongly coloured, with black predominant after 1911.

The influence of the Vienna Kunstgewerbeschule was enormous, for Moser and Powolny's students, when not themselves teaching, opened studios where they put into practice the new methods they had learned. At Langenzersdorf Eduard Klablena made figures with crackled glazes, Ernst Wahliss established himself at Turn (Trnovany) near Teplitz (Teplice) and won admir- [70] ation for his 'Serapis-Fayence' decorated in bold high-temperature colours, while at the same time (from 1912 with this title) the Vereinigte Wiener und Gmundner Werkstätte were showing their simple black and white wares.

It was in Prague that the most revolutionary designs were created, the work of the Artel group founded in 1908 in imitation of the Wiener Werkstätte. The shapes of its vases of simple struc- [68] ture were based on geometric elements such as the circle, pyramid and line. One might be tempted to call them Cubist, despite their violent opposition of colours—usually only two clashing ones were used—barely toned down by the ivory softness of the crackled white ground. They show a three-dimensional quality that the Cubist painters also tried to produce.

However original their ideas may have been, there remained one point which still tied the Viennese designers to the past. This was the small craft enterprises which they used to carry out their projects. One more step into the twentieth century had to be taken, and this was taken by the Deutscher Werkbund. Founded in 1907 around the architect H. Muthesius, it brought together architects, artists, craftsmen and industrial potters such as Richard Riemerschmid, Josef Hoffmann and Henry van de Velde. The [64, 67] Deutscher Werkbund sought to give new life to the applied arts and pleaded for an alliance of designers with industry, while reminding the latter to respect the actual nature of their materials. The first example of 'total design' was Peter Behrens's work for the AEG company after 1907. The members of the association [66] accepted that machines had to be used for the mass production of

(continued on p. 42)

52

52 **LICHTE** (Germany, Heubach Bros). *Great Crested Grebe,* before 1910. Porcelain. H. 12 cm. Kunstgewerbemuseum, Berlin (Staatliche Museen Preussischer Kulturbesitz); WA 89.
This factory, founded in 1822 in Thuringia, one of the major German ceramic-producing centres, passed into the hands of the Heubach brothers in 1840. It originally manufactured useful wares, and after 1876 began to make decorative objects such as painted plaques and vases; later, especially from *c.* 1900, it concentrated on sculpture: figures, especially animals, in biscuit or decorated with underglaze colours. The finest pieces are by the sculptors Paul Zeiler and Max Esser, who later worked for Meissen and Berlin.

53 **KARLSRUHE** (Germany, Grossherzogliche Majolika-Manifaktur). *Fruit Bowl,* 1908–10. Earthenware. H. 15 cm. Kunstgewerbemuseum, Cologne; E 4350.
Although the *Jugendstil* period saw the triumph of porcelain and the reappearance of stoneware in Europe, influenced by Japanese and national traditions, curiously enough, earthenware, although it had been used at the beginning of the ceramic revival, was largely neglected except in some Italian and German factories. One of these exceptions was the firm founded by the painter Wilhelm Süs in 1899, which then moved to Karlsruhe where Hans Thoma, the designer, was already established. The factory specialized in animal and human figures, either on their own or integrated with vessels, as here.

54 **BERLIN** (Germany, Königliche Porzellan-Manufaktur). *The Fiancée,* 1908–10. Porcelain. H. 40.5 cm. Schloss Charlottenburg, Berlin; WA 23.
The table centrepiece entitled 'The Marriage Procession' was created by Adolph Amberg for the marriage of the Crown Prince in 1905. It depicts representatives from all nations of the world assembled to offer their gifts to the betrothed couple, rendered respectively as a Roman cavalier and as Europa riding on the Bull. The set consists of twenty figures accompanied by ornamental pieces, candelabra, bowls and vases. Rejected by the court on the grounds that the figures were too scantily clad, the centrepiece was not purchased and issued until some time between 1908 and 1910.

55

55 **VIENNA** (Austria, Wiener Keramik). *Rearing Horse, c.* 1911–12. H. 26.2 cm. Österreichisches Museum für Angewandte Kunst, Vienna; W. I. 1128.
The Wiener Keramik, founded in 1905 by Berthold Löffler and Michael Powolny, who were joined by the sculptor Lang, merged in 1912 with the Gmunder Keramik, which was founded in 1884 and taken over by Franz Schleiss in 1909. The Wiener Keramik, most famous for its figures and decorative objects, produced some of the first ceramics decorated in strong colours and even gilt highlights. The decoration, combined with highly stylized geometric forms, was characteristic of the 'Austrian reaction'.

56 **WALTERS,** Carl (U.S.A., 1883–1955). *The Stallion,* 1921. Earthenware. H. 26.7 cm. Whitney Museum of Art, New York; 1883–1955.
After a promising start as a painter, Carl Walters took up ceramics after 1921. At first he made painted pottery, then specialized in sculpted works, mainly animal figures which, lacking any pretensions to realism, were quite clearly intended to be decorative. The museum acquired this work, which characteristically rejected the affectations of Art Nouveau, on the occasion of Walters's first public exhibition at the Whitney Studio Club in 1924.

56

57

58

59

57 **SELB** (Germany, Rosenthal AG). *'Donatello' Coffee Service,* c. 1905–10. Porcelain. H. of coffee-pot 18 cm. Kunstgewerbemuseum, Cologne; E 4071 a.-w.
In 1880 Philip Rosenthal founded a porcelain-painting studio at Erkersreuth, and then around 1890, with his brother Max, set up a factory at Selb, where many firms were already established. The firm, which became a limited company in 1897, initially only made services; later it produced decorative objects. This service, designed by Philip Rosenthal, was one of the first to be issued 'in the white', in deference to the radical theories which equated ornament with 'crime'. However, bowing to the reluctance of their customers to purchase the white service, several decorative schemes were adapted for it, such as the 'Alice' pattern shown here.

58 **SCHMUZ-BAUDISS,** Theodor-Hermann (Germany, 1859–1942). *Soup-tureen,* 1912–13. Porcelain. H. 26 cm. Kunstgewerbemuseum, Cologne; E 4159 a, b.
Theodor Schmuz-Baudiss was one of the first designers to work in a variety of materials. After a period spent in direct modelling and collaboration with Swaine & Co. at Hüttensteinach and with J. J. Scharvogel in Munich and Darmstadt, from 1902 he worked for the Berlin factory, of which he was artistic director from 1908 to 1925. Here he created such forms as this 'Ceres' service, produced with three different types of decoration.

59 **MANCHESTER** (England, Pilkington Tile & Pottery Co.). *Dish, c.* 1910. Earthenware. D. 48.2 cm. Victoria and Albert Museum, London; C. 32–1964.
This factory was established in 1891. Its art pottery department, which developed rapidly, concentrated on *flambé* and crystalline glazes and lustres. The painter and decorator Gordon Mitchell Forsyth, creator of this decorative scheme, was artistic director from 1906 to 1915; he had previously been art director of Minton, Hollins & Co. After 1908 decoration became more varied and, as a result of royal patronage, the firm's products were marketed under the name 'Royal Lancastrian'. The company closed down in 1938.

60

60 **MEISSEN** (Germany, Staatliche Porzellan-Manufaktur). *Soup Plate,* 1920. Porcelain. D. 25 cm. Bröhan Collection, Berlin.
In the same way as *Jugendstil* was adopted by Meissen in a tardy and half-hearted fashion, since the factory preferred to devote its major efforts to the reproduction of its former creations, the application of the new functional theories preached by the Bauhaus was rare, although Meissen did call on the services of the painter and architect Adelbert Niemeyer. The latter, who created the form and decoration of this plate, had helped to found the Deutscher Werkbund in 1907 and provided designs for a great number of ceramic companies; he worked in stoneware as well as porcelain.

61 **METTLACH** (Germany, Villeroy & Boch). *Water Jug and Wash Basin,* c. 1900. Stoneware. H. of jug 29.5 cm. Museum Bellerive, Zurich; 1974–29.
The company founded by François Boch in 1788, which became Villeroy and Boch during the 19th century, had by 1900 set up branches in several European countries. It produced a number of ceramic materials, including some of its own invention. Most of its wares were made by highly industrialized methods, although collaboration continued with designers capable of accepting the demands inherent in mass production. The designer here is Joseph Maria Olbrich, architect and co-founder of the Vienna Secession, which from the outset stressed the value of collaboration with industrial concerns, decried the use of unnecessary ornament and insisted on the absolute priority of structure and functionalism.

61

62 **FINCH,** Alfred William (Belgium–Finland, 1854–1930). *Cup, c.* 1900. Earthenware. H. 10 cm. Bethnal Green Museum, London; C 759–1966.
Having commenced his career as a painter and engraver, this Belgian of English origin, a pupil of Whistler, became part of the 'Groupe des Vingt' and introduced neo-Impressionism into Belgium. In order to earn his living, Finch became a decorator for Boch at La Louvière before opening his own studio in 1896. In the following year he took over as director of the Iris studios at Borgå (Porvoo) in Finland. He taught ceramics at Helsinki from 1902 to 1930, which earned him the name of 'father of Finnish ceramics'. He used incised and slip decoration on restrained, utilitarian forms, before eventually devoting himself entirely to high-temperature glazes.

63 **BROUWER,** Willem Coenrad (Netherlands, 1877–1933). *Coffee-pot,* 1905. Earthenware. H. 11.9 cm. Gemeentemuseum, The Hague; MC 35-zj.
After studying drawing and spending some time in J. A. Loeber's design studio (1894) and then at the Goedewaag pipe factory at Gouda, Brouwer opened a pottery studio at Leiderdorp in 1901, which was later to expand greatly. All the pieces made there, including architectural ceramics, were designed by him. They are distinguished by restrained forms and stylized decoration, often realized by the traditional process of incised slip, usually on a monochrome ground.

64 **RIEMERSCHMID,** Richard (Germany, 1868–1957). *Coffee-pot, c.* 1905. Stoneware. H. 22.2 cm. Hetjens-Museum, Düsseldorf; Sp. 228.
The architect and painter Richard Riemerschmid played a considerable role in the development of the decorative arts in Germany through his participation in many societies and his teaching, first at Nuremberg (1902–5) and then in Munich (1912–24). In the field of ceramics, he adapted his technique perfectly to the various materials, designing a service for Meissen (1903–4) with underglaze blue geometric decoration. He also created some wares of restrained form for the stoneware manufacturer Reinhold Merkelbach of Höhr-Grenzhausen. Their geometric or linear relief decoration was ideally suited to traditional techniques.

65

66

65 **MENDEZ DA COSTA,** Josef (Netherlands, 1863–1939). *Coffee-pot,* 1901. Salt-glazed stoneware. H. 18.5 cm. Gemeentemuseum, The Hague; MC 177-zj.
After studying sculpture and applied arts, Josef Mendez da Costa designed ceramic schemes for the Amsterdam shop Het Binnenhuis (1888–1902), while teaching at the same time. In 1912 he went to Laren, where he produced work that differed radically from that of his compatriots: first, he was the only Dutch potter to work in stoneware and, second, he specialized in animal and human figures, as well as making useful wares.

66 **BEHRENS,** Peter (Germany, 1868–1940). *Coffee-pot with Handle, c.* 1903. Salt-glazed stoneware. H. 25.9 cm. Badisches Landesmuseum, Karlsruhe; 70/46.
Peter Behrens was one of the most versatile German designers, since he designed typefaces, furniture, fabrics, book-bindings, glassware and silverware as well as ceramics for many factories. He was very influential by virtue of his teaching and founded many decorative arts societies. He was one of the first to work closely with industry, becoming artistic consultant to the Allgemeine Elektrische Gesellschaft combine in 1907.

objects, but they intended to preserve standards of quality. But within the movement itself opposition developed between Muthesius, who accepted standardization, and Van de Velde, who considered that it inhibited artistic creativity. This showed how complex working relationships between industry and artists were likely to be. The movement was very influential and instigated the formation of similar associations in Austria in 1910, in Switzerland in 1913 and in England in 1915.

As far as ceramic factories were concerned, two important traits marked the production of these years of reflection between 1905 and 1914. The more important of these was the amazing increase, particularly in Scandinavian and German factories, in the production of enamel-painted figures, mostly of animals. The modellers were Carl-Frederick Lijsberg at the Royal Danish Porcelain Company in Copenhagen, Waldemar Lindström of Rörstrand, Theodor Karner at Nymphenburg, and Paul Walther and Otto Pilz at Meissen. We also find human figures, often in contemporary dress and striking contemporary attitudes, modelled by Christian Thomsen in Copenhagen, Rudolf Marcuse and Paul Schley in Berlin, Joseph Wackerle at Nymphenburg, and Konrad Hentschel in Meissen. In a class apart are the allegorical figures by Paul Scheurich, who worked for Meissen and then for Berlin. Their Baroque feeling is quite foreign to the generally prevailing style. The most characteristic group made in this period is perhaps the monumental centrepiece commissioned in 1905 from Adolph 54 Amberg for the marriage of the Crown Prince. This was at first rejected as the figures were judged to be too scantily clad, but the first concern of Schmuz-Baudiss, when he took up his duties as artistic director in Berlin in 1908, was to put it into production. The predominance of sculpture at porcelain factories accounts for the works of the Grossherzogliche Majolika-Manufaktur, 53 founded at Karlsruhe in 1901, where among the decorative pieces were figure sculptures whose massive quality recalls those of Michael Powolny. The Sèvres factory was the sole exception. It did not reject its long sculptural tradition, but instead honoured it by re-issuing a large number of eighteenth-century models. Whatever new work was going on at Sèvres, the old traditions were kept up and the factory was now in the unique position of producing biscuit porcelain wares, predominantly of contemporary figures, as well as a few table centrepieces.

Another characteristic of the period was the appearance of a certain weariness with the languid Art Nouveau decoration. This was perhaps more strongly felt by those aware of Viennese works. The reaction manifested itself in a return to the decorative formulae of the past and a simultaneous adoption of heavier forms. This was particularly apparent in Berlin and at Sèvres. The immense 'Ceres' 58 service designed in 1912 by Schmuz-Baudiss for Berlin is the perfect counterpart to Lucien d'Eaubonne's creations for Sèvres in the massiveness of its forms and the stiffness of its floral decoration, which henceforth served simply to emphasize the shape. Decorative processes used in the past, and supposedly abandoned, such as transparent enamels or gilding, were to reappear at both enter-

(continued on p. 44)

67

67 **VAN DE VELDE,** Henry-Clemens (Belgium, 1863–1957). *Vase,* 1903–1904. Stoneware. H. 25.8 cm. Kestner Museum, Hanover; 1968, 11.
One of the most versatile personalities of the early part of this century, this architect was an interior designer, painter, graphic designer and teacher, who also produced designs for silver, glass-ware and ceramics. He endeavoured to respect the true nature of each medium, and the fluid arabesques of his porcelains are quite different to the restrained and powerful forms which he created for Reinhold Hanke at Höhr-Grenzhausen, whose aim it was to revive the German stoneware tradition.

68 **PRAGUE** (Czechoslovakia, Artěl). *Vase*, before 1914. H. 30.5 cm. Österreichisches Museum für angewandte Kunst, Vienna; W. I. 1482.

Founded in 1908 in imitation of the Wiener Werkstätte, Artěl set up its own production studios in 1919 and became the S.A.R.L. The society took part in the 1925 international *Exposition des Arts décoratifs* in Paris and was dissolved in 1935. This vase, designed by Vlastislav Hofman, was purchased by the museum in 1915. Its bold geometric structure and witty colour scheme demonstrate how artistically advanced the lands of the Austro-Hungarian Empire were at this time, when they were strongly influenced by the radicalism of the Vienna Secession.

69 **JANÁK,** Pavel (Czechoslovakia, 1882–1956). *Objects*, 1911. Earthenware. H. 9 cm.

After attending the Technical University of Prague, Janák studied architecture in Vienna under Otto Wagner, a member of the radical Secessionist movement. From 1921 to 1941 Janák taught architecture at the Prague Academy of Applied Arts, specializing in town planning and the restoration of historic monuments. These pieces were produced in the Rydl studio at Ton.

68

69

prises. The use of massive forms, emphasized by rearrangement of the decorative motifs, is evident on some Nymphenburg vases.

One can already detect signs of forthcoming independence. Some factories, foreseeing the dominating role that freelance potters were to play, resumed certain lines of research. In 1912 the Royal Copenhagen factory took on the potter Patrick Nordström, who, after reading the recipes of Carriès and of Sèvres, taught himself to make stoneware. The factory undertook mass production of this new material, for which Nordström perfected an exuberant series of glazes obtained by the use of several layers of colour. The production of stoneware was launched at the same time by Bing and Grøndahl. In another field the Manifattura Fornaci S. Lorenzo, owned by the Chini brothers, became fascinated with lustre glazes; so, too, did the Pilkington Company (which in 1913 received authorization to call itself Royal Lancastrian), which also investigated the decorative possibilities of incised slip. Another innovative step was Philip Rosenthal's opening in 1908 of an art department at the Selb factory, which he entrusted to the Dane Julius von Guldbransen of Copenhagen.

So far little mention has been made of Russia, but during the years of the revolution questions were raised which were only partly linked to the innovative ideas of the Deutscher Werkbund. The development of the plastic arts, which passed through Fauvism, Cubism and Futurism to the beginnings of Abstractionism, had repercussions in that country. In 1915 Kazimir Malevich published the *Suprematist Manifesto,* in which he affirmed his desire to free himself from objects so that feeling could be expressed. He stated that painting must abandon representationalism in order to express sensations directly by means of elementary geometric forms and pure colours. About the same time Vladimir Tatlin was creating abstract compositions from various materials and was building up his theory of Constructivism, based upon an analysis of the relationship between form, volume and space.

On the other hand, the revolution caused a rethinking of the social role and function of the artist, enshrined in slogans such as 'Art in Life' or 'Art in Production'. A new public was emerging, affected by the vast changes brought about by the destruction of the old order, which wanted an improvement of living conditions. After the first post-revolutionary years, during which the essential function of art in general and the decorative arts in particular had been to spread propaganda on behalf of the new ideas, it became obvious that people had to be trained to design and produce common domestic objects. The Vkhutemas, founded in 1920 towards this end, becoming the Vkhutein in 1927, owed much to V. Tatlin's Constructivist theories. These theories leaned towards rationality, and emphasized logical construction in design and the importance of function. Simplicity of form and ornamentation was recommended. Like the Bauhaus group, the Vkhutemas artists insisted on the necessity and manner of conceiving products intended for mass production, but this synchronization occurred in a country that was still without an industrial infrastructure.

In the field of ceramics the 1917 revolution led to nationalization of the former Imperial Factory, which in 1917 became the National Porcelain Factory of Petrograd and then, in 1925, the Lomonosov National Porcelain Factory of Leningrad. The only concern in the Soviet republic to produce porcelain, it found itself confronted with a completely new production programme, to make utilitarian objects available to all who could afford and appreciate them. Lacking all the usual machinery, the factory found the second of these aims difficult to achieve. But the porcelain made very quickly showed itself to be an efficient propaganda vehicle: slogans and emblems were freely used on tablewares and ornamental pieces and were confidently mixed with more traditional decoration. As for porcelain figures, Red guards, revolutionary sailors or women embroidering a banner replaced poetic representations of peasants. Moreover, at the request of the artistic director Nikolay Suetin, many artists, painters or sculptors designed objects such as K. Malevich's coffee-pot. Decoration schemes, often influenced by Suprematism, were devised by Vasiliy Kandinsky, Alexander Rodchenko and Ilya Chashnik.

The same spirit of purity, simplification and geometry, evident in early twentieth-century architecture, and in the Constructivist style, affected all those artists who were to express their views in the revue *De Stijl.* This was founded in 1917 by Piet Mondrian with the aid of J.J.P. Oud, Vantongerloo, Van Doesburg and Van der Leck. Their influence on the Bauhaus was to be felt at the same time as that of the Deutscher Werkbund. The Bauhaus was established in 1919 by Walter Gropius who, after succeeding H. van de Velde as director of the Kunstgewerbeschule founded in Weimar in 1906, merged it with the Weimar Art School. This institution experienced two distinct periods of activity and played a fundamental role all over the world in developing architecture and the decorative arts, since a number of its members were forced to leave their homeland when the Bauhaus was closed down by the Nazis in 1933, and propagated its theories in their work as well as their teaching. In its first so-called 'craft' period, which lasted until its removal to Dessau in 1925, the avowed aim of the institution, like that of the Deutscher Werkbund, was to unite art, crafts and industry to produce work of good quality *en masse* without sacrificing quality. In his manifesto of 1919 Gropius declared: 'Architects, sculptors and painters must all return to craftsmanship. For there is no such thing as a professional artist. There is no essential difference between the artist and the craftsman... The roots of the *métier* are... indispensable to each artist; they are the source of creation...' The students received a double training: a

(continued on p. 58)

70 **TURN near TEPLICE** (Czechoslovakia). *Vase,* date unknown. Earthenware. H. 22 cm. Bröhan Collection, Berlin.
The Amphora factory, founded in 1892, produced luxury porcelain in one of the important centres of 19th-century German ceramics. It received the Highest Award in Chicago in 1893. Soon afterwards the factory opened a terracotta studio which also produced earthenwares, often decorated in the *cloisonné* technique with strong colours on a matt ground. The shapes were generally simple but were often supplied with elaborate handles or ornamented with naturalistic motifs that were sometimes rather overdone. In 1900 the proprietors were Hans and Karl Riessner, Rudolf Kessel and Eduard Stellmacher.

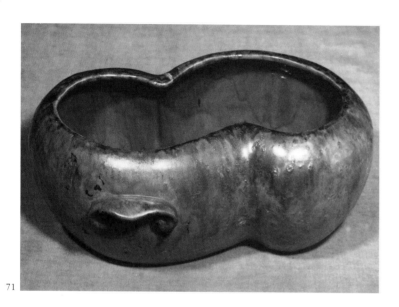

71

71 **JOHNOVA,** Helena (Czechoslovakia, 1884–1962). *Jardinière*, 1935. Earthenware. L. 37 cm.
Helena Johnova studied at the Academy of Applied Arts in Prague (1899–1909), then in Vienna (1909–11) with Michael Powolny and from 1919 to 1942 taught ceramics at the former institution. Her very varied work includes ceramic portraits, zoomorphic and floral sculpture and many pots, often of majestic proportions.

72 **SCHARVOGEL,** Johann Julius (Germany, 1854–1938). *Tankard,* c. 1900. Stoneware. H. 16.5 cm. Museum Bellerive, Zurich; 1970–17.
After working for Villeroy and Boch at Mettlach, Scharvogel went on to open a studio in Munich, where he was associated with such artists as Theodor Schmuz-Baudiss, the painter W. Magnussen and the graphic designer Paul Haustein. He created pieces , whose decoration in underglaze and *flambé* colours reveals Oriental influence, but he was also ever conscious of the demands of form. After directing the new factory at Darmstadt from 1906 to 1913, he returned to work permanently in Munich.

72

73 **BINNS,** Charles Fergus (England—U.S.A., 1857–1934). *Vase,* 1916. Stoneware. H. 26.5 cm. Detroit Institute of Arts, Detroit, Michigan (gift of Mr. George G. Booth).
Born in England, Binns was the son of the director of the Royal Worcester Porcelain Works. He studied chemistry in Birmingham and arrived in the United States in 1897 to take up the directorship of the Technical School of Sciences and Art at Trenton, and then of the New York College of Clay Working and Ceramics at Alfred University. He belonged to numerous artistic societies and became a missionary for the cause. He wrote many textbooks and was perhaps even more important as a teacher than as a creative artist.

74 **COPENHAGEN** (Denmark, Royal Danish Porcelain Factory). *Vase,* c. 1914–1916. Stoneware. H. 27.5 cm. Royal Danish Porcelain Factory Museum.
The success of stoneware at the *Exposition Universelle* of 1900 induced factories throughout Europe to attempt its manufacture. The first trials at Copenhagen were carried out by the chemist Waldemar Engelhardt and the artist Knud Kyhn around 1903–4, but full-scale production was only launched when Patrick Nordström joined the firm in 1912. He had studied the formulae devised by Carriès and by the staff at Sèvres and familiarized himself with the practical techniques. He created new effects by using glazes derived from local raw materials.

73

74

75 **BRADEN,** Norah (England, 1901–). *Bowl, c.* 1938. Stoneware. D. 23 cm. Victoria and Albert Museum, London; Circ. 304–1938.
After studying ceramics in London, Norah Braden was for a year a pupil of Bernard Leach at St. Ives. In 1928 she set up a studio with one of the master's other students, Katherine Pleydell-Bouverie, at Coleshill in Wiltshire, where they both experimented with glazes made from wood and plant ash. Norah Braden began to teach pottery at Brighton in 1936. She continued teaching after the War, but no longer produced her own pots. Little of her very limited output remains, as she destroyed much of it herself.

76 **PLEYDELL-BOUVERIE,** Katherine (England, 1895–). *Roc's Egg,* 1929–30. Stoneware. H. 25.5 cm. Victoria and Albert Museum, London; 236–1930.
After studying at the Central School of Arts and Crafts in London, Katherine Pleydell-Bouverie worked with Bernard Leach at St. Ives in 1924 before opening a pottery at Coleshill in Wiltshire. She was joined there from 1928 to 1936 by Norah Braden and they both conducted research into glazes made from wood and plant ash. In 1946 she moved to Kilmington Manor, also in Wiltshire.

75

77 **BURSLEM** (England, Royal Doulton). *Vase,* 1925. Porcelain. H. 18 cm. Victoria and Albert Museum, London; C. 66–1972.
During the 1920s and 1930s the firm of Doulton perfected a spectacular range of glazes inspired by Chinese pieces (called 'Song', 'Chang' and 'Chinese Jade', for example), alongside a more modest palette of monochrome glazes; at the same time the firm developed its production of decorated wares, calling on the services of both designers and artists. At this period a number of studio potters were also interested in coloured glazes.

78 **COWAN,** Guy R. (U.S.A., 1884–1957). *Ginger Jar,* 1917. Earthenware. H. 35.7 cm. Cowan Pottery Museum, Public Library, Rocky River, Ohio.
Born into a family of industrial potters, Cowan studied ceramics with Charles Fergus Binns (cf. Pl. 73) before establishing himself first at Cleveland, then in the suburb of Rocky River. He is particularly well known for his sculptural figures, which were produced by employees to his designs. The powerful structure of his piece, which has a glaze more typical of Chinese than of Japanese ceramics, shows that Cowan soon abandoned the Art Nouveau aesthetic.

76

77

78

79

80

81

79 **LIMOGES** (France, Haviland & Co.). *Tea-pot,* 1925. Porcelain. H. 11 cm. Haviland Factory, Limoges.
The various factories in the Limoges region had to adapt to changing taste and often called on the services of outside designers. The painter Jean Dufy (1888–1964) worked for Haviland from 1915, providing many decorative schemes of which the best known is the series of *Châteaux de France* of 1924 and *Pivoines,* shown here, of 1925. He also designed incrusted borders and figural decoration for vases.

80 **ALBISSOLA** (Italy, Manifattura Fenice). *Tea-pot, c.* 1922–5. Maiolica. H. 13 cm. Private collection.
This region, where a ceramic tradition had existed since the Renaissance, underwent a revival from the 1920s onward. Many old factories modernized their products. One of these was the Giuseppe Mazzotti factory. Mazzotti's son Tullio designed countless pieces before allying himself with the Futurist Marinetti. Others which were established at this time divided their output between wares inspired by early models and modern creations. The Fenice factory, founded in 1922 by Manlio Trucco, followed this course. Trucco, who had worked with Paul Poiret, designed stonewares and also decorated some pieces modelled on his premises by the sculptors Arturo Martini and Francesco Messina.

81 **ETRURIA** (England, Josiah Wedgwood & Sons). *Jug, c.* 1920. Earthenware. H. 17.8 cm. Victoria and Albert Museum, London; C. 711–1921.
The factory established at Etruria in Staffordshire in 1769 by Josiah Wedgwood was famous for its stoneware. Bone china was a later development. From 1902 new impetus was provided by the artistic director John E. Goodwin, who developed new forms, particularly for 'Queen's Ware'. He introduced some new decorative methods including matt and spattered (sponged) glazes or, as here, metallic lustres. He entrusted the ceramic decoration studio to Alfred and Louise Powell, who designed this pattern.

82 **HANLEY** (England, A. E. Gray & Co.). *Vase, c.* 1926–30. Earthenware. ▷
H. 34.2 cm. Victoria and Albert Museum, London; C. 193–1977.
As well as creating models and decorative schemes for her own production unit (cf. Pl. 89), and adapting the 'Jazz style' to mass production, using strongly geometric figurative patterns and lively colours, 'Susie' Cooper was working for various factories, supplying them with designs for shapes and decoration. A number of English firms endeavoured to introduce the new style; the most successful were those which employed good professional designers.

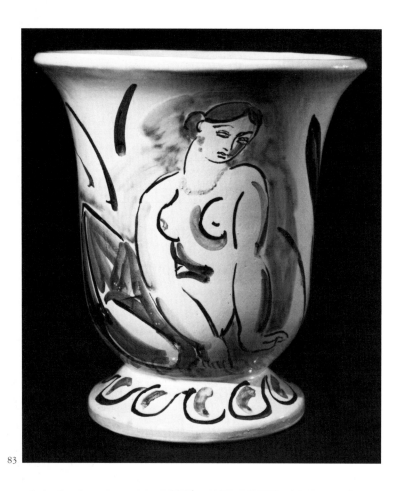

83 **GRANT**, Duncan (England, 1885–1978). *Vase, c.* 1937. Earthenware. H. 25.8. Victoria and Albert Museum, London; Circ. 389–1954.
Form 1913 to 1919 the designer Duncan Grant was one of the co-directors of the Omega Workshops, for which he designed textiles and ceramics. While continuing his painting career, he produced schemes for interior decoration, rugs and table services. This vase, made by Phyllis Keyes, demonstrates the influence of his painterly technique upon his decorative work.

84 **BUTHAUD**, René (France, 1886–). *Vase, c.* 1928. Stoneware. H. 39 cm. Musée des Arts décoratifs, Bordeaux; 78.3.7.
A former pupil of the Ecole des Beaux Arts in Bordeaux, Buthaud worked with ceramics from 1919. In 1923 he was appointed by the Primavera studio at the *Printemps* store to direct a modern ceramics factory near Tours. From 1928 to 1965 he exhibited faïence and earthenware pots at the Rouard gallery. Their simple forms left ample scope for the figurative decoration which he preferred. After 1940 most of his exhibits were figures.

83

85 **PONTI**, Gio (Italy, 1891–). *'Donatello' Dish,* 1924. Maiolica. D. 48 cm. Museo di Doccia, Sesto Fiorentino; 7037/27.
The architect Gio Ponti demonstrated his interest in design by founding the influential review *Domus* in 1928. From 1923 he had worked in association with the Richard-Ginori company, principally creating figural decorative schemes that the factories later adapted by varying the colours and scale of the designs, or by freely combining his designs with purely ornamental motifs. This dish is part of a series, with the theme *'Le mie donne'*.

86 **LIMOGES** (France, Haviland & Co.). *Plate, c.* 1925. Porcelain. D. 25 cm. Manufacture Haviland, Limoges.
Suzanne Lalique, daughter of the glass artist René Lalique, designed textiles, wallpaper and screens and also produced some strongly geometric designs for plates made at Sèvres. She married Paul Haviland and worked for William Haviland from 1925 to 1931, creating a great many decorative schemes, including one entitled *Paquerette*. At the same period Jean Dufy, brother of Raoul, also produced some fine decorative designs for the Haviland factory.

87 **BURSLEM** (England, Arthur J. Wilkinson & Co.). *Plate,* 1934. Earthenware. D. 27.5 cm. Victoria and Albert Museum, London; C. 168–1972.
Between 1916 and 1920 the artistic director of the Wilkinson factory was Clarice Cliff. She herself designed the range known as 'Bizarre ware', and was also responsible for commissioning artists from outside the factory. Generally she sent out the blanks for decoration. The painter Laura Knight actually designed both shapes and decoration for the 'Circus' service. Later she also designed ceramics and glass for Wedgwood.

88 **PARIS** (France, Jean Luce). *Plate,* 1925. Porcelain. D. 25 cm. Musée des Arts décoratifs, Paris; 25,011.
The 1920s saw the arrival of a large group of dealers who either designed or marketed goods for interior decoration such as glassware, silver, table services and so on. In the wake of pioneers such as Bing in Paris, studios sprang up in department stores and dealers such as Georges Rouard or Jean Luce adopted the geometric style which triumphed at the 'Arts décoratifs' exhibition held in 1925.

84

85

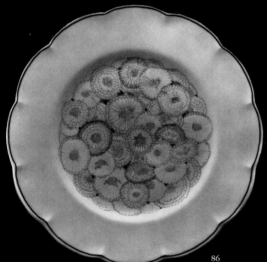

86

87

88

89

89

90

54

91

92

89 **BURSLEM** (England, Susie Cooper Pottery). *'Kestrel' Service, c.*1935. Earthenware. D. of vegetable dish 20.6 cm. Victoria and Albert Museum, London; Circ. 143 & A (vegetable dish), Circ. 145 & A (soup-bowl).
Susan Vera Cooper began her career in ceramics as a decorator before opening her own studio, rented from Doulton & Company. She bought pieces 'in the white', frequently made to her own designs, and decorated them initially by hand and later by lithographic transfer. This decorative scheme is of a later date than the form. With Eric Slater, Susie Cooper was one of the few to transpose the 'Jazz style' tastefully to industrial production. She has worked for various chain-stores and official organizations. Her production unit, though largely autonomous, is now part of the Wedgwood group.

90 **BURSLEM** (England, Royal Doulton). *Tea Service,* decorated *c.*1928. Earthenware. H. of tea-pot 16.5 cm. Victoria and Albert Museum, London; Circ. 748/55–1968.
The firm of Doulton, which became industrialized early in the 19th century and produced sanitary and everyday wares, was one of the first to open an art department in liaison with the local art school and to encourage collaboration with artists from outside. This decorative scheme is the work of Frank Brangwyn, the well-known painter, who began his career as a designer by working for William Morris. The service is characteristic of the revival of painted art pottery and stoneware that occurred even in industrial concerns during the 1930s.

91 **OHR,** George E. (U.S.A., 1857–1918). *Tea- and Coffee-pot,* after 1900. Earthenware. H. 18.7 cm. National Museum of American History, Smithsonian Institution, Washington, D.C.
George Ohr, who worked at Biloxi in Mississippi, was the first American studio potter. As a precursor of later developments he was misunderstood by his contemporaries. His free and skilful handling of vigorous forms, as well as his way of ridiculing utilitarianism and introducing a dreamlike quality into his work, anticipated many future artistic trends.

92 **VIENNA** (Austria, Augarten). *Tea Service, c.*1925. Porcelain. H. of tea-pot 14.2 cm. Kunstgewerbemuseum, Cologne; Ov. 101 a–h.
The establishment founded in 1717 by Claudius du Paquier, which closed in 1864, is the best known Viennese factory, but a great number of other concerns, particularly decorating workshops, opened there at the end of the 19th century. They were soon profoundly influenced by the Secessionists Koloman Moser and Josef Hoffmann, who both taught at the Kunstgewerbeschule and were ardent adherents of 'undecorated form'. This service with 'grotesque' decoration, designed for the firm of Augarten which was founded by Franz von Zülow in 1922, shows how the traditional Viennese style survived.

93

94

93 MAYODON, Jean (France, 1883–1967). *Bowl,* 1943. Stoneware. D. 21.5 cm. Musée national de céramique, Sèvres; MNCS 20,816.
From his training as a painter Mayodon retained his characteristic taste for figurative decoration on ceramics, in which he first showed an interest around 1912. He produced pottery with painted or modelled decoration and small decorative objects as well as monumental works (sculpture, chimney-pieces and fountains). In 1941–2 he was artistic director of the Sèvres factory, for which he created several vase shapes.

94 CECCARONI, Rodolfo (Italy, 1888–   ). *Little Bowl,* 1933. Terracotta. D. 19.4 cm. G. Ribe Collection, Recanati.
After gaining his diploma at Camerino Technical College, Ceccaroni began his art training in Rome in 1909. He also took courses at night-school in drawing, and then in interior decoration and restoration. He became assistant lecturer at the Istituto Leonardo da Vinci and then professor at the Grottaglia and Sesto Fiorentino ceramic schools, while visiting as many ceramic establishments as possible. In 1917 he constructed his first wood-fired kiln. He still approaches his work in the spirit of a craftsman when choosing clay, mixing colours and carrying out decoration. Renewing the figurative tradition of Italian ceramics, he has managed to depict the customs and flavour of his native land as well as to represent religious scenes in a style that respects its historic legacy, yet is modern.

95

95 NONNI, Francesco (Italy, 1885–1976). *Figurine,* 1927. Maiolica. H. 7 cm. Museo internazionale delle Ceramiche, Faenza.
Having studied cabinet-making, wood-carving and drawing, in 1915 Nonni began to teach sculpture at Faenza, and then xylography in Rome. His interest in ceramics goes back to 1919 when he provided designs for Pietro Melandri, but he was most active in this field in the 1920s and again after the Second World War. He created a great many lively coloured figures of contemporary or theatrical personalities. Their immediate success explains the countless copies which were soon made. Xylography, painting and sculpture are the key to his career.

96 GOLIA, working name of Eugenio **COLMO** (Italy, 1885–   ). *Dish,* 1924. Porcelain. D. 42 cm. Madame E. Mozo Collection, Turin.
Golia very soon revealed his talents as a caricaturist and founded the review *Numero* in 1914. Ceramics was his hobby and between 1922 and 1935 he decorated more than fifteen hundred pieces of porcelain which he purchased 'in the white'. He produced several types of decoration including elaborate traceries of flowers and leaves, filled with birds and animals, closely related to his textile designs, a fabulous bestiary of oriental inspiration filled with the peacocks, parrots and monkeys so popular at this period, as well as figures of *bayadères* recalling the Russian ballet, Spanish dancers, ladies in crinolines and saucy girls. His work is typical of the decorative aspect of the Art Deco style, both in its strong colours and in its choice of themes.

craftsman taught them to know the 'tricks of the trade', and an artist taught them design and the theory of form. In 1925 the school was transferred to the building at Dessau designed by Gropius. He left the establishment in 1928. In 1932 the Bauhaus had to move to Berlin, where the Nazis put an end to it the following year under the pretext of its alleged 'Bolshevism'.

From 1923, in the so-called 'industrial' period, the teaching followed a new direction: henceforth men were to be trained to design, in close liaison with industry, objects that were both functional and aesthetically rewarding. This stage corresponded with a training programme which emphasized the practical side. The students drew up designs which were put into production by industry at the same time as they experimented with new forms and techniques. Ceramics were taught at the Bauhaus by Gerhard Marcks, before a studio was opened at Dornburg in 1920 under the direction of Theodor Bogler and Otto Lindig. It lasted until 1930. Here pieces were made which were perfectly adapted to their function, which was further emphasized by simple forms. In this way the functionalism of the Bauhaus and the Werkbund easily gained ground in Germany, where the war had allowed only those factories that were sufficiently industrialized and well organized on business lines to survive.

In France the situation of the decorative arts and their development in the period between the two world wars were much more complex. On one hand, there was a revival of craftsmanship around Emile-Jacques Ruhlmann. Artists, designers and craftsmen worked in precious materials for a luxury market encouraged by a bourgeoisie that wished to be dazzled in order to forget the horrors of the war and the troubles of the time: inflation, the rise of Fascism and the economic crisis. The 1925 Exhibition des Arts Décoratifs et Industriels was a triumph for this sort of art. Forms were simplified and geometric in outline, without becoming functional, and decoration was consistently based upon stylized floral and animal motifs. The sinuous arabesque had given way to geometric simplification, which might be said to reveal Cubist influence. Faced with traditionalist tendencies, a new school had been attempting to make its voice heard. Emphasizing the social importance of art, it felt the necessity of producing objects accessible to all, which involved industrialization and the manufacture of simple, austere and functional shapes. Francis Jourdain, a forerunner of this movement, had been exhibiting furniture suitable for mass production since 1902, and founded the Ateliers Modernes in 1912 in order to make suites of furniture available to the general public. The journal *L'Esprit Nouveau,* founded in 1920 by Le Corbusier and Ozenfant, expressed similar ideas but was even more radical in approach. As a result their pavilion at the 1925 Exhibition was greeted with absolute incomprehension. Other followers of Functionalism, such as René Herbst, Robert Mallet-Stevens and Pierre Chareau, whose work was rejected by protagonists of the dominant 'decorative' movement, united in 1930 to form the Union des Artistes Modernes, declaring: 'Modern art is truly an art of the people, a pure art available to all...' These men worked in a spirit akin to that of the Bauhaus.

Similar social preoccupations arose in England, where in 1934 the Prince of Wales himself exhorted architects to 'design and work for the great majority instead of attending to the needs of a minority'.

In the ceramic factories there was obvious uncertainty as to what measures to adopt at the moment when their creative role was being strongly questioned by the increasing importance of independent potters. Some factories had already thought it opportune to resume independent research, since they feared that otherwise they might be eclipsed by such potters. The Royal Copenhagen Porcelain Factory continued its research into glazes and began to produce a phosphatic porcelain known as 'ironstone porcelain', as well as earthenware from 1924, while maintaining production of stoneware vases decorated by Jais Nielsen and the more traditional figures. Wilhelm Kåge, who joined the factory at Gustavsberg in 1917, perfected his inlaid silver on a green ground (Argenta), a particularly translucent porcelain body (Cintra) and a copper glaze (Farsta), and designed forms of remarkable sobriety. In the same way, in England, the Burslem subsidiary of Doulton's factory, under the artistic direction of Charles J. Noke (assisted after 1900 by Cuthbert Bailey), perfected a series of new bodies and rich glazes called 'Flambé', 'Song' and 'Chang', names which clearly affirm their Chinese ancestry. The same attention to glazes and firing was evident at the Shelley Potteries, as well as in the Carter, Stabler and Adams (at Poole) and Pilkington factories. Aiming to rival the studio potters, industrial companies such as the Denby Pottery and Doulton started to make stoneware with monochrome glazes, sometimes simply adopting traditional forms restored to favour at that time by Michael Cardew, or creating sophisticated shapes similar to Scandinavian work, whose fame was beginning to spread. Among these original pieces were some designed for Doulton by Vera Huggins in the 1930s and by Doris Johnson.

Ceramic work was imbued with fresh vitality as a result of modifying volume, outlines and surfaces for purely decorative purposes, as distinct from functional ones. In Germany geometric patterns were designed in the 1920s by Adelbert Niemeyer for the Karlsruhe factory, directed after 1920 by Max Laeuger, and for the factory at Meissen. But it was in France that the new movement triumphed. The Sèvres factory brought its production up to date with the help of contemporary interior designers and artists. Architects such as Henri Patou and Eric Bagge and interior designers such as E.-J. Ruhlmann created forms based upon geometric figures; decorations which included the human figure, long barred as a subject, were highly stylized and arranged in a more logical manner than before; and polychrome enamelled sculpture made its appearance in the form of statuettes or decorative panels. Similarly, at Limoges William Haviland produced pieces with pure outlines and used the long-neglected celadon ground; he called on Jean Dufy and Suzanne Lalique to decorate pieces and on Maurice-Edouard Sandoz to model animal figures. Paris dealers such as Georges Rouard and Jean Luce designed, issued and dis-

(continued on p. 60)

97 LENINGRAD (Petrograd) (U.S.S.R., State Porcelain Factory). *Suprematist Ink-stand,* 1922–3. Porcelain. H. 12 cm. Kunstgewerbemuseum, Cologne; Ov. 89 a, b.

The former Imperial Factory, founded at St. Petersburg by Peter I, was nationalized in 1917, initially under the name of the Petrograd State Porcelain Factory (1917–24). An entirely new work force was brought in and attempted to produce forms and decoration that were based on the functionalist theories of the Bauhaus, the Vkhutemas and the Constructivists. The iconographic vocabulary is based principally on revolutionary symbols, occasionally combined with traditional motifs, but the influence of avant-garde pictorial theories is noticeable on some pieces.

98 CHASHNIK, Ilya (Russia/U.S.S.R., 1902–29). *Soup-tureen,* 1924. Porcelain. Galerie Jean Chauvelin, Paris.

After studying under Malevich at the Vitebsk Institute of Plastic Arts, Chashnik took part in 1919 in the foundation of the UNOVIS (Declaration and Foundation of the New Art), of which this tureen bears the mark. In 1922 he worked with Suetin at the Lomonosov factory, providing decorative schemes that were strongly influenced by the Suprematist theories of his teacher.

97

98

tributed typical works in the Art Deco style, as did the *ateliers* opened by the large department stores.

In the same way in England the big companies occasionally showed the same desire for change, despite their tendency to carry on with their old lines, which they modernized by means of a simple alteration in the glazes. Sometimes their innovations were backward-looking, like the 'Fairyland Lustre' of Daisy Makeig-Jones for Wedgwood, which enjoyed enormous success even though metallic lustres were now out of fashion. More contemporary accents can also be discerned, in Eric Ravilious's decorative schemes as well as in the pared-down shapes conceived by the architect Keith Murray, both of whom worked for Wedgwood. After the Paris Exhibition of 1925 the Modern Jazz style spread. This then gave way to the lively patterns conceived by Eric Slater 82, 89 for the Shelley Potteries and by Susie Cooper in her Burslem studio. Just as in France, artists were associated with certain industrial concerns. Thomas A. Fennemore was employed by E. Brain 83 and Co.; Clarice Cliff obtained the services of painters like Duncan 87 Grant or Laura Knight for A. J. Wilkinson's factory; and Knight designed the forms of her 'Circus' service instead of simply decorating pieces in current production as was the usual practice.

85, 126 In Italy the architect Gio Ponti, who founded the important journal *Domus* in 1928, worked for the firm of Richard-Ginori, allowing it complete freedom in the use of his design projects. These were altered in both format and colouring, and they were even cut up and the pieces fitted together in combinations unforeseen by the artist. The Art Deco style also penetrated centres of traditional ceramics, one of the most typical being that of Albissola in Liguria. The founders of the Casa del'Arte appointed Manlio Trucco as artistic director in 1921. After extensive travels through Europe and the Americas he collaborated with Paul Poiret in designing textiles for the 'Martine' studio. He immediately introduced the new decorative style exemplified in his repertoire of motifs, with their strong colouring and geometric composition. In 1922 Trucco went into partnership with the painter 80 Geranzani and founded the new Fenice studio. Their work was soon imitated by all the local factories: those of Dario Ravano, of Giuseppe Mazzotti (whose son Tullio designed most of its work), and of Bartolomeo Rossi. This was a former pipe factory; Rossi applied the new vocabulary mainly to sweetmeat dishes in the form of Easter eggs or little bells. Albissola played an important role in the history of modern ceramics because collaboration with artists was encouraged there at a very early stage. The painters Orlando Grosso and Pietro Dodero supplied decorative schemes, and the sculptors Francesco Messina and Arturo Martini modelled freely-conceived figures which were then painted by Manlio Trucco.

These decorative inventions had a tendency to burn themselves out quickly. In the case of Art Deco the style became progressively less and less well defined; the human figure and perspective reappeared, while the rule that decoration should be subordinated to form was gradually forgotten. At the same time one can find evidence of research into functional and disciplined forms: at Gus-

tavsberg under the influence of Wilhelm Kåge, artistic director 105 from 1917 to 1949, the creator of the standardized and stackable 'Praktika' service (1933); at the Bing and Grøndahl factory, which enjoyed the services of Ebbe Sadolin; and in Berlin, where stylistic development was under the direction of Günther Freiherr von Pechmann. In 1927 Marguerite Friedländer-Wildenhain, a former Bauhaus student, designed the 'Halle' service, with its massive forms, for the Berlin factory, and in 1930-2 Trude Petri created the 'Urbino' service, followed in 1938 by the 'Arcadian' 107 tea service; these works were characterized by their elegant form, which was perfectly suited to mechanically-produced porcelain.

In fact most of the characteristics of the period after the Second World War had appeared before the conflict broke out, so that the disruption created by the war and its material and economic consequences did more to accelerate current transformations than to inspire new ones. Yet they also led to the total abandonment of a decorative style that was already breathing its last.

Major changes resulted from the introduction of a new technology that progressively infiltrated all the stages of the manufacturing process. We have already remarked on the progress in this direction since 1900, and the movement towards modernization had, if anything, now expanded: tunnel-kilns and continuous tunnel ovens, heated by fuel oil, were now in general use. Henceforth mechanization would affect every operation, the fashioning process being undertaken by powerful, fast jollying machines complete with dryers, and decoration almost universally printed, using a lithographic or silk-screen process. The latest innovation is the installation of equipment making possible the application and firing of underglaze patterns which are unique in that they are dish-washer-resistant.

In order to fight competition by making a rapid changeover to the new machines, firms found themselves involved in heavy investments. These financial obligations only accelerated, once

(continued on p. 62)

99 **KANDINSKY,** Vasiliy (Wassily) (Russia–France, 1866–1944). *Cup and Saucer.* Porcelain. H. 5.6 cm. Private collection.
After living in western Europe from 1896 onwards, in 1914 Kandinsky returned to Moscow where he taught at the Academy of Fine Arts and founded the Academy of Artistic Sciences in 1921. In 1922 he returned to Germany to take up a teaching post at the Bauhaus at Weimar, where Klee was already teaching, and in 1933 settled at Neuilly-sur-Seine. The model for these pieces was created for the Leningrad factory in 1922. An original version is in the collection of the Centre Georges Pompidou. In 1972 Karl Flinker issued a limited edition of 190 examples for the Haviland Studio, using the chromolithographic process in thirteen colours.

100 **VAN DER LECK,** Bart Anthony (Netherlands, 1876–1958). *Plates,* 1939. Earthenware. D. 30 cm. Rijksmuseum Kröller-Müller, Otterlo.
The painter Van Der Leck joined the *De Stijl* group in 1917, after meeting P. Mondrian and T. Van Doesberg, but left it in 1919. His primary training at the School of Decorative Arts perhaps explains why he became interested, as well as in painting, in everything capable of transforming the environment: he designed tapestries and murals, and also concerned himself with advertising, typography and industrial design. In the 1930s he began to work with ceramics, designing vases, plates and tiles, using the same primary colours that he employed in his paintings. These pieces are unique examples of his work.

99

100

again, a process that had begun in the nineteenth century: the progressive combination of firms into large groups with a diversified output such as the Società Richard-Ginori in Italy, Doulton and Wedgwood in England, Rosenthal and Lorenz Hutschenreuther in Germany, Upsala-Ekeby and the Swedish Co-operative Union and Wholesale Society in Scandinavia. These companies often have one or more art pottery departments working in varied materials and different styles, as well as departments making sanitary or insulator products alongside heterogeneous materials such as plastic or glassware.

The last characteristic feature of the industry today is that the spirit of intensive competition, which forces factories to adapt rapidly to the development of techniques and taste, also obliges them to compete in dreaming up new commercial themes and searching for new outlets and a new clientèle. This is the reason why Scandinavian and German companies launched the fashion for Christmas plates. The emergence of collectors of commemorative wares stimulated the manufacture of pieces intended as reminders of special events, such as a country joining the Common Market or a princely marriage. The reasons which led to the development of architectural ceramics at the turn of the century have in our own day, the age of prefabricated materials, resulted in numerous mural panels integrated into architectural schemes, in both public and private buildings.

The factories' main way of reaching the majority of the general public clearly depends on the aesthetic and practical quality of their production. Nevertheless an establishment's image depends to a large extent on the interest it takes in pure artistic creativity, even if this relates only marginally to the factory's overall production. This interest can be shown in different ways. Factories sometimes call on the services of designers trained in various techniques. They may open studios for research, which may be applied to current production, or may collaborate with potters or artists.

This is not the first time that we have come across 'designers'. The awareness, first felt towards the end of the nineteenth century, of the necessity to establish and respect the principles of decoration best suited to forms and materials, encouraged a new profession. As early representatives of these 'new men' one can point to such multi-talented decorators as Eugène Grasset or, in England, Christopher Dresser, who from 1879 designed shapes and decoration for the Linthorpe Pottery.

From the time when architecture, including interior as well as exterior design, was seen as an ensemble in which all elements must harmonize, it became normal practice to entrust one man with the design of each of these elements. Logically, architects dominated this first stage in the setting up of this new profession. 67 The most famous of all was Henry van de Velde, who, apart from designing furniture, fabrics, dress ornaments and embroidery motifs, also created ceramics. In stoneware he undertook schemes in 1903 for everyday wares and vases for the Bürgeler Töpfereien and in 1905 for Reinhold Hanke at Höhr-Grenzhausen; in 1908 and 1909 he was at the Kunstgewerbeschule at Weimar. In porcelain he designed decoration for Meissen in 1905 or thereabouts,

around 1908 for the porcelain factory at Burgau near Jena and for Bing and Grøndahl, and in 1933 a service intended for the Belgian railways for the Baudour factory. There were many such creatively-minded artists at this period. In Belgium the goldsmith Philippe Wolfers designed ceramics made in the Guérin stoneware pottery. In England the painter Frank Brangwyn worked for several factories. In France Samuel Bing secured the services of Georges de Feure and Edouard Colonna, and Julius Meier-Graefe those of Maurice Dufrêne. 90 20, 39 12

In Germany the painter and architect Richard Riemerschmid, 64 who was responsible for the interior decoration of the Munich Opera House in 1901, designed furniture and worked for Reinhold Merkelbach at Höhr-Grenzhausen; in 1903–4 he designed patterns for Meissen which could be manufactured at the lowest cost. Adelbert Niemeyer worked for all the largest factories. But 60 the most important development occurred when Peter Behrens, 66 painter, graphic artist and architect, one of the founders of the Deutscher Werkbund in 1907, became in that same year artistic consultant for the A E G combine, for whom he designed all their projects: buildings, fittings, products and packaging. From then on the new profession of designer was linked with industry, a trend further accentuated by the teaching of the Bauhaus and then its diffusion across the world.

In the field of ceramics the root of the problem was whether having recourse to the designer could benefit the industry. For the restrictions imposed by a material which had to undergo the hazardous process of firing are crucial and are often unforeseen by a trained designer who is a complete stranger to this particular medium. Thus a certain amount of specialization was inevitable.

It would be tedious to list here the names of all those designers who dedicated their activity wholly or mainly to ceramics. Among the best known are Heinrich Löffelhardt, who created the 'Arzberg 2075' service in 1963 for the factory of that name, and the 123 Finn Tapio Wirkkala, designer of ornaments and numerous services for Rosenthal, including 'Variations', 'Polygon' and 'Century'. The use of such designers is comparatively rare in France, where the small number of factories has prevented the emergence of specialists; this undoubtedly is explained by the existence of an unadventurous public with a taste for the traditional. The first attempt to employ a non-specialist designer was in 1966–7, when the 'Aries' service was designed by the Paris office of one of the 125 pioneers of the profession, Raymond Loewy, who on this occasion was to discover that his slogan 'The ugly will not sell' was quite accurate, while the counter-claim 'Beauty will sell well' does not always hold.

Another possibility for the factories was to open a studio where potters could carry out artistic research. Since the end of the nineteenth century we have seen several such initiatives. This type of studio is nowadays found mainly in Scandinavian establishments. In most cases the group of researchers has a double objective: they are undoubtedly expected to produce a large amount of original work, but also to help the factory staff produce new forms

(continued on p. 64)

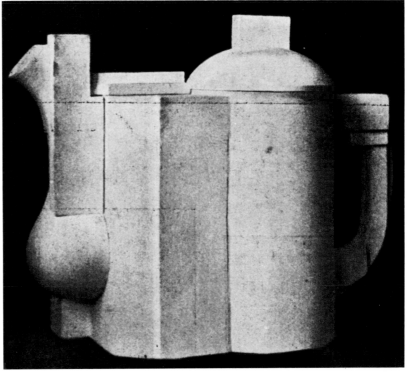

101   101

101 MALEVICH, Kazimir (Russia/U.S.S.R., 1878–1935). *Coffee-pot and Coffee-cup,* 1922. Porcelain. H. of coffee-pot 16.5 cm. Lomonosov National Factory Museum, Leningrad.

A pioneer of abstract art with Kandinsky and Mondrian, Malevich attended the Kiev Academy in 1895 and went to Moscow at the beginning of the century. He is known to have seen the paintings of Picasso and Braque before 1914. In 1915 he published the Suprematist Manifesto, painting his *Black Square on White Ground* and then his *White Square on White Ground.* At the end of his life, unable to paint as he wished, he executed decorative schemes and became involved in architecture. This design was used by the former Imperial Porcelain Factory, which had been nationalized in 1917.

102 BOGLER, Theodor (Germany, 1897–1968). *Tea-pot,* 1924. Stoneware. H. 12.5 cm. Kunstgewerbemuseum, Berlin (Staatliche Museen Preussischer Kulturbesitz); 1970, 28.

After studying architecture and history of art at the Bauhaus, Bogler became commercial director of the ceramic studio which the Bauhaus opened at Dornburg. In 1925–6 he directed the workshop, producing models and shapes at the Velten-Vordamm stoneware factory. He was subsequently in charge of the print-works and art workshops at Maria Laach Abbey from 1927, while continuing to design forms for the Staatliche Majolika-Manufaktur at Karlsruhe and for various factories at Höhr-Grenzhausen. This tea-pot was made by the Bauhaus studio.

102

and patterns in order to broaden the range of current output. This is the case at the Royal Copenhagen factory, where in 1970 Anne-Marie Trolle designed the 'Domino' service. In 1975, on the occasion of the factory's anniversary, Gertrud Vasegaard created the 'Capella' service, whereas the only reminders of the work of Axel Salto in the 1950s are some bold single pieces. Similarly, the Gustavsberg studio, opened in 1942, witnessed the decorative creations of the artistic director Stig Lindberg, as well as the research into glazes carried out by Berndt Friberg, who was first employed around 1935 as an assistant thrower to Wilhelm Kåge; another such work was the 'Vardag' service, conceived by Karin Björnquist about 1950. A workshop of this type existed at Rörstrand until this factory was taken over by the Upsala-Ekeby group. Here stoneware and sculptures were made by Carl-Harry Stalhane, who also designed services for restaurants and large ceramic wall decorations. In the 1950s a 'Moka' service was created here by Hertha Bengston, who now works with the German factories of Thomas and Rosenthal. Marianne Westmann also worked at Rörstrand.

These studios are sometimes completely cut off from current production: for instance, the studio of the Arabia factory, opened in 1932 by the artistic director Kurt Ekholm, gradually tended to produce nothing but original works not intended for mass production. Since it brought the Russian sculptor Michael Schilkin under its roof in 1936, the studio has included among its creative personnel Toini Muona, then Peter Winquist and today it employs Rut Bryk and Francesca Lindh-Mascitti.

As well as these permanent studios, which could seem a rather expensive item in the factory's budget, as it is easier to justify a salary in the accounts than to estimate the prestige conferred by well-known names, factories are able from time to time to call on the temporary services of outsiders, including potters. In this way in the 1950s the Gustavsberg factory called in Anders Liljefors, who used his original sand-casting technique there. In 1963 Karl and Ursula Scheid were approached by the firm of Lorenz Hutschenreuther at Selb to make their porcelain decorated with underglaze relief. Wedgwood welcomed the research of the potter Jacqueline Poncelet and the sculptor-ceramist Glenys Barton, who worked in commercial-quality bone china. Some of her work contrasts white biscuit china with the same material decorated by lithographic transfer, and made possible the commercial production of almost ethereal work. In France the Sèvres factory opened its workshops to the American Fance Franck and the Canadian Louis Gosselin. The former designed and decorated herself several series of pots and *jardinières* and a goblet with engraved decoration under a celadon glaze for current production. The latter made a relief pattern with decoration recalling the traces left by the sea upon sand. Used first on a bowl, this pattern was also employed to decorate a series of boxes and vases with irregular sides. Gosselin is presently studying vase forms inspired by little spiral-shaped shells. In 1979 the directors of the Rosenthal Studio-Linie commissioned the Scheid husband-and-wife team to develop the finest formula of stoneware possible and also to produce a range of glazes suitable for industrial production.

The last possibility open to pottery and porcelain factories, at once the more prestigious and most risky, was to collaborate with famous artists who, in general, had never worked with ceramics. This kind of partnership had great precedents: Boucher, Falconet and Jean-Jacques Lagrenée the Younger had worked for Sèvres in the eighteenth century, as had Jean-Auguste-Dominique Ingres and Eugène Delacroix in the nineteenth century, while John Flaxman and William Blake had done the same for Josiah Wedgwood. This arrangement could also be set up indirectly by dealers who commissioned designers and then undertook to issue and distribute the work. The house of Christofle commissioned projects in this way from a number of artists between 1940 and 1950. But, attractive though this policy might seem because of the renown of these associates, in practice it presents many problems. The artists are primarily concerned to see their work faithfully reproduced and are insufficiently aware of the constraints and special nature of the medium—for example, they sometimes try to work with forms or colours that are impracticable in the material. Such difficulties as these can in the end be beneficial, since they force new problems to be posed and solved. This type of collaboration is usually of an episodic nature: for instance, the sculptor and graphic artist Eduardo Paolozzi designed a pattern for a plate for Wedgwood in 1970. A deliberate policy of working with artists can only be found in two establishments which, paradoxically, are situated at almost opposite ends from each other as regards the relative extent of industrialization: the powerful firm of Rosenthal and the Sèvres factory. Since the 1950s Rosenthal has launched a series of limited editions of sculpture, bas-reliefs and decorative schemes designed by a great number of artists, among whose names one might pick out those of Henry Moore, Etienne Hajdu, Lucio Fontana, Gio Pomodorro and Victor Vasarely. The factory alone is responsible for the production in a limited edition. In contrast, at Sèvres the collaboration between artist and factory is more complete. Granting commis-

(continued on p. 80)

103 **SELB** (Germany, Rosenthal AG). *Tea Service 'Tac1',* 1968–70. Porcelain. H. of tea-pot 12 cm.
The Rosenthal factory operates a most varied creative policy, for besides wares in current production designed by its own studio, it issues limited editions of pieces by artists, works in association with ceramists and employs professional designers. This service, illustrated with the pattern in black, was designed by Walter Gropius and Louis A. McMillen in 1968 and shown for the first time the next year, when the factory was among those awarded a gold medal at Faenza.

104 **VIENNA** (Austria, Porzellan-Manufaktur Josef Böck). *Breakfast Service,* *c.* 1901–2. Stoneware. H. of tea-pot 15.5 cm. Österreichisches Museum für angewandte Kunst, Vienna; Ke 9775.
Josef Böck Junior, who inherited a china shop, founded the firm which bears his name in 1898. He worked closely with the Kunstgewerbeschule, especially with its founders, Josef Hoffmann and Koloman Moser, as well as with their pupils, including Jutta Sika, who designed this model; the pieces were made by various factories, in this instance the Wächtersbacher Steingutfabrik. In his death in 1935 the company passed to his children, Karl and Ferry, who in 1960 sold it to the firm of Haas and Czjzek.

103

104

105

106

105 GUSTAVSBERG (Sweden). *Tea Service,* 1935. Earthenware. H. of tea-pot 14 cm. Nationalmuseum, Stockholm; NM Khv. 7.8 and 14/1935.
This factory was founded in the mid-17th century, and made faïence and phosphatic porcelain in the English taste. Under the direction of Wilhelm Kåge there was a complete change of policy. He designed this service, enhanced by its cadmium glaze, one of many glazes perfected in the 1920s. The renown of the Scandinavian style owes much to the Gustavsberg factory.

106 STABLER, Harold (England, 1872–1945). *'Studland' Coffee Service, c.* 1933. Earthenware. H. of coffee-pot 17.5 cm. Victoria and Albert Museum, London; Circ. 306 & A, 30788, 308, 309 & A–1954.
Harold Stabler was an enameller, jeweller and designer as well as a potter. He arrived in London in 1900, after working in wood and metal, and taught at the Royal College of Art, and then in the ceramics department of the Sir John Cass Technical Institute. In 1921 he became a partner with Charles Carter and John Adams in the pottery at Poole, which then became Carter, Stabler and Adams Ltd., for which he designed garden figures, tiles and services.

107 BERLIN (Germany, Staatliche Porzellan-Manufaktur). *'Urbino' Table Service,* 1930–32/1970. Porcelain. H. of soup-tureen 15 cm. Kunstgewerbemuseum, Cologne; E 4714 a–h.
The Berlin factory resumed the tradition of great table services by commissioning the designer Trude Petri (1906–68) to design this set in 1930–2, together with a coffee-service, produced in celadon, black and white. The service won a grand prix at the Milan Triennale and the *Exposition Internationale* in Paris in 1937. Trude Petri completed the set in 1948 by adding a mocha service.

108

108 DECŒUR, Emile (France, 1876–1953). *Dish,* 1933. Stoneware. D. 32.5 cm. Musée national de céramique, Sèvres; MNCS 24,291.
After setting up at Fontenay-les-Roses, Decœur worked in porcelain and stoneware, combining the two by sometimes blending kaolin with his stoneware body (after 1927). At the Salons he regularly exhibited works which initially were ornamented with restrained carved or painted decoration intended to enhance the forms; but he soon abandoned all ornament when he began to experiment with sophisticated glazes. Between 1939 and 1942 he designed a series of bowl and vase shapes for the Sèvres factory, for which he was artistic consultant from 1942 to 1948.

109 BESNARD, Jean (1889–1958). *Dish,* date unknown. Earthenware. D. 28 cm. Musée national de céramique, Sèvres; MNCS 20,746.
Son of a painter and sculptor, Jean Besnard originally studied folk pottery, in the Savoy at the outset, and remained interested in it throughout his life, during which he travelled widely. Working with a thrower and glaze specialist, he became well known for his very individual glazes, such as the 'lace series' and the 'white retracted glaze', an example of which is shown here.

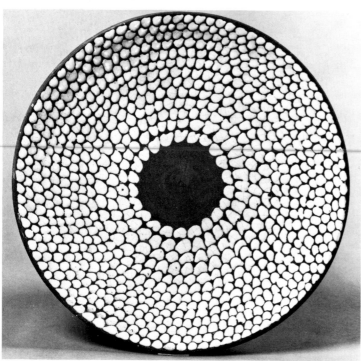

109

110 SIMMEN, Henri (France, 1880–1963). *Vase, c.* 1905. Salt-glazed stoneware. H. 34 cm. Bethnal Green Museum, London; C. 13–1970.
Attracted to traditional pottery, Simmen learnt the technique of stoneware and faïence from Edmond Lachenal. After producing salt-glazed stonewares, he left to study the methods used for this medium in the Far East and, on his return to France, produced some very restrained pieces, hand-modelled, decorated with monochrome glazes, sometimes over sculpted decoration; occasionally they were enriched with pieces of horn or ivory from the hand of his Japanese wife, an ivory-carver.

111 LENOBLE, Emile (France, 1875–1940). *Vase, c.* 1912. Stoneware. H. 29.5 cm. Musée des Arts décoratifs, Paris; 38,284.
After working in the ceramic industry, in 1903 Emile Lenoble entered the studio of his grandfather by marriage, Ernest Chaplet, at Choisy-le-Roi. Strongly influenced by Korean and Chinese ceramics, he made stoneware with carved decoration under monochrome glazes, concentrating increasingly on the glazes. His son Jacques was also a potter.

112 SERRÉ, Georges (France, 1889–1956). *Vase,* 1939. Stoneware. H. 28 cm. Musée national de céramique, Sèvres; AD 117.
Georges Serré began as an apprentice, then became a ground colourist at the Sèvres factory before being sent in 1916 to Saigon, where he taught at the local art schools. This explains the influence of Far Eastern ceramics upon his work. On his return in 1922 he opened a studio at Sèvres; using a wood-fired kiln, he produced one-off thrown pieces, simply decorated with glazes or engraved decoration. From 1940 to 1950 he directed the ceramic studios of the Ecole des Arts appliqués, Paris, and then continued his glaze experiments.

▽112   111△

113 **MURRAY,** William Staite (England, 1881–1961). *Bowl, c.* 1930. Stoneware. D. 24 cm. Victoria and Albert Museum, London; C. 954–1935.
After Bernard Leach, William Staite Murray was the second great English pioneer studio potter, but his ideas differed radically from those of Leach. Staite Murray, who was head of the Ceramics Department at the Royal College of Art, and had a studio at Bray in Berkshire, considered potting as a truly artistic creative venture and was quite uninterested in useful wares. He exhibited his pieces, which were titled, in galleries alongside paintings. In 1940 he left to settle in Southern Rhodesia.

114 **METTHEY,** André (France, 1871–1920). *Plate,* before 1923. Earthenware. D. 25.8 cm. Musée des Beaux-Arts, Grenoble; 2283.
While on military service André Metthey took part in a regional sculpture competition and won as a prize Garnier's treatise *La Céramique,* which led him to his vocation. After various fruitless attempts, this self-taught potter produced his first stonewares around 1901, and set up at Asnières. In the initial period, up to about 1907, he mostly made earthenwares which he had decorated by many painters. He eventually devoted himself exclusively to lead-glazed earthenwares, decorating his pieces with geometric or figurative patterns, often inspired by Middle Eastern ceramics.

113

115 **LEACH,** Bernard (England, 1887–1979). *Vase,* 1931. Stoneware. H. 26 cm. Victoria and Albert Museum, London; Circ. 147–1931.
Born in Hong Kong of English parents and influenced by his training in drawing and etching, Bernard Leach was the leading English studio potter. He played a considerable role worldwide through his teaching, books, lectures and original work. He combined English ceramic tradition with Japanese ideas, maintaining that a potter must be totally responsible for his work, and must base himself on tradition in order to create, however modern his work. After establishing his St. Ives pottery in 1920 with Shoji Hamada, which is continued today by his son David, he opened a new studio in 1936 at Shinner's Bridge, near Dartington Hall in Devon, until he was obliged to give up potting in 1972.

114

116

117

116 **CARDEW,** Michael (England, 1901–). *Jug, c.* 1938. Earthenware. H. 28.5 cm. Victoria and Albert Museum, London; Circ. 310–1938.
Michael Cardew was Bernard Leach's first and most notable English pupil. In 1926 he revived an old pottery at Winchcombe in Gloucestershire, intending to give new life to traditional slip decoration. Nowadays he divides his activities between England, where he has a pottery at Wenford Bridge in Cornwall, and Africa where he has been teaching since 1942, continuing to write and lecture.

117 **GENSOLI,** Maurice (France, 1892–1973). *Pot with cover,* before 1939. Stoneware. H. 41 cm. Musée national de céramique, Sèvres; MNCS 24,358.
Born in Oran, Gensoli lived in France for most of his career; he worked both in his own studio and for the Manufacture nationale de Sèvres, which he joined in 1921 as a decorator, before taking charge of the faïence studio, later becoming head of the decorating studio (1928–58). He created monumental works such as the door for a school at Creil (1941) and showed a consistent predilection for sculptural works of varying sizes.

118 **BEYER,** Henri-Paul-Auguste (France, 1873–1945). *Saint Bon,* date unknown. Stoneware. H. 50 cm. Musée national de céramique, Sèvres; MNCS 18,135.
Beyer was a master glass-blower at Lyons before becoming a stoneware potter. Working in the folk pottery tradition, he used salt-glaze and some other very simple glazes for domestic wares, and also produced busts and figures, which are impressive in the simplicity of their modelling.

119 **SOUDBININE,** Seraphin (Russia–France, 1870–1944). *Tortoise-terrine,* date unknown. Stoneware. H. 20 cm. Musée national de céramique, Sèvres; MNCS 19,475.
Born in Russia, Soudbinine was inspired by Rodin during a visit to Paris, where he decided to settle and to become a sculptor. After seeing some Far Eastern pots at the Metropolitan Museum in New York, he determined to concentrate on ceramics. He produced sculptural pieces in stoneware and porcelain, many of which were wittily conceived.

120

121

122

123

120 **ETRURIA** (England, Josiah Wedgwood & Sons). *'Harvest Moon' Tea Service, c.*1940. H. of tea-pot 14 cm. Victoria and Albert Museum, London; Circ. 4, 6, 8–1941.

The Wedgwood factory was a pioneer of industrialization and proved that it intended to remain so by adopting the oil-fired tunnel kiln in 1918. During the 1930s many artists, such as Eric Ravilious and Keith Murray, were commissioned to produce designs under the impetus of Victor Skellern, who was artistic director from 1935 to 1965. In 1940 the factory moved from its original buildings to Barlaston, to newly-equipped premises benefiting from the most up-to-date techniques, but never lost sight of its creative purpose. The restrained form of this service is shown to best advantage by the monochrome glaze.

121 **SCHEIER,** Edwin and Mary (U.S.A.). *Coffee Service,* 1947. Stoneware. H. of coffee-pot 20.4 cm. Everson Museum of Art, Syracuse (gift of Richard B. Gump); P.C. 48, 551, 1–19.

When Edwin and Mary Scheier started to work with ceramics, they set up in Virginia before going to teach at the University of New Hampshire until 1950, when they left for Oaxaca in Mexico. The annual exhibitions of American ceramics organized at Syracuse made no distinction between studio pieces and those intended for mass production, and at the twelfth exhibition this service won the Richard B. Gump prize for the best design suitable for mass production.

122 **BERLIN** (Germany, Staatliche Porzellan-Manufaktur). *'Crocus' Tea and Coffee Service,* 1956/72. Porcelain. H. of coffee-pot 23.2 cm. Kunstgewerbemuseum, Cologne; E4715 a–w.

The Berlin factory was quick to recognize the need to adapt its production to the dictates of mechanization in order to become profitable, and continued to create forms adapted to the modern way of life, from both a functional and an aesthetic viewpoint. After commissioning the first generation of specialized designers in the 1930s, in 1956 the factory turned to the potter Hubert Griemert to design this service, which was complemented in the following year by a dinner service.

123 **ARZBERG** (Germany). *'Arzberg 2075' Tea and Coffee Service,* 1963/72–6. Porcelain. H. of coffee-pot 23.5 cm. Kunstgewerbemuseum, Cologne; E4890 a–g.

During the 19th century the opening of many small factories transformed Arzberg into one of the centres of the Bavarian ceramic industry. By 1900 production methods had become to a large extent industrialized and this led to a reorganization of the companies concerned, most of which are now part of the great Hutschenreuther group. Besides hotel wares, some original works are still made, such as this service created by Heinrich Löffelhardt in 1963, with its matching dinner service.

124

125

124 **LIMOGES** (France, Coquet, Porcelaine de Limoges). *Service,* 1972. Porcelain.

The various factories of the Limoges region have from time to time attempted to create contemporary shapes by employing staff or outside designers, among them Marc Held, whose work is shown here. These experiments are the more praiseworthy since the French public is notably conservative and prefers to invest in copies of early pieces. This service is produced in white and celadon.

125 **LIMOGES** (France, Bernardaud). *'Aries' Service,* 1966–7. Porcelain.
Limoges, the most important French porcelain centre, has made great efforts, especially since the Second World War, to modernize its machinery and plant. One of the first attempts to update the product itself occurred in 1966, when Pierre Bernardaud commissioned the Compagnie de l'esthétique industrielle Raymond Loewy of Paris to design the 'Aries' service. Various subsequent attempts to decorate these forms demonstrate how this short-lived association between designer and factory, unless carefully controlled, can present unforeseen problems.

126 **PONTI,** Gio (Italy, 1891–   ). *Bowl,* 1927. Porcelain. H. 11 cm. Museo di Doccia, Sesto Fiorentino; 5354/1275.
The decorative schemes created by the architect Gio Ponti for the well-known Richard-Ginori factory are essentially figurative, but some purely geometric designs were created that depended either on the play of lines emphasizing the form of objects or, as in this case, on a subtly calculated *trompe-l'oeil* effect; the apparent failure to acknowledge a structure while respecting its proportions creates a fascinating intellectual game.

127 **BARLASTON** (England, Wedgwood and Co.). *'Graphic Permutation 1',* 1970. Slip-cast porcelain. H. of each cube 5 cm. City Museum and Art Gallery, Stoke-on-Trent.
In 1940 the Wedgwood factory moved to a modern location at Barlaston where production was highly industrialized. However, this did not mean an end to its artistic endeavours. Glenys Barton, the sculptor and potter, was invited to carry out some free-ranging investigations into bone china. Her research led to the production of a series of pieces with frequently combined casting and modelling, mixed sculpted and smooth parts, and biscuit and decorated zones; it drew on industrial techniques of photolithographic or silk-screen transfer to create limited editions of highly personal works.

126

127

128

129

128 **MILAN** (Italy, Richard-Ginori Società Ceramica Italiana). *Table Service,* 1973. Museo internazionale delle Ceramiche, Faenza.
The largest Italian factory, now highly industrialized, could not but take an interest in design, so higly regarded in that country. Joe Colombo, well known as a versatile designer, assisted by Ambrogio Pozzi and Ignazia Favata, was commissioned to design this service, made in both monochrome and two-tone versions. The service was awarded the gold medal of the President of the Republic for functional and utility products at Faenza in 1973.

129 **SARTORI,** Cesare (Italy, 1930–   ). *Vessels,* 1965. Maiolica. Max. h. 15.5 cm. Museo internazionale delle Ceramiche, Faenza.
After studying at Nove, his native town, and then in Venice, Sartori began to work principally as a designer. As artistic consultant to factories and as a teacher of drawing, he is one of those very rare independent potters who, in his studios at Nove, concentrates on the creation of pieces intended for mass production. These vessels won him the industrial design prize at Faenza in 1965.

130

130 **COPENHAGEN** (Denmark, Royal Porcelain Factory). *Butter-dish,* 1962–9. Porcelain. H. 7.25 cm. Kunstgewerbemuseum, Cologne; E 4706.
Scandinavian factories were the first to adopt a dual production system: they mass-produced by highly industrialized methods services, pots and figures which made their reputation and ensured their financial stability, while maintaining experimental studios and occasionally calling in independent potters on a temporary basis. The 'Gemina' service was created in this way by Gertrud Vasegaard in 1962.

131 ZAO, Wou-Ki (China, 1921–   ). *'Diana' Dish,* 1979. Porcelain.
D. 26 cm. Archives, Manufacture nationale de Sèvres.
This painter first worked at the Sèvres factory in 1969, painting in watercolours
a decorative scheme for a dish produced in low-temperature colours. For the
complete set of dishes which the artist created for the Ministry of Culture in
1979–80 the lithographic transfer process was used, as it was the best means of
preserving the delicacy of the original watercolours on the numerous pieces in
the service.

132 DOWNING, Joe (United States, 1925–   ). *'Diana' Dishes,* 1976. Porcelain. D. 26 cm. Archives, Manufacture nationale de Sèvres.
From 1973 to 1976 this painter created a maquette, or model, for three dishes,
painting directly on to porcelain after completing preliminary projects in oils on
canvas. The dishes were subsequently produced using low-temperature colours,
so reviving in a felicitous and sensitive manner the use of the traditional Sèvres
blue ground. Joe Downing is currently in the process of painting a series of
designs for small plaques directly on to porcelain.

131

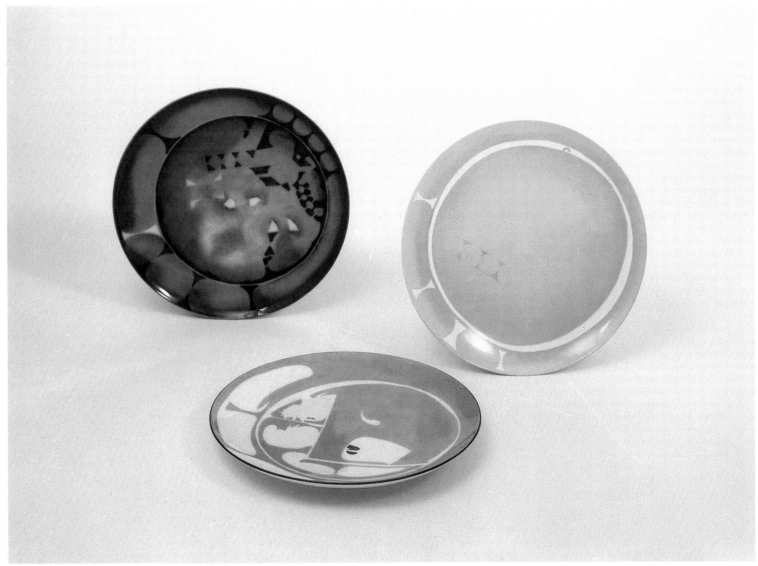

132

sions to contemporary artists, a policy resumed in 1964 at the instigation of André Malraux, minister responsible for the arts, had the aim of producing editions of various kinds of work created by the artists concerned. These included designs for gilt decoration by André Beaudin, Georges Mathieu, Roger Vieillard, Marcel Fiorini and James Guitet; designs for painting in *petit-feu* (low-temperature) colours by Serge Poliakoff, Alexander Calder, Alicia Penalba and Geneviève Asse; and designs for bas-reliefs, vases or wares with relief decoration or sculpture by Arthur-Luiz Piza, Etienne Hajdu, Marc-Antoine Louttre, François-Xavier Lalanne, and Anne and Patrick Poirier. But the artists were given the freedom to participate directly in the manufacturing process. Thus Hajdu himself painted all the biscuit pieces in a service intended for the Elysée Palace; Fiorini engraved the linoleum which served as the mould for his 'photophore' (a lamp which uses the translucency of porcelain); and Georges Jeanclos was given facilities to model the drapery of fine white porcelain which envelops each of his *Dormeurs*.

Artists

During the first three decades of this century factories dominated the field of ceramics. Afterwards the work of studio potters, whose number and creative originality were both remarkable, began to attract the attention of collectors. Before examining their work, we shall discuss the contribution made by artists (i.e. painters and sculptors) who, at one time or other in their career, chose clay as their medium of expression.

Their experiments, although short-lived, have been essential to the evolution of ceramic art, because they were of short duration and only formed one stage in a creative effort which was not fundamentally concerned with ceramic art. Potters became aware of a whole new dimension to their work: the traditional production of useful and decorative objects was no longer their sole objective, and that creative effort which for a certain number of artists had constituted only an element in their career became an end in itself for a whole new generation of potters.

Independent potters who worked with the factories will not be discussed at this point. We have already dealt with this aspect of relations between the world of 'fine art' and that of ceramics. A later chapter will be devoted to the activity of artists who, having encountered ceramics at a given moment in their career, were to become true art potters. We will consider here only those painters or sculptors for whom this branch of art was always an intermittent activity.

Some sculptors either used the facilities offered by practical potters to translate their work into clay or else allowed the potters themselves to produce clay versions of their models. The potters had the dual advantage of working on well-conceived models and of having their name linked with that of a famous artist. The sculptor could thus ensure that his work was more widely available than was possible if he used marble or bronze cast by the lost-wax method, for example, even though ceramic versions of sculptures were only produced in limited numbers.

Rodin was one of the earliest sculptors to utilize ceramics. He was not a total stranger to the medium since he had been summoned to the Sèvres factory by his teacher, Albert Carrier-Belleuse, who became artistic director of the establishment in 1877. Rodin worked there from 1878 to 1882, initially assisting in the manufacture of the centrepiece known as the *Triomphe de la Chasse* by Carrier-Belleuse. Later he decorated some vases using a new technique which involved incising and finishing processes that called upon his sculptural skills. The group known as *La Faunesse,* bought by the State in 1891, was issued in porcelain by Chaplet.

In 1895 Edmond Lachenal produced two examples in stoneware of the *Tête de Douleur* and Jeanneney obtained authorization in 1903 to reproduce in stoneware a bust of one of the 'Burghers of Calais' and the 'Head of Balzac' which he exhibited in 1904 at St. Louis. Dalpayrat made ceramic versions of the works of Constantin Meunier and Ferdinand Faivre, while Edmond Lachenal translated into stoneware the works of Dejean, Fix-Masseau, Prosper d'Epinay and Sarah Bernhardt. Georges Serré made stoneware versions of sculptural works by Gimond, Dejean and Contesse.

This type of relationship between 'artist' and 'potter' is not fundamentally different from that which exists between a factory and the artist who creates a model which is then manufactured. In both cases the creator is not involved with his creation. The situation is quite different when artist and potter co-operate. The artist suggests an idea which the second realizes. The artist often merely decorates a piece that the potter has formed and will fire. Even large murals are created in this way. Alternatively, the artist can handle the clay, seeking advice from the potter and calling on his knowledge of the necessary techniques.

The independent artist potter, acting as a creator of pieces intended to be seen as works of art, is, as we shall see, a fairly recent phenomenon. One of the first of them, Théodore Deck, quickly understood how he could benefit from the policy adopted by commercial concerns which worked in collaboration with artists. He managed to collect together painters such as Eléonore Escallier, Jean-Louis Hamon and Emile-Auguste Reiber, who understood how to exploit all the possibilities offered to them by Deck's technical ingenuity. He was able to create sumptuous dishes imitating maiolica decorated with floral patterns in Japanese style, delicate scenes in the antique manner or portraits on a gold ground.

About the same time Félix Bracquemond and Ernest Chaplet made faïence and peasant pottery decorated by the *barbotine* method in the studio opened at Auteuil by the Haviland brothers. This involved the use of coloured liquid clay, according to a process perfected by Chaplet in 1871. Although the work of the Auteuil artists is scarcely known today, it deserves mention in so far as it constitutes one of the very rare instances where a connection has existed between a movement in painting, in this case Impressionism, and a contemporary type of ceramic design.

The studio run by Chaplet was important for another reason: it introduced two great artists to ceramics. Jules Dalou, on his return from exile, was introduced to Chaplet by Félix Bracquemond and produced some sculptures and bas-reliefs in faïence and stoneware. The shock created by these works in a markedly realistic style led to a profound change in the style of Chaplet's studio. From then on it concentrated on the manufacture of stoneware decorated with naturalistic motifs in polychrome enamels. To prevent the colours from blending, the coloured areas were contained within an incised outline. These stonewares attracted the attention of Paul Gauguin, who was the first great artist to turn potter.

Gauguin was introduced to Chaplet in 1886. At first (in 1886–7) he worked with him to produce thrown pieces, while concurrently modelling his own vases of asymmetrical and unbalanced form, in sombre colours, which were strongly influenced by Japanese and pre-Columbian ceramics. On his return from Martinique in 1887 Gauguin worked for a while with Delaherche, Chaplet's successor, but they soon parted company. During this period he produced pots of simpler form, accentuating the contrast between the unglazed stoneware surface and the glazed areas. He enclosed his designs within deeply incised lines. This practice was technically necessary and was similar to the *cloisonné* technique that he was employing at that time in his paintings. In the years 1889 and 1890 his subjects became progressively more symbolic and sorrowful; at this time he moved on from vases to sculpture, creating three models between 1893 and 1895 before giving up this form of expression.

Following on from Ernest Chaplet, André Metthey enjoyed a privileged relationship with a new group of painters. A self-taught potter, he set up a studio around 1901 at Asnières where he devoted himself principally to the production of tin-glazed earthenware. Ambroise Vollard introduced to him the Fauves and their friends who then came to work at his studio and to paint on crude stanniferous glazes. At the Salon d'Automne of 1907 Metthey exhibited about a hundred pieces decorated by artists who were still little known: Auguste Renoir, Odilon Redon, Pierre Bonnard, Maurice Denis, André Derain, Aristide Maillol, Pierre Laprade, Jean Puy, Georges Rouault, Maurice de Vlaminck and Henri Matisse. One might wonder why this group of men of diverse talents wanted to work directly with clay. Painting on a tin glaze is clearly more difficult than working on canvas, since it allows no correction. Besides, the tones of the glazes change during firing to a greater extent than the colours of a painting that is drying off and, even though the painters might be shown a sample palette to demonstrate the colours after firing, the method remains hazardous. One might conclude in Metthey's case that he feared he was not sufficiently competent as a draughtsman, although his later work amply contradicts this. The painters' motives are more difficult to determine. They were perhaps tempted by the opportunity to escape from the easel. Pottery decoration allowed them to break openly with the constraints of rendering perspective and the illusion of three dimensions, at the very moment when their paintings were coming to grips with this fundamental problem. Moreover, the very simple and limited forms offered by Metthey—tall narrow vases, globular vases, plates, plaques, bowls—gave them the opportunity to experiment with new formats and shapes, at a time when the role of canvas as the proper ground for painting had not yet been questioned. The painters may also have been attracted by the intensity of colour available in pottery decoration, as they were on the point of adopting colour for its own sake in their easel-paintings. From this point of view it is interesting to note that another group of painters obsessed with colour, the members of 'Die Brücke', became involved with ceramics around 1912. It is equally possible, as has been suggested by Michel Hoog, that painters, at a period when their role and function were beginning to be questioned, wanted to get closer to their public and chose to work with ceramics because of their privileged role 'as part of daily life. Ceramics played a more important role than any other art in the domestic setting, and were also used in mural decoration'. (Hoog, M., 'Peintres et céramistes en France au début du XXᵉ siècle', *Cahiers de la céramique, du verre et des arts du feu*, Nᵒ. 50 (1971), pp. 12–18.)

Whatever their motives, the artists must have been disappointed by the results, for very quickly this collaboration came to an end. Only Georges Rouault, who had been the first to join up with Metthey in 1906, continued to work regularly with him until 1910, exhibiting faïence and then lead-glazed pottery along with his paintings. It was Rouault who was the most interested in the very substance and texture of colour.

Henri Matisse had contributed traditional objects—vases, plaques, dishes and plates—to Metthey's stand in 1907. It was undoubtedly at this time or a little later, and probably in Metthey's studio, that he painted a triptych on ceramic tiles intended for the house of Karl-Ernst Osthaus, which Henry van de Velde was building at Hagen at the time. It appears that one of the aims of this project had been to allow young artists to try their hand at new materials. Osthaus was an admirer of the paintings of Matisse—he had bought several of his works—and, just as Van de Velde had entrusted the realization of his schemes to many factories, Osthaus became involved with ceramics. He was anxious to accompany Matisse, whom he had met on a train in 1909, to visit a new crematorium built by Peter Behrens, for which Osthaus had commissioned a ceramic panel from the painter E. R. Weiss. The design of a faun and nymphs produced by Matisse, like the vine shoots surrounding the panels, is related to the ink sketches for woodcuts which he executed in 1906. In the same way, when Matisse, who had worked on twenty or so plates at Vallauris, returned some forty years later to work on the panels of painted ceramic tiles for the church on the plateau of Assy (1946–7) and the chapel at Vence (1954), their uncluttered design paralleled his great contemporary studies in Indian ink. (Neff, John H., 'An Early Ceramic Triptych by Henri Matisse', *Burlington Magazine*, 104 (1972), pp. 848–53.)

In 1912 André Mare presented his *Maison cubiste* at the Salon d'Automne. This included faïence by Georges Rouault and designs on porcelain by Jacques Villon that, strangely, were still very traditional in conception. *(continued on p. 85)*

135
142
141
139

139

133 **RODIN**, Auguste (France, 1840–1917). *Head of Balzac,* 1903 edition. Stoneware. H. 47 cm. Musée du Petit Palais, Paris; PPS 1145.
Rodin was one of many sculptors whose work was produced by potters, always in limited editions. Right at the outset of his career he worked for a period at the Sèvres factory, endeavouring to devise a decorative process using carving and finishing techniques that would display his sculptural talents to their best advantage. This piece was produced by Jeanneney in 1903, at the same time as the *Burghers of Calais,* and exhibited in 1904 at St. Louis. Chaplet had already issued the *Satyress* in 1891 and Lachenal had cast two proofs in stoneware of the *Head of Sorrow* in 1895.

134 **KOKOSCHKA**, Oskar (Austria, 1886–1980). *Mask,* 1962. Porcelain. H. 19 cm. Schloss Charlottenburg, Berlin (on loan).
Both the artist's tragic expressionism and his ability as a portraitist to reveal the soul of the sitter, are recognizable in this poignant work. It was begun by the painter's sister and completed by him.

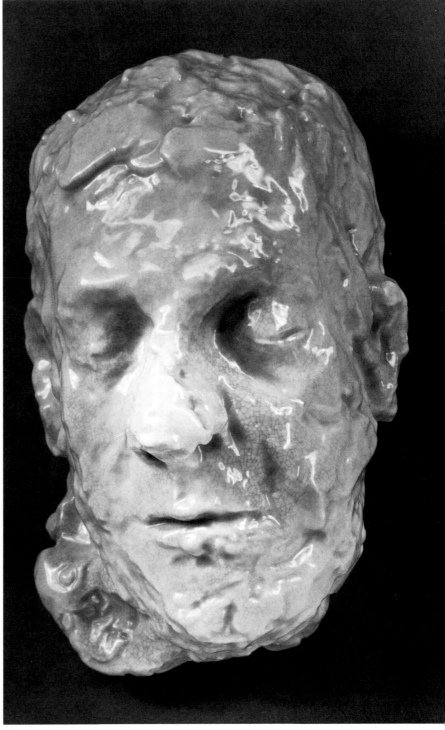

133   134

135 **RENOIR,** Pierre-Auguste (France, 1841–1919). *Vase,* 1900. Earthenware. H. 55 cm. Musée d'art moderne de la Ville de Paris (Henry-Thomas Bequest).
Contrary to what is often written, Renoir did not paint porcelain at Limoges, his birthplace, which he left at the age of four. When in Paris, aged about eighteen, he began by painting blinds and porcelain. It is not known where this vase was decorated.

136 **CASSATT,** Mary (U.S.A., 1845–1926). *Vase,* date unknown. Earthenware. H. 53.5 cm. Musée du Petit Palais, Paris; PPSA 1835.
This American who worked in Paris was a good friend of the Impressionists with whom she exhibited. She also helped to make them known and admired in the United States, at a time when no one in France was yet buying their paintings. Besides being famous as a painter she is also well known for her skilful engravings, strongly influenced by Japanese prints, as is evident from their bold composition and stylized simplification of motifs. Neither of these characteristics are recognizable in this vase which belonged to Ambroise Vollard. It seems to be a rare example of her incursion into the field of ceramics, which undoubtedly took place early in her career.

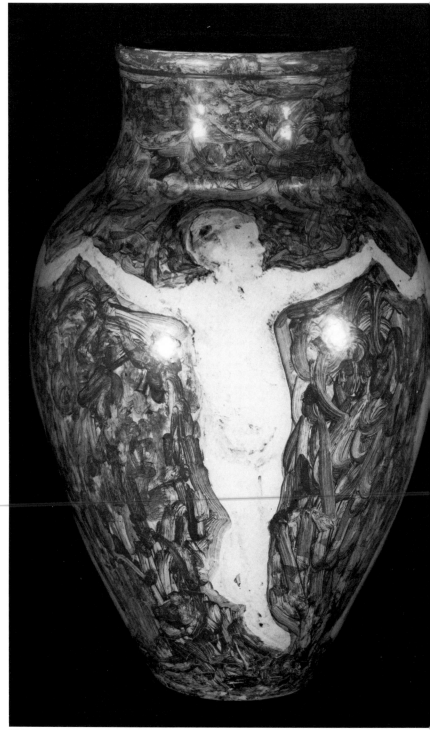

135   136

Although French and Italian artists were particularly interested in the possibilities offered by ceramic materials, the Dutch painter Jan Toorop worked at Delft, where he painted some frescoes on tiles for the Amsterdam Exchange built in 1900 by Berlage. In England the potter Bernard Moore, like Metthey, opened wide the doors of his workshops to a great number of artists between 1905 and 1915. These painters signed their work.

We have seen that many Russian painters were associated with the former Imperial factory between 1917 and 1920. During the 1920s Alexander Archipenko modelled a series of busts at the Grossherzogliche Majolika-Manufaktur at Karlsruhe, which at that time was directed by Max Laeuger. The earliest example of a sculptor working directly with clay, no longer as a preliminary medium intended to be replaced in the final work by a nobler material such as marble, stone or bronze, but to be used for the definitive work, seems to date from the renewed fashion in Italy at the end of the nineteenth century for small decorative statuettes in terracotta inspired by the Antique. This fashion was encouraged 150 by the 'Ritorno all'ordine'. The sculptor Arturo Martini provided a range of forms influenced by the Vienna Secession for the Gregori pottery of Treviso from 1908 to 1912, and chose terracotta for some very original work, using clay as a direct means of expressing feeling. In 1920 he joined a movement called 'Valori plastici' which stressed the importance of a return to classical ideals and formal values, espousing classical naturalism and the use of antique materials such as stone and terracotta. Many Italian artists followed in Martini's footsteps: Marino Marini used clay for nude studies and portraits, Romano Romanelli for portraits, and Quinto Martini for classical figures. At that time terracotta held a special position. As a mutable medium, with more malleability than bronze or marble, it seemed better able to reflect a period of crisis and experimentation.

Terracotta was not the only ceramic material employed by Italian artists. Many were attracted to tin-glazed earthenware. Arturo Martini worked during the 1920s at Albissola, a centre of traditional ceramics. He was joined there by many Futurists such as Prampolini, Fili and Munari, who experimented with geometric stylization. In 1927 Filippo Tommaso Marinetti drew up *Il manifesto futurista ceramica e aeroceramica* with Tullio, the potter from Albissola; it was published in 1938.

It is possible that the sculptors' familiarity with clay, which was used in all art schools, and its low cost in a period of grave economic crisis contributed to its adoption, as much as its malleability and versatility. In any case it ceased to be regarded with 170 scorn. In the 1920s the Catalan potter José Llorens Artigas and his painter friends first began to work together. Artigas arrived in Paris in 1923 and joined forces with Picasso, who then carried out with him his first experiments in the field of ceramics, as did Raoul 138 Dufy and Albert Marquet. With Dufy Artigas produced a series of small gardens and fountains for apartments, as well as table ornaments decorated by the painter and planted by the landscape gardener Nicolau Maria Rubio Tuduri. These miniature gardens were first exhibited in 1927 at the Galerie Bernheim jeune, and

were later shown in Brussels and London. Albert Marquet came 137 to see Artigas to ask him to make some tiles for his new bathroom and eventually, after having made some vases and trial plaques, was persuaded to paint them himself. (Marquet, Marcelle, 'Céramiques d'Albert Marquet', *Cahiers de la céramique, du verre et des arts du feu,* No. 18 (1960), pp. 135–45.)

Apart from these attempts at collaboration and the interest shown around 1935 by Bart van der Leck, one of the painters of 100 the 'De Stijl' group, it is true to say that artists only discovered ceramics in the 1940s.

The collaboration between the potter Artigas and Joan Miró *Frontispiece* commenced in 1941. Their first joint works—vases, dishes, plaques and sculpted pieces—were shown in 1945 at Pierre Matisse's gallery in New York and in 1948 in Aimé Maeght's recently-opened gallery in Paris. We will come across extensive 276 evidence of Maeght's interest in ceramics. While he was aware of the possibility of fruitful experimentation, he also certainly knew that his designs could be reproduced by means of engraving, too.

In 1946–7 Picasso made his first ceramics at the pottery of 145–8 Madoura (Suzanne Ramié), having experimented with Artigas in 328 the early 1920s. After completing her studies in Lyons, Madoura established herself at the Atelier du Plan at Vallauris, and in 1936–8 was introduced to ceramics by potters who were working with the local clay, experimenting with traditional techniques and forms. After the war she and her husband Georges Ramié opened the Atelier de Vallauris. This old centre was already recovering its former character before Picasso arrived.

In 1946 Picasso visited an exhibition of works by the Vallauris potters organized by Madoura. Intrigued by what he saw, he contacted her and made some pots. Returning the following year, he became so passionately involved with this new field of experiment that he stayed for two years. 'Madoura taught him, at his own request, the eleven traditional methods she practised of firing and glazing clay. He was interested in everything: alquifou (green glazes), slips, etc. He used existing forms as well as designing other unusual shapes. Pots were thrown for him; then he transformed them, modelled them, sculpted them and invented new techniques of incising, of using paraffin wax resist, reliefs, playing with clay surfaces etc. The painter and the sculptor in him were expressed alternately or even simultaneously, utilizing the unexpected qualities inherent in clay glaze and firing. He was amused and enchanted by the 'blown shape', long sought after and now finally caught.' (Moutard-Uldry, Renée, 'La Renaissance de la céramique à Vallauris', *Cahiers de la céramique, du verre et des arts du feu,* No. 3 (1956), pp. 21–9.)

At roughly the same time as Picasso's infatuation was encouraging the revival of ceramics at Vallauris, a similar movement was under way in Italy at Albissola. In the wake of Arturo Martini and the Futurists a great number of artists went to work there. From 1936 onward Lucio Fontana produced his series of sculpted works, 151 and after the Second World War it attracted Italian sculptors such as Manzu, Garelli and several members of the 'Cobra' group, *(continued on p. 96)*

137 **MARQUET**, Albert (France, 1875–1947). *Tiles,* 1932–3. Earthenware. For the bathroom of his new apartment Albert Marquet commissioned Artigas to decorate some ceramic tiles. Artigas succeeded in persuading him to paint them himself, after he had completed two trial vases, thus transforming the bathroom into a veritable album of travel souvenirs. These are the only ceramic works by the painter.

138 **DUFY**, Raoul (France, 1877–1953). *Scheme for an Apartment Garden,* 1927. H. 20 cm. Centre Georges Pompidou, Paris; AM 11,040.A.
Around 1923 the painter was initiated into the mysteries of ceramics by Artigas. This association led to the creation of a series of fountains and little indoor gardens decorated by the artist and planted by the architect and landscape gardener Nicolau Maria Rubio Tuduri. These gardens were a Western counterpoint to Japanese bonsai. André Malraux dreamed of reproducing them.

139 **MATISSE**, Henri (France, 1869–1954). *Triptych* (central panel), 1908–9(?). Earthenware. Hohenhof, Hagen; K 2632.
Matisse was one of a group of young painters who came to try their hand at decorating pots at André Metthey's studio in 1906–7. He appears to have also worked with Metthey on this triptych, commissioned by Karl-Ernst Osthaus for the house being built for him at that time at Hagen by Henry van de Velde. Osthaus allowed several artists to work in materials that were relatively new to them. Awkwardly situated in a room that was too narrow and had insufficient space for it to be viewed properly, this triptych is a good deal less well known than later works by Matisse of the same type, such as the panels for the church on the plateau of Assy or for the Rosary Chapel at Vence.

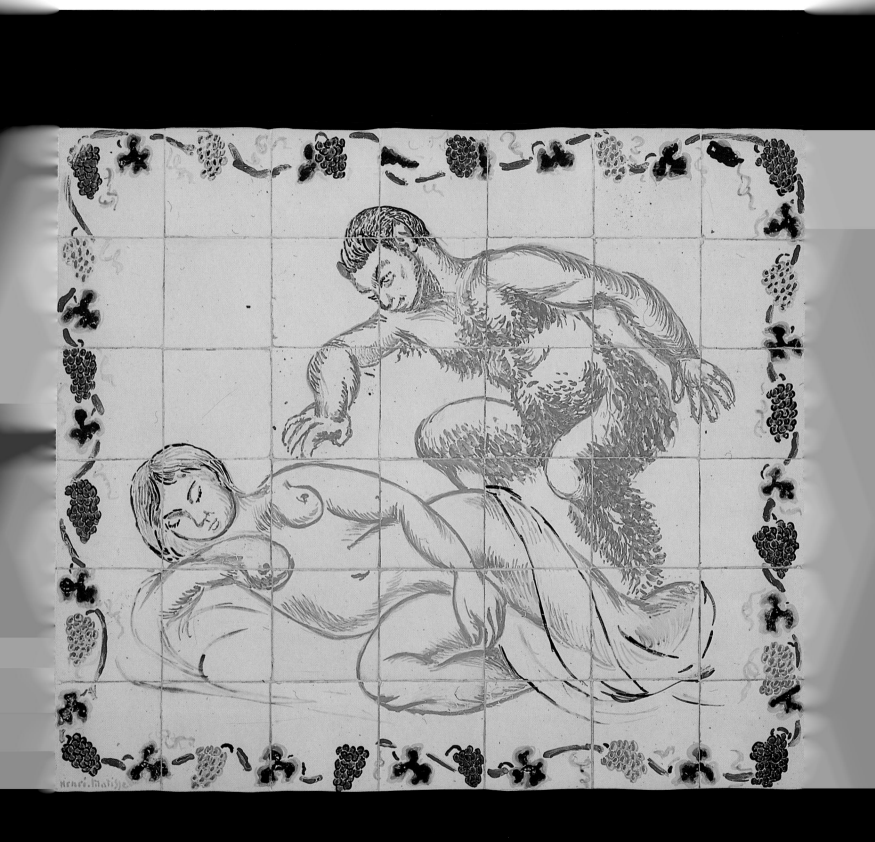

140

140 VAN DONGEN, Kees (Holland–France, 1877–1958). *Dish with Three Nude Figures,* 1907–9. Earthenware. D. 35.5 cm. Musée d'art moderne de la Ville de Paris; AM AD 258.
The picture dealer Ambroise Vollard became interested in ceramics and particularly in André Metthey who was indeed an excellent potter. From 1905 to 1907 Vollard brought 'his' painters to Metthey's studio at Asnières. Later the artist created designs for Bernardaud at Limoges.

141 VLAMINCK, Maurice de (France, 1876–1958) and **METTHEY,** André (France, 1871–1920). *Tube Vase,* 1907–9. Earthenware. H. 54 cm. Musée d'art moderne de la Ville de Paris; AM 203; PPSAD 1967.

142 DERAIN, André (France, 1880–1954). *Tube Vase with Three Seated Nude Figures,* 1907–9. Earthenware. H. 54 cm. Musée d'art moderne de la Ville de Paris; AM 128; PPSAD 1878.

The picture dealer Ambroise Vollard became interested in ceramics and particularly in André Metthey who was indeed on excellent potter. From 1905 to 1907 Vollard brought 'his' painters to Metthey's studio at Asnières. Later the artist created designs for Berardand at Limoges

141

142

143 **DUFY**, Raoul (France, 1877–1953). *Vase,* 1930. H. 42 cm. Centre Georges Pompidou, Paris; AM1157 oA.
Decorated with a portrait of the famous picture dealer Ambroise Vollard, this vase demonstrates the painter's enduring interest in ceramics. Dufy became involved in the decorative arts in the 1920s, when he worked for Paul Poiret, for whom he decorated his Seine barges, *Délices, Amours* and *Orgues,* and also for the textile firm of Bianchini-Férier. He executed the Bœuf woodcuts in 1920, and from 1921 made a name for himself as a designer as much as a painter by exhibiting regularly at salons.

144 **CHAGALL**, Marc (Russia–France, 1887–). *A Midsummer Night's Dream,* 1952. Ceramic. H. 32 cm. Galerie Maeght, Paris.
From 1950 the ceramics of Chagall were made by several different potters including Madame Bourreau at Antibes, Ramel at Vence, Lhospied at Golfe-Juan and especially by Georges and Suzanne Ramié at Vallauris. Ninety-two of his ceramics were shown in the exhibition devoted to him at the Grand Palais in Paris from December 1969 to March 1970. 'Ceramics', said Chagall, 'are an alliance of clay and fire; if you deliver something noble into the fire, then some small part of it will be returned to you, but if the piece is bad, then it will be destroyed, and nothing will remain. The judgement of fire is pitiless.'

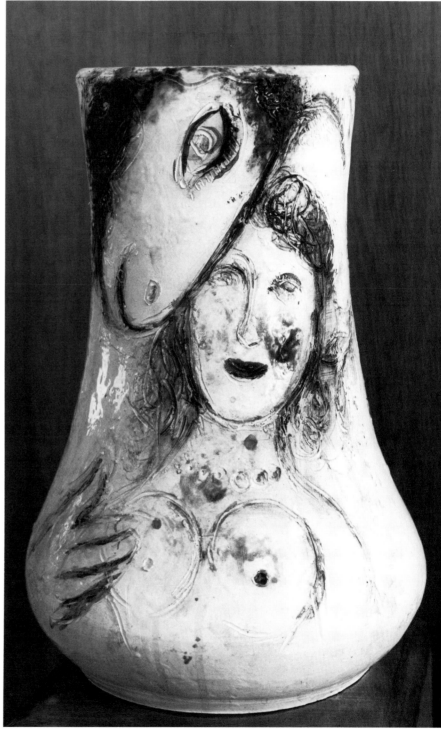

143 144

147

PICASSO, Pablo (Spain, 1881–1973).

145 *Crouching Female Figure,* 1953. Terracotta. H. 30 cm. Musée Picasso, Paris; MP 683.

146 *Woman,* 1950. Terracotta. H. 16 cm. Musée Picasso, Paris; MP 673.

147 *Seated Musician,* 1950–1. Terracotta. H. 14. cm. Musée Picasso, Paris; MP 678.

148 *Vase in the Form of a Female Figure,* 1947. Terracotta. H. 45 cm. Musée Picasso, Paris; MP 377.

During the summer of 1946 Picasso, intrigued by an exhibition by the Vallauris potters, paid a visit to Madoura and made some objects in her studio that he left to be fired. He returned one year later to the day and then discovered ceramic technique. He conceived such a passion for it that he was to remain at the pottery for two years, creating two thousand pieces in the first year. In 1949 the Maison de la Pensée française exhibited 149 of them for the first time. Picasso's contribution was highly personal, but although working freely with the material he respected its 'laws'—in contrast to Joan Miró, who worked with ceramics before Picasso. Miró made more fundamental innovations, producing pieces divorced from the ceramic tradition.

145

149

150

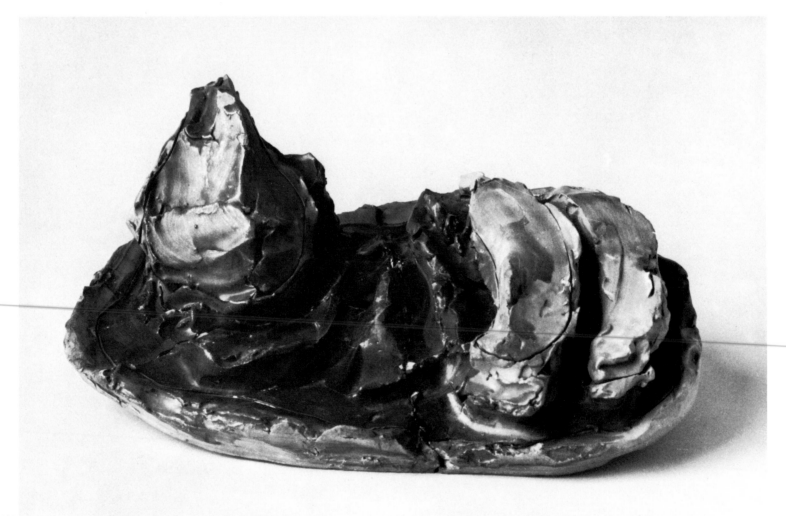

151

152

153

149 **PORTELETTE,** François (France, 1936–). '*A Very Gentle Trembling*', 1981. Fireclay. H. 62 cm. Artist's collection.

After training as an engraver, Portelette became a sculptor producing *bas-reliefs,* initially on metal and then on paper moulded on to clay; quite recently he became involved with clay for its own sake. Because of the narrowness of his kiln, he made this *bas-relief* in ten pieces, chamfered before drying and assembled after firing on a rigid panel with the aid of a mortar. The work exemplifies his interest in the association of realistic landscape with a human figure in movement.

150 **MARTINI,** Arturo (Italy, 1889–1947). *Woman at the Window,* 1930. Terracotta. H. 32 cm. Galleria nazionale d'arte moderna e contemporanea, Rome.

Martini studied ceramics at Faenza, attended the Munich Academy and worked in Paris before learning sculpture at Treviso and Venice. His work as a sculptor very soon procured him employment with ceramic factories (Gregori of Treviso and Manlio Trucco of Albissola) where he used clay for some very innovative work. From the early 1920s he was a member of the *Valori Plastici* group, which advocated a return to the past and the revival of classical styles and materials. This must have contributed to his choice of terracotta as his favourite medium.

151 **FONTANA,** Lucio (Argentina–Italy, 1899–1968). *Pear and Bananas,* 1938. Earthenware. H. 11 cm. Museo internazionale delle Ceramiche, Faenza; 2571.

Born in Argentina, Lucio Fontana attended a technical institute in Milan in 1914–15. In 1922 he returned to Argentina, where he produced his first figurative sculptures before registering in 1928 at the Brera Academy in Milan. In 1931–2 he produced some small pictures painted and scratched on cement. He

was particularly involved with ceramics between 1936 and 1938, when he worked at the Tullio Mazzoti factory at Albissola. He again returned to Argentina from 1939 to 1946 and worked mainly on sculpture. Once more coming back to Italy, he developed his spatial theories which found typical expression in his notched and fissured work of the 1950s. However he did not completely abandon ceramics, for in 1959 he completed his *Nature* series in terracotta and another series entitled *Small Theatres* in 1964.

152 **MELANDRI,** Pietro (Italy, 1885–1976). *Bas-relief,* 1939. Terracotta. H. 78 cm. Museo internazionale delle Ceramiche, Faenza.

Melandri, who was a painter and stage producer before becoming a potter, never rejected the rich Italian ceramic tradition. 'Historiated' maiolica was the forerunner of his figurative designs, even though his iconography is resolutely innovative, while his *bas-reliefs,* often produced in association with architects, recall the art of the Della Robbias. This panel was awarded the grand prix at the second Faenza competition, which was at that time organized on a national basis.

153 **BERTI,** Antonio (Italy, 1904–). *Annunciation,* 1947. Terracotta. H. of the Virgin 92 cm.

The return of classical art in Italy which began in the 1920s was marked by the revival of terracotta sculpture. The movement was greatly encouraged by the Mussolini régime which whole-heartedly allied itself with an iconography that extolled national grandeur. The style survived the fall of the régime, and some important artists adopted it. This group representing the Annunciation, designed to stand on the bridge of San Piero at Sieve, inside a wooden structure, eventually had to be replaced by a bronze version, because of the effects of atmospheric pollution.

93

154

154 SCHRECKENGOST, Victor (U.S.A., 1906–). *Punch-bowl,* 1931. Porcelain. H. 29.2 cm. Cowan Pottery Museum, Public Library, Rocky River, Ohio.

The son of a potter, Schreckengost studied at Cleveland (1924–8), then at Vienna with Michael Powolny. On his return to the United States he taught at Cleveland, while working for G. Cowan (cf. Pl. 78). It was at that time that he designed a series of twenty punch-bowls, which seem to display Cubist influence, for a reception by Eleanor Roosevelt. A commercial edition of these was enormously successful. He eventually designed for many factories while producing ceramic sculptures and numerous architectural works.

155 ARCHIPENKO, Alexander (Russia–U.S.A., 1887–1964). *Walking Woman,* 1937. Earthenware. H. 64.4 cm. Perls Galleries, New York.

After studying in Kiev and then in Paris, in 1923 the sculptor Archipenko settled in the United States, where he played an important role through his teaching and creative work. During the Depression a number of sculptors made use of ceramic materials, which were less costly than bronze or marble. Perhaps more important, their lively colours formed a visual antidote to the contemporary gloom. Archipenko managed to exploit the textural qualities and colour possibilities of this medium. He exhibited on many occasions at the Ceramic Nationals at Syracuse, N.Y.

156 LÉGER, Fernand (France, 1881–1955). *Composition in Red and Black,* 1951. H. 45 cm. Galerie Louise Leiris, Paris.

While in New York in 1945 Léger attempted some polychrome sculpture. Throughout his life he was concerned with architectural problems, theatrical set design, carpets and typography. He designed a mosaic for the church on the plateau of Assy by Novarina in 1949. This year marks the dawning of his interest in ceramics. His works in this medium were made in Roland Brice's studio at Biot.

155

157

299 including Karel Appel, Corneille and Asger Jorn as well as some artists influenced by Surrealism, such as Wilfredo Lam and Roberto E. Matta.

In 1947–8, as we have already seen, Matisse made some dishes at the Atelier du Plan before undertaking his great panel for the church on the plateau of Assy. In the following year Artigas began 159 to work with a painter from the Galerie Maeght, Georges Braque. 144 Soon afterwards he became associated with Marc Chagall, about whom Gaston Bachelard wrote: 'What a wonderful period we are living in, when the greatest painters wish to become ceramists. Here are men who fire colours, and with fire they create light. Marc Chagall immediately became a master of this satanic kind of painting which penetrates the surface of things and is inscribed in the depths of chemistry.'

The 1950s saw a huge increase in the number of ceramic artists. In 1954 Matisse decorated the walls of the Rosary Chapel in Vence, and in 1956–8 Miró and Artigas together completed the first of a long series of decorative wall-panels for the UNESCO building in Paris.

At the same period Fernand Léger was working on sculpture 156 and coloured *bas-reliefs* at his pupil Roland Brice's studio at Biot. 179 Jean Lurçat was also involved with ceramics at this time. He worked at the Sant-Vicens pottery at Perpignan, producing several murals. The first was made in 1959 on the theme of the 'Four Elements' for the Radio-Télévision studios at Strasbourg; a second

157 **NEVELSON,** Louise (Russia–U.S.A., 1900–   ). *Moving-Static-Moving Figures,* 1945. Terracotta (partial view). Whitney Museum of American Art, New York; 69,159.
Born in Kiev, Nevelson studied in New York and Munich, and then worked with the Mexican muralist Diego Riviera. She is now considered to be one of the most important contemporary American sculptors. She was particularly involved with ceramics during the 1940s. This group of eighteen figures, in Constructivist style, is her major work in this genre. She took full advantage of the medium, exploiting its massive character, exploring the possibility of impressing the soft clay, and contrasting brilliantly glazed areas with others left in the biscuit state.

was created in 1961 for the Sant-Vicens pottery and two more were completed in 1965 for the Préfecture de la Seine. His compositions resembled a tapestry, their broad flat areas of colour enclosed by strongly defined outlines.

Edouard Pignon had already thrown and painted his first pots at Vallauris with Picasso around 1949, and then went on to tackle monumental ceramics. He decorated the French Pavilion at the World Fair in Brussels, and then did the *Les Plongeurs* ('The Div- 282 ers') mural in fire-clay and lava for the Lumini School of Fine Arts near Marseilles, and created the façade of the Cultural Centre at Argenteuil, in collaboration with the architect Dubrulle.

Since 1945 experiments in ceramics by artists have taken place on an ever-increasing scale, especially as potters, thanks particu-

(continued on p. 98)

158

159

158 **LAURENS**, Marthe (France, 1886–1957). *Dish,* 1950. D. 43.5 cm. Private collection.
Marthe Laurens, painter and potter, wife of the sculptor Henri Laurens, was amazingly self-effacing. Her ceramics were exhibited only once, at the Palais Rumina in Lausanne in 1951, at the exhibition *Céramiques des Maîtres.* Her pieces are worthy of their present environment, where they seem to watch over the works of Henri Laurens and Georges Braque.

159 **BRAQUE**, Georges (France, 1882–1963). *Dish,* 1949. Stoneware. D. 48 cm. Galerie Maeght, Paris.
Braque worked with Artigas from 1949. He was a master of still lifes and was highly skilled at depicting objects, which appear in his lithographic works, tapestry cartoons, stained glass and ceramics, as well as in his paintings. He was typically French and kept alive the classical tradition. This bird, also depicted on a limited edition of thirty plates (24 centimetres in diameter) in 1960, shows both Greek and French inspiration.

160 **HAILE**, Thomas Samuel (England, 1909–48). *'Triumphant Procession' Vase,* 1937. Stoneware. H. 40.5 cm. Art Gallery, Southampton.
Haile, like Henry Hammond, was a pupil of William Staite Murray, and shared his belief in the importance of decoration; in his case this was very similar to contemporary painting. Although he left for the United States in 1939, he returned for war service in England and then resumed his ceramic activities in 1947, but was killed in an accident the next year.

160

161

162

161 **DANGAR,** Anne (Australia–France, ?–1951) and **GLEIZES,** Albert (France, 1881–1953). *Dish,* 1936. Glazed earthenware. D.45 cm. Musée d'art moderne de la Ville de Paris; AM 132, PPSAD 1882.
Having trained as a painter in her native country, Anne Dangar went to Paris in 1926 to continue her studies with André Lhote, before taking up ceramics at the Viroflay pottery. Attracted by the theories of Albert Gleizes, she established herself as a potter around 1930 in the craft centre which the painter and his wife set up on their property, Molly Sabata (Isère). In order to assure the survival of ancient crafts she taught children from the village, while producing traditional useful wares alongside works inspired, like this one, by the compositions of Albert Gleizes.

162 **MOORE,** Henry (England, 1898–). *'Moonhead',* 1971. Porcelain. H.26 cm.
Moore is certainly one of the most important sculptors of the twentieth century, and the human figure, either realistically rendered or conventionalized almost to the limits of abstraction, is one of his favourite themes. He agreed to participate in the policy, launched by the Rosenthal factory at Selb, of issuing works by contemporary artists, and furnished the model of this sculpture which was cast in three examples. The smooth whiteness of the porcelain is particularly well suited to this work with the lunar associations contained in its title.

larly to Picasso, have discovered the freedom of working communally. Some of these experiments have been encouraged by patronage. For instance, Aimé Maeght and Jean-Louis Prat, of the Maeght Foundation at Saint-Paul-de-Vence, not only integrated the ceramics of Miró and Artigas into the Foundation's buildings and garden, but after 1970 also encouraged certain artists to work

in the *atelier* created by Muraour under the guidance of Joan Gardy Artigas.

Since 1978 Hans Spinner has placed his technical skill at the 345 disposal of various artists. In 1973 Chillida completed a series of 269 massive sculptures in fire-clay, and in 1977 he produced a series of chamotte works painted with copper oxide and fired in an

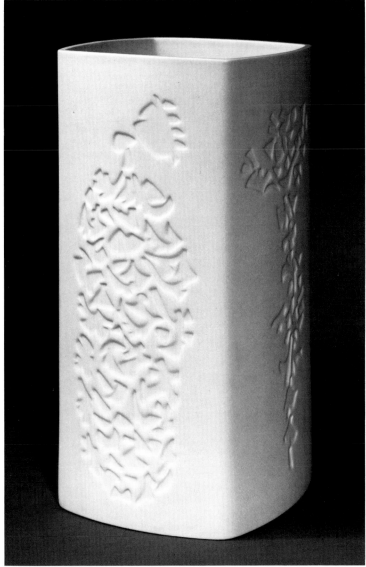

163 **PIZA**, Arthur-Luiz (Brazil–France, 1928–). *'Luis' Vase,* 1975. Porcelain. H. 58 cm. Archives, Manufacture nationale de Sèvres.
Piza, a highly skilled engraver, lived in France for twenty-five years and exhibited at more than two hundred one-man shows or group exhibitions. The work he carried out at Sèvres, including dishes, panels, and the 'Luis' and 'Clelia' vases, ensured the factory's success at exhibitions all over the world from Finland to Korea and the U.S.S.R. to the U.S.A. Piza maintained close ties with the head of the firm, Antoine d'Albis.

164 **HAJDU**, Etienne (Rumania, 1907–). *'Mary Magdalen' Vase,* 1974. Porcelain with semi-matt glaze. H. 45 cm. Archives, Manufacture nationale de Sèvres.
As a child, the sculptor Hajdu was fascinated by potters, and after making several works in terracotta was invited in 1965 to work for the Sèvres factory. He created a series of forms ornamented with impressed designs illustrating the play of light and shade, as well as decorative schemes, which he either painted in high-temperature colours directly on to unfired pieces or else designed moulds from which the pieces could be slip-cast. A true virtuoso, Etienne Hajdu, a sculptor by training, has experimented with all the Sèvres techniques.

oxidizing atmosphere; these are decorated with carved, cut, grooved or painted symbols. Among others, the painter Jean-Michel Meurice also worked in this studio. Recently the Canadian painter Jean-Paul Riopelle, who had already completed some large sculptures in plaster, became infatuated with pottery. In 1980 he finished a mural composed of porcelain plaques and a series of

lamp sculptures; encouraged by these first steps, he is planning to decorate the ceiling of the Canadian National Bank in Montreal.

This interest in the sculptural possibilities of ceramics seems almost to be confined to France, with the exception of some Italian sculptors. However, in present-day Germany the painter Julius Bissier, for example, has collaborated with Richard Bampi, 177

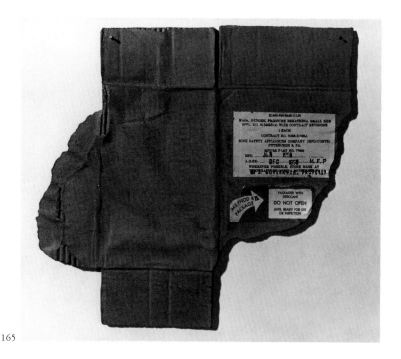

165 **RAUSCHENBERG,** Robert (United States, 1925–). *Tampa Clay Piece 1,* 1972. Earthenware. H. 37 cm. Graphic Studio, University of South Florida, Tampa, Florida.

After studying at Kansas City, in Paris and then at Black Mountain College under the direction of Joseph Albers, Rauschenberg became known as a defender of the status of artists and for his paintings reflecting the environment which incorporated rubbish and other miscellaneous objects. He worked in ceramics in 1972 during a stay at the University of South Florida, creating a series of five pieces whose theme linked them with a contemporary series of engravings; they were issued in a limited edition by Allen Eaker and Julio Juristo.

166 **NOLAND,** Kenneth (United States, 1924–). *Ceramic Relief No. 3,* 1978. Stoneware and porcelain slip. L. 68.8 cm. Artist's collection.

After studying in North Carolina and then in Paris, Noland returned to the United States, where he became a leading figure in the post-war abstract–impressionist movement, exploring the expressive power of colour. From May to November 1978 he created sixty-five works, most of them in porcelain, at the Syracuse Clay Institute in an extension of his quest into the nature of colour.

and in the United States there are many artists working in clay. The economic crisis and the Depression induced artists to employ cheap materials whenever possible. It was in this way that Alexander Archipenko returned to ceramics for his experiments 155 with surface textures, as did Isamu Noguchi. Elie Nadelman, a sculptor specializing in monumental works, hard hit by the economic situation, began to make small figures, first using plaster and papier-mâché, then clay, which he enamelled in white, grey, yellow and black colours. Between 1934 and 1939 Jackson Pollock decorated porcelain, especially vigorous bowls and plates.

In 1945 Louise Nevelson created a Constructivist work, *Mov-* 157 *ing-Static-Moving Figures,* in terracotta. It comprises fifteen totems based upon simple geometric forms assembled together. Her work is usually characterized by accumulations of elements. Here she adds a game with space and texture, playing with the space separating the figures themselves as well as with the space separating them from the spectator, and contrasting the matt areas with the glazed or decorated parts.

After the Second World War the sculptor Manuel Neri became interested in ceramics during his studies at the California College of Arts and Crafts (1956–7). He produced a series of sculptures in the form of arches decorated with brilliant glazes which had a profound influence on West Coast ceramic sculpture. Right at the outset of his career, in 1956, Roy Lichtenstein worked with the 331 ceramist Ka-Kwong-Hui. They produced traditional domestic wares in terracotta, piling them up so that they looked ridiculous. They also made moulded heads and decorated them with dots, bands and flat patterns in primary colours borrowed from popular comic strips. These clearly relate to Lichtenstein's later paintings. In 1972 Robert Rauschenberg paid a three-month visit to the 165 Department of Art of the University of South Florida, Tampa, where with the assistance of Allen Eaker and Julio Juristo he created five clay works and a series of engravings. In 1976 the potter Margie Hughto organized an exhibition of sculpted work in terracotta at the Everson Museum of Art. It included the work of ten contemporary artists. In 1978, aided by her and his students, Kenneth Noland made sixty-five pieces at the Syracuse 166 Clay Institute.

We have discussed painters and sculptors, but there is another category of artists who ought to become involved more often with ceramics: that is engravers.

Some traditional potters are critical or even jealous of the intrusion of great artists into the field of ceramics, even if they all pursue the same ideal with the same dedication.

No one has expressed the creative aim more ably than Paul Valéry, in his *Pièces sur l'Art*: 'Of what use are these arts of the fire if not to proclaim man's victory over this element? Man's earliest products were made using fire. No sooner had he tamed fire and enslaved its heat, and through it mastered clay and metal to create tools, arms and utensils, than he channelled it into producing objects created for pleasure and contemplation. There must once have been a man who, idly caressing some commonplace pot, felt moved to create another one purely for pleasure.'

Potters

The changes of taste and outlook which took place in the second half of the nineteenth century had a profound influence on the products of art pottery manufacturers. These changes also led to the birth of a totally new kind of craftsman, the 'studio potter'.

Several factors contributed to his appearance. In the first place, the reaction against the shortcomings of industry, led in England by John Ruskin and William Morris and in France by E. Viollet-le-Duc, was accompanied by a eulogy of the craftsman and a rehabilitation of medieval techniques. This attitude encouraged the revival of tin-glazed earthenware and traditional stoneware.

The second important factor was the European discovery of the arts of other parts of the world. After the sensation caused by the Japanese stand at the Universal Exhibitions of 1862 and 1867, countries with a rich ceramic tradition, such as China, Korea and the Middle Eastern lands, were rediscovered; later primitive African and South American pottery came to be appreciated as well.

Artist potters also benefited from a series of favourable circumstances. At this time there was a widespread and passionate interest in chemistry. Knowledge of this science was indispensable for the preparation of glazes and clay bodies (Alexandre Bigot was at first a physics and chemistry teacher). A number of potters carried out systematic researches into glaze effects in the latter half of the nineteenth century. One of the earliest and best known was Ernest Chaplet, but there were also some remarkable pioneers in England, such as the chemist William Burton, who worked for Wedgwood before becoming, from 1892 to 1915, manager of the Pilkington Tile and Pottery Company, where he produced some superb shaded and crystalline glazes as well as lustres. In 1898 another pioneer, William Howson Taylor, opened a studio at Smethwick, first making pottery and then porcelain. Influenced by his admiration for the theories of Ruskin (after whom he named his factory) and for Chinese ceramics of the Song and Ming dynasties, he produced three different types of glaze: *soufflé* wares with monochrome shaded glazes; lustres, also in a wide range of shades and colours; and above all so-called 'high-temperature' glazes, which combined unusual, variegated colours. At that time everyone guarded jealously the secret of their glazes. Chaplet burned all his recipes when blindness forced him to stop his experiments, and William Howson Taylor did the same before his death.

However, a reaction soon set in. In 1897 Charles Fergus Binns arrived in the United States, and in 1900 became director of the New York School of Clay Working at Alfred University where he stressed the technical aspect of ceramics. From the early years of the century Bernard Moore gave technical assistance to several English factories. Indeed, he devised the formula for copper-red used by Doulton's. Michael Powolny, teaching in Vienna, strongly emphasized the importance of glazes and knowledge of chemistry, as did Richard Lunn, professor of ceramic techniques at the Royal College of Art in London from 1903. It seems that the traditional secrecy surrounding ceramic techniques has disappeared nowadays, to judge from the number of publications of articles or popular works about them, although in some cases authors neglect to mention little tricks of the trade that are indispensable for successful results using the given formulae.

Another circumstance that has encouraged the development of new types of ceramics is the modern practice of designing a building as a coherent ensemble in which all elements must harmonize. Every aspect now has to be considered with a fresh eye, so that even the details can constitute works of arts in their own right. Panels of architectural ceramics adorn façades or interior areas, and various ornamental or utilitarian objects lose their strictly functional status.

Before the First World War the most striking feature in the activity of European art potters is the predominance of stoneware. In some cases it was adopted as part of a national tradition, while in other instances it gradually supplanted more traditional materials. The techniques vary according to the degree of Far Eastern influence, especially Japanese, which had the effect of displacing traditional techniques. Signs of current decorative trends can also be discerned in the work of some stoneware potters. Once again it should be noted that although the burgeoning Art Nouveau movement had a rapid and extensive effect on the production of factories, influenced as they were by the caprices of fashion which determined their customers' taste, artist potters, like other artists, remained untouched by merely transient influences.

Traditional stoneware appears to have been rediscovered before the general craze for all things Japanese set in. The adoption of this material was also aided by the fact that it was in common use for mass-produced sanitary and domestic wares, so that production processes had been highly developed.

The painter and potter Jean-Charles Cazin seems to have been one of the first to choose to work with stoneware. He left France for England in 1870 and worked for the Fulham Pottery, which made useful and decorative brown stonewares decorated with

(continued on p. 115)

167

168

167 **MASCARIN,** Mario (Italy–Switzerland, 1901–66). *Bowl,* 1959. Stone-ware. D. 29.5 cm. Musée Ariana, Geneva; 501.
Mario Mascarin followed several different careers. Originally an accountant, he then became a correspondent for the paper *Il Mondo* at Bergen in Norway. Towards 1928 he tried his hand at pottery with traditional Norwegian potters before going on to study the subject in 1929 at Nove. He emigrated to Switzer-land in 1930 and in 1935 founded a studio near Zurich. He worked in faïence with the sculptor Arnold d'Altri before going on to become associated with manufacturers. He continued teaching and producing his own work. He was one of the first potters in Switzerland to work in stoneware.

168 **BONTJES VAN BEEK,** Jan (Germany, 1899–1969). *Vase, c.* 1940. Stoneware. H. 11.4 cm. Hetjens-Museum, Düsseldorf; 1941–331a.
Jan Bontjes van Beek studied pottery and the chemistry of ceramics and glazes before producing architectural ceramics. In 1933 he opened a studio in Berlin which was destroyed during the war. After the war he played an important part in the revival of German pottery, particularly through his teaching which emphasized the study of glazes.

169 **BONIFAS,** Paul A. (Switzerland, 1893–1967). *Vase,* date unknown. Earthenware. H. 21.2 cm. Musée Ariana, Geneva; AR 6269.
Paul Bonifas studied various crafts (engraving, jewellery, enamelling) before tak-ing up ceramics and its chemistry, as well as mineralogy. In 1915 he opened his first studio at Versoix near Geneva which was destroyed by fire in 1919. He was appointed technical director at the factory of Achille Bloch and Sons (1920–1), before becoming secretary-general of *l'Esprit nouveau,* the review edited by Amédée Ozenfant and Le Corbusier (1921–2), who were at that time passion-ately interested in portraying original ceramic forms in their drawings and paint-ings. He opened a second studio at Ferney-Voltaire before leaving in 1946 for the U.S.A. (Seattle, Logan), where he taught until 1959. He subsequently devoted all his time to his own creative work.

170 **ARTIGAS,** José Llorens (Spain, 1892–1980). *'Moonlight' Vase,* 1927. Stoneware. H. 25.5 cm. Museu de Ceramica, Barcelona; 8679.
Born in Barcelona, Artigas was taught by Joan Miró at the art school run by Fran-cesc Galé in that city. He went on to study drawing at the School of Fine Arts, and then ceramics with Francesc Quer at the Higher School of Applied Arts. From 1923 to 1941 he lived in Paris, where he associated with many artists whom he taught ceramics (cf. Pls. 137, 138), giving them the benefit of his immense technical expertise. His continuous association with various great artists tends to overshadow the potter's own work.

169

171 **KREBS,** Nathalie (Denmark, 1895–1978). *Vase, c.* 1956. Fine stoneware. H. 40 cm. Dr. H. Thiemann Collection, Hamburg.
Nathalie Krebs studied chemistry and from 1919 to 1929 worked for Bing and Grøndahl of Copenhagen. In 1929–30 she shared a studio with Gunnar Nylund, and then from 1930 to 1968 ran the independent 'Saxbo' studio. This was historically of great importance since it was the first in Denmark to make stoneware. There she carried out research into form, firing and glazes. This vase, by Eva Staehr-Nielsen, was glazed by Nathalie Krebs.

172 **GRIEMERT,** Hubert (Germany, 1905–). *Jug with Narrow Neck.* 1961. Stoneware. H. 43 cm. Dr. H. Thiemann Collection, Hamburg.
Hubert Griemert studied painting and ceramic modelling. Throughout his career he created designs for factories (Fürstenberg, 1934–6, Berlin, *c.* 1950, Bauscher Brothers at Weiden, 1958) while carrying out research in his own workshop. His teaching is his most important contribution to contemporary German ceramics.

173 **LINDIG,** Otto (Germany, 1895–1966). *Jug,* 1957. Stoneware. H. 27 cm. Dr. H. Thiemann Collection, Hamburg.
After studying drawing, modelling and sculpture, Otto Lindig directed the ceramic workshop at the Weimar Bauhaus (1919–20); he then taught pottery (1920–2) and became technical director (1922–30) of the ceramic studio which the Bauhaus set up at Dornburg. From 1930 to 1947 he continued to direct the workshop, by now independent, before going on to teach in Hamburg until 1960.

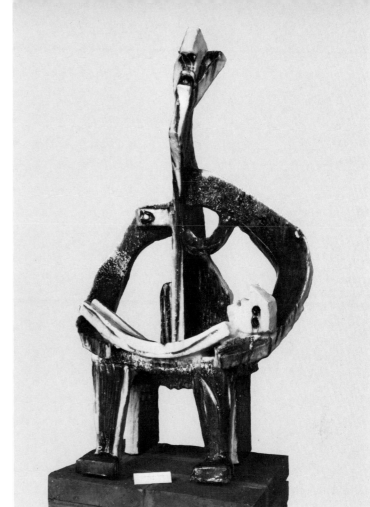

174

175

174 **LEONCILLO,** called Leoncillo **LEONARDI** (Italy, 1915–68). *The Typist,* 1952. Earthenware. H. 72 cm. Museo internazionale delle Ceramiche, Faenza.
After studying at the Perugia Institute of Art and then at the Fine Art Academy in Rome, Leonardi participated in the 7th Triennale in Milan in 1940, at the request of the architect Gio Ponti. His exhibition of twenty-two works at the Del Fiore Gallery in Florence in 1949 was highly praised by Roberto Longhi. In 1948 he took part in the first Venice Biennale. In 1955 he created a monument entitled *Alla partigiana Veneta* and another in 1957 at Albissola Marina, an important centre of modern Italian ceramics.

175 **GAMBONE,** Guido (Italy, 1909–69). *Mother and Child,* 1954. Earthenware. H. 119 cm. Museo internazionale delle Ceramiche, Faenza; 13,664.
Gambone entered the Avallone studio at Vietri sul Mare around 1925 and subsequently taught himself the craft of pottery. From 1950 he worked in Florence. He won several awards at Faenza and elsewhere in Italy, as well as a silver medal in 1955 at Cannes. He played an important role in freeing Italian pottery from the weight of traditions by showing that clay could be used in a totally new fashion.

176 **LEONCILLO,** called Leoncillo **LEONARDI** (Italy, 1915–68). *Winter Meeting,* 1961. Earthenware. H. 154 cm. Museo internazionale delle Ceramiche, Faenza; 13,753.
Although all figurative allusion has disappeared from this piece, the disposition and structure of the coloured areas remain fundamentally the same as in Leonardi's earlier realistic works.

176

177

178

177 **BAMPI,** Richard (Brazil–Germany, 1896–1965). *Egg, c.* 1953. Earthenware. H. 20.8 cm. Hetjens-Museum, Düsseldorf; 1962–31.
Bampi studied architecture at Munich, then at the Bauhaus, where he worked as a sculptor and graphic designer. Later, while on a visit to Italy, he learnt the technique of enamelling on metal. From 1923 to 1927 he worked in Rio de Janeiro as a sculptor and graphic designer. He also set up a pottery workshop, which in 1927 he transferred to Kandern, where he worked in earthenware until 1938. His fame dates from the 1950s. He was one of the first in Germany to produce non-functional forms, freely modelled and asymmetrical.

178 **SALTO,** Axel (Denmark, 1889–1961). *Vase,* 1957. Stoneware. H. 23.3 cm. Dr. H. Thiemann Collection, Hamburg.
Salto studied ancient languages and then painting and in 1923 produced his first ceramic works for Bing and Grøndahl. In 1929–30 he worked with Carl Halier and Bode Willumsen and in 1931–2 with Nathalie Krebs. From 1934 he worked for the Royal Copenhagen Factory while continuing his career as a painter, graphic artist and fabric designer. He was one of the first potters in Denmark to be interested in sculptural rather than functional forms.

179

179 **LURÇAT,** Jean (France, 1892–1966). *Catalan 'dourque' Jug,* 1956.
H. 37 cm. Firmin Bauby Collection.
Lurçat studied under Victor Prouvé, a leading figure in the Nancy school of decorative arts, and from 1919 to 1936 devoted himself to painting. He was influenced by Matisse, and also by Cubism and Surrealism. He became concerned with tapestry in 1933 and in 1939 set out to revive this art at Aubusson, and was totally successful. In the 1950s he applied himself with equal passion to the decoration of innumerable dishes and pots at the Sant-Vicens studios at Perpignan. These are unique pieces or appeared in limited editions. Lurçat also designed for Haviland and created several murals, including some in 1961 which were destined for the Sant-Vicens pottery. These were designed in the same way as his tapestries, having strictly defined areas of colour.

180 **CAILLE,** Pierre (Belgium, 1912–   ). *The Tower,* 1958. Stoneware, partly enamelled. H. 71.5 cm. Musées royaux d'Art et d'Histoire, Brussels; CR. 254.
Born at Tournai, Caille studied at the National School of Architecture and Decorative Arts in Brussels, where he later taught. Following the advice of Henry van de Velde he took an interest in ceramics, while continuing to paint, design and create jewellery. His first ceramic murals date from 1949 and in 1953 he decorated the casino at Ostende. He played an important part in the history of Belgian ceramics through his work, since he was the first potter to be liberated from traditional functionalism, and through his teaching.

180

181

182

183

181 **NATZLER,** Gertrud and Otto (Germany–U.S.A., 1908–71 and 1908–). *Earth Crater Bowl,* 1956. Earthenware. D. 30.5 cm. Everson Museum of Art, Syracuse; P.C. 59.26 (gift of U.S. Potters' Association).
Gertrud and Otto Natzler belonged to a group of artists who were already well known in their own country (they were awarded a Médaille d'argent in Paris in 1937) who came to the fore during the 1940s in the United States, whither they had emigrated. Gertrud had studied at the School of Decorative Arts in Vienna; her neo-classical pieces were glazed by Otto. They both rapidly became famous for their technological expertise. Since Gertrud's death, Otto continues to work on his own, now also making the pots.

182 **PRESSET,** Claude-Albana (Switzerland, 1934–). *Bowl.* 1978. Porcelain. H. 19.2 cm. Musée Ariana, Geneva; AR 5831.
After studying painting, Claude-Albana Presset took a course in ceramics in the Sordet-Bonifas workshop (1954), then became a pupil of Philippe Lambercy in Geneva. She had a workshop from 1955 to 1960; she then went on a study trip to Japan in 1960–1 (she returned to the Far East in 1973), and then to India. In 1963 she opened a studio near Geneva, where she teaches pottery at the School of Decorative Arts. She took part in the exhibition of miniatures organized at Kyoto in 1980 by the International Academy of Ceramics.

183 **GROTELL,** Maija (Finland–U.S.A., 1899–1973). *Vase,* 1949. Stoneware. H. 31.2 cm. Everson Museum of Art, Syracuse; P.C. 50.641 (gift of G. R. Crocker & Co.).
Maija Grotell was born in Helsinki, where she studied painting, design and sculpture and worked for six years as a potter with Alfred William Finch (cf. Pl. 62). In 1927 she emigrated to the United States where she made an important contribution through her teaching, particularly at Rutgers University, N.J. (1936–8) and at Cranbrook Academy of Art at Bloomfield, Mich. (1938–66), as well as through her own work.

184 **CHAPALLAZ,** Edouard (Switzerland, 1921–). *Vase,* 1968. Stoneware. H. 38 cm. Fina Gomez Collection, Paris.
After studying at the Swiss School of Ceramics at Chavannes-Renens (now moved to Vevey), Chapallaz set up his own studio in 1953. He has also worked in the ceramic industry, and continues to act as an occasional technical consultant. From 1958 to 1968 he taught ceramics at the School of Decorative Arts in Geneva. Many of his works have been incorporated into buildings in Switzerland and Mexico. In 1980 he participated in the exhibition of miniatures organized by the International Academy of Ceramics in Kyoto.

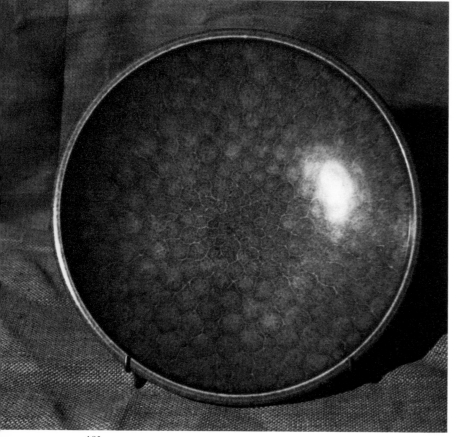

185

186

185 FOUQUET, Pierre (France 1909–). *Bowl,* 1955. Stoneware.
D. 38 cm.
After completing his studies at the Applied Arts School and the College of Arts
and Crafts in Paris, Pierre Fouquet started to practise his craft in 1927, first casting, modelling and glazing, and then creating models. He was responsible for
establishing and organizing the pottery workshop at the Paris École Supérieure
des Arts Appliqués et des Métiers d'Art, and today teaches ceramics at the Institut
National de Restauration des Œuvres d'Art. He designs new shapes and is
interested in glazes, which he treats with a high degree of technical skill. This
bowl, painted in a rare mottled copper-blue, is a fine example of his technique.

186 SEKA (Venezuela, 1923–). *Ceramic,* 1972. H. 27.5 cm. Victoria and
Albert Museum, London; Circ. 511–1972.
Born in Zagreb, Yugoslavia, Seka studied sculpture at the Academy of Fine Arts
from 1942 to 1945. She then went to the Grande Chaumière in Paris, where from
1946 to 1948 she studied sculpture and drawing. In 1948, while taking a degree
in art history, she began to show an interest in pottery and since 1952 has had
her own studio in Caracas.

187 RAIDEL, Anton (Austria, 1943–). *Vase,* 1976. Stoneware. H. 18 cm.
Anton Raidel studied at the School of Decorative Arts at Graz and then at the
Academy of Modern Art in Vienna. He graduated in 1968 and became an independent member of the 'H' group from 1969 to 1973, when he set up his own
studio. He has taken part in numerous symposia and exhibitions and has received
many awards. He also works as a designer.

187

110

188 MONTMOLLIN, Frère Daniel de (France, 1925–). *Vase,* 1979. Stoneware. H. 15 cm. Private collection, Germany.

Frère Daniel de Montmollin set up the Taizé community pottery studio in 1950. He was no stranger to the technique and allowed his readers the benefit of his experience in his works *Le poème céramique* and *L'art de cendres.* Frère Daniel successfully experimented with iron-red derived from straw, used straw ashes on a felspathic cobalt glaze, and created glazes containing ashes from cereal crops. His work is permanently on exhibition in Paris at the home of his friends Jeanine and Raymond Sauvaire. He is one of the leading representatives of a fundamental trend in French ceramics, and is renowned for his glaze effects; among his colleagues are Agathe Ruffe, Annie Fourmanoir, Paul Badié, Alain Girel and Jean-Pierre Cluzel.

189 MERCHAN, Cristina (Venezuela, 1926–). *Vase,* 1976. Stoneware. H. 12 cm. Fina Gomez Collection, Paris.

Cristina Merchan studied low-fired ceramics at Caracas (1953–6), then stone-ware at Barcelona with Francesc Albors and José Llorens Artigas (1958–61). Since 1958 she has been living in Barcelona and Paris. Her work demonstrates her constant pursuit of the most subtly varied glazes and surfaces. The surface of her pots can be roughly textured in high relief, skilfully modelled with striations and bands, or else smooth and plain.

190 DEL PIERRE, Francine (France, 1913–68). *Box,* 1965. Earthenware. H. 7.5 cm. Fina Gomez Collection, Paris.

Francine Del Pierre took up ceramics in 1946 and joined the Vallauris pottery in 1947, at a time when its fame was increasing. She opened her first studio in Paris in 1949; her workshop in rue Bonaparte was set up in 1961. She made several journeys to England, where she struck up a friendship with Bernard Leach and Shoji Hamada; she exhibited regularly with them and undertook many lecture tours. She worked in stoneware as well as faïence and was concerned with volume and decoration; her sensitive designs were always inspired by nature.

188

189

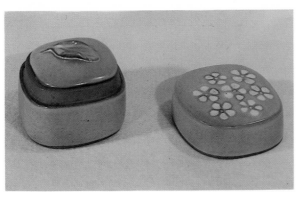

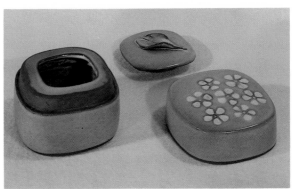

190

191

192

191 **STOCKER,** Monika (Switzerland, 1950–). *Double-walled Vase,* 1979. Thrown stoneware. H. 17 cm. Musée Ariana, Geneva; AR 6061.
Monika Stocker studied pottery in Berne and then in Geneva with Philippe Lambercy. She works with the ceramist Dominique Grange at Lovatens. As well as producing domestic wares, each artist conducts his or her own research. Monika Stocker creates double-walled vases with glazes which emphasize the volume of the pieces. Many of her works are initially thrown and achieve their final form through hand-modelling.

192 **ZAHNER,** Arnold (Switzerland, 1919–). *Vase,* 1976. Porcelain. H. 17 cm. Musée Ariana, Geneva; AR 5791.
The son of a potter with whom he trained from 1934 to 1936, Zahner was a pupil at the Swiss School of Ceramics at Chavannes-Renens and later, for a few months in 1938, attended the School of Ceramics in Berne. From 1938 to 1941 he studied kiln construction and from 1934 to 1942 learned drawing and modelling at Basle. In 1942 he became the proprietor of the family firm, which was later merged with a large ceramic group enterprise and was finally sold in 1977. He also had his own studio where he produced ceramics as well as mosaics. He has made several study trips in Europe as well as to Japan, where he worked with local potters. He has exhibited all over the world.

193 **BEN LISA,** René (France, 1926–). *Vase,* 1979. Stoneware. H. 12 cm. Fina Gomez Collection, Paris.
Ben Lisa studied at the School of Fine Arts at Marseilles, where he has taught pottery since 1972, producing wonderful glazes on a restricted range of shapes. He says of his work: 'I take quartz from the bowels of the earth and combine it with clay, artificially renewing the thousand-year-old mysterious marriage between mineral and earth and confronting forces which are for ever ready to escape me. This seems to me terrifying ... I feel that I am handling forces more powerful than myself. I feel unworthy of subduing them, of succeeding in my

quest. A humble potter, I manipulate these forces to give rein to my feelings, while they seek only rest. Forcing this encounter is frightening...'

194 **DEJONGHE,** Bernard (France, 1942–). *Plaque* (detail), 1979. Stoneware. 30 × 30 cm.
Dejonghe studied at the School of Arts and Crafts in Paris and has always dreamed of making large mural panels with stunning glazes. His murals at Gennevilliers are examples of his technique. His shields and plaques are fine achievements. Thirty shades of the same red are produced in a single firing. For the sake of his work Dejonghe lives in the Briançon region. He is a master-potter whose reputation does not extend outside France, but by the turn of the century this will have changed.

195 **CHAMPY,** Claude (France, 1944–). *Bowl,* 1979. Stoneware. H. 9 cm. A.D.M. Sarver Collection.
After completing his training at the School of Arts and Crafts in Paris in 1975, Champy participated in the exhibition organized by Noella Gest at Saint-Rémy de Provence, *Eighteen Artists in Pottery,* which marked the revival of French ceramics. His wife, Catherine Champy, prefers to work on objects connected with the domestic setting. 'By remembering houses, bedrooms, attics, cellars, we learn to remain ourselves' (Gaston Bachelard).

196 **SCHOTT,** Margarete (Germany 1911–). *Double-walled Pot,* 1978. Porcelain. H. 10 cm.
After taking a course in philology Margarete Schott studied ceramics with Fritz Theodor Schroeder at Heppenheim from 1947 to 1948 and then at Darmstadt from 1948 to 1951. From 1951 to 1952 she worked in Harry C. Davis's studio in England. Since 1952 she has been teaching ceramic technology at Darmstadt, where she opened a studio ten years later. She is particularly concerned with reduction firing on thrown stoneware and porcelain.

193

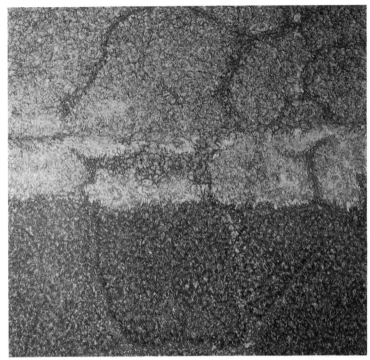

194

195

196

197 **DEL PIERRE,** Francine (France, 1913–68). *Flat Oval Vase.* 1966.
Earthenware. H. 38 cm. Fina Gomez Collection, Paris.
In 1976 an exhibition was organized at the Museum of Fine Arts, Caen, by F.
Debaissieux and Fance Franck, the latter an excellent potter who was a pupil of
Francine del Pierre. This exhibition brought together 140 of her pieces, among
them five vases, forty bowls, thirty boxes and flasks and twenty panels or tiles.
About one hundred pieces were in faïence and the remainder in porcelain or
stoneware. Watercolour drawings were another highlight of this wonderful
exhibition. About one hundred earthenware pieces were shown, the remainder
being of porcelain or stoneware.

197

198 **LEACH**, Bernard (England, 1887–1979). *Incised Jar,* 1972. Stoneware. H. 29.2 cm.

The main characteristic of Bernard Leach's work is its synthesis of Eastern and Western ideas. Throughout his life he has tirelessly pursued this one objective, which he felt to be his vocation.

relief patterns or coloured slips. During his stay Cazin also taught at the Lambeth School of Art, where one of his pupils was Robert Wallace Martin, a pioneer in the revival of stoneware in England. On his return to France in 1871 Cazin set up a studio at Boulogne-sur-Mer where he made stoneware showing a much stronger Japanese influence. His pieces have incised, modelled or pierced decoration.

In 1881 Ernest Chaplet made his first stoneware pots with Albert Dammouse and Frédéric Hexamer. At this time he was in charge of the Haviland studio at Auteuil, where the potters were losing interest in the *barbotine* process. The workshop moved to rue Blomet in Paris in 1882, making stonewares with matt glazes and naturalistic decoration, which greatly attracted Gauguin and probably influenced his later work. 37

Théodore Deck, after working with faïence for a long period, also became interested in stoneware.

In England, as we have already seen, the earliest artist potters to work in stoneware were the four Martin brothers who established themselves in Fulham in 1873 and moved to Southall in the spring of 1877. They made vases with incised or modelled decoration, in a great variety of colours, in addition to the highly popular 'face jugs', birds and grotesque animals, using a very fine salt-glaze that allowed the modelling to show through. 17

In Germany a revival of traditional salt-glazed stoneware occurred at Höhr-Grenzhausen in the Westerwald region. Reinhold Hanke took over his father's firm in 1859. His first Art Nouveau pieces were designed by Henry van de Velde and Peter Behrens around 1900. Hanke became interested in French stoneware which showed Japanese influence and designed some restrained and powerful forms, decorated with linear incised patterns intended to show off the flow-glazes or crystalline effects. In the other Höhr-Grenzhausen factory which belonged to Reinhold Merkelbach, Richard Riemerschmid designed pieces in an idiom that was much closer to the traditional one, although his geometric decoration was unmistakably modern. 67, 66

64

Josef Mendez da Costa, who worked in Laren from 1912, was the only Dutch potter to use stoneware decorated in the traditional way with motifs incised through a layer of slip. He also modelled animals and figures in stoneware. 65

The work of all these stoneware potters, who were strongly influenced by Japan, shares certain characteristics. Collections of Oriental art were gradually assembled in Europe, by the Goncourt brothers, by Paul Jeanneney, and by Justus Brinckmann, who some time after 1880 began to build up his collection for the Hamburg Museum. Initially European craftsmen attempted to reproduce the outward appearance of Oriental pieces, without understanding their underlying theoretical principles, even though, as we now know, these factors were undoubtedly of prime importance. Flecks of gold which were intended to conceal a blemish became for the Europeans purely ornamental devices just as asymmetry, which was the result of spontaneous creation and internal tension, was perceived as purely ornamental. It was only

(continued on p. 128)

199 **CASSON,** Michael (England, 1925–). *Jug.* Salt-glazed stoneware. H. 61 cm.
Michael Casson started teaching in 1946 and experimented with traditional stonewares, glazing them with salt and firing them in a reducing atmosphere. He has also worked in porcelain, using gas, oil or wood to fire his kiln. He has made an important contribution as a teacher and lecturer both in England and the United States, and his involvement with the Craftsmen Potters Association of Great Britain has helped to maintain the continuing vitality of British ceramics.

200 **ECKERT,** Otto (Czechoslovakia, 1910–). *Vase,* 1945. Stoneware. H. 102 cm. Artist's collection.

201 *Vase,* 1973. Stoneware. H. 36 cm. Private collection.
Eckert studied sculpture at the School of Decorative Arts in Prague before taking up ceramics, and first worked with a large number of industrial concerns. His repertoire is wide and varied and includes sculpture on naturalistic or social themes as well as domestic wares, *bas-reliefs* and pots. He is concerned with new relationships between form and decoration, and also seeks fresh decorative solutions. He has made a fundamental contribution through his teaching. Since 1946 he has directed the ceramic studio at the Prague School of Decorative Arts, which has trained several generations of Czech and foreign potters.

199

202

203

202 **KOSTANDA,** Alexandre (Poland–France, 1921–). *Vase,* 1974. Stoneware. H. 67 cm.
After a period of teaching at the School of Applied Arts at Beaune and also at Longchamp, Alexandre Kostanda settled at Vallauris in 1949 and established the Vallauris Biennale. He has participated in numerous exhibitions in the U.S.A. In reproducing a work by Kostanda we also pay homage to all the potters in the Vallauris region who are endeavouring to preserve its artistic production, among them Bessone, Roger Capron, Jean Derval, Roger Collet, Gilbert Portanier and Jean-Paul van Lith; and at Biot the Swedish potter Hans Hedberg.

203 **BRENNAND,** Francisco (Brazil, 1927–). *Vase with Opening.* 1977. H. 92 cm.
The *Antiga Ceramica Sao Joao* was founded by Ricardo Lacerda de Almeida Brennand in 1904. This vast factory, in keeping with the size of Brazil itself, was revived in 1971 by Francisco Brennand who produces monumental vases as well as tiles for walls and floors. Francisco studied painting in France with André Lhote and Léger from 1949 to 1952 and ceramics in Umbria in 1953. He is also responsible for numerous wall panels, the first, in the airport at Recife, dating from 1958. His floral panels (Miami, Brasilia) can reach up to 700 square metres in extent.

204 **WEIGEL,** Gotlind (Germany, 1932–). *Form,* 1978. Porcelain. ▷ H. 14 cm.
Gotlind Weigel studied ceramics from 1949 to 1952 at Plankenfels near Bayreuth and from 1952 until 1956 at Hanover, while also working on architectural projects. From 1956 to 1958 she was taught by Hubert Griemert at Höhr-Grenzhausen, and in 1958–9 she worked in the studio of Rolf Weber. In 1959–60 she became artistic director of a small factory.

118

205

207 VASSOS, Demetriou (Cyprus, 1954–). *Vase,* 1980. *Raku* ware. H. 27 cm.

Vassos was born in Famagusta and studied ceramics bevore being forced to flee to Larnaca in 1974. A grant from the Cyprus government enabled him to study for three years from 1978 at the Istituto Statale d'Arte per la Ceramica at Faenza. He took part in his first international exhibition there in 1981 before returning to Larnaca to open a studio there. His pots, somewhat reminiscent of those of classical Greece, are thrown, then incised, touched up and partially glazed using a brush. The glaze is fired at 980° and, while the kiln is still hot, the pieces are removed and immediately transferred into a strongly reducing atmosphere (i.e. an atmosphere deprived of oxygen).

208 SMITH, Derek (England–Australia). *Spherical Thrown Form.* Porcelain. H. 17 cm.

Derek Smith was born in England, and studied design and ceramics at Loughborough and Leicester before emigrating in 1956. From 1962 to 1972 he taught and directed the Australian branch of Doulton and in 1977 opened the Blackfriars Pottery, where with a small team he produces domestic high-fired stonewares, alongside individually-created stonewares intended for exhibition or commissions; they are thrown or modelled by hand, and are as a rule decorated with matt glazes.

205 MOHY, Yves (France, 1925–). *Vase,* 1973. Stoneware. H. 52 cm. Collection of l'Atelier d'Amon, Paris.

After studying at the Ecole des Métiers d'Art in Paris, Yves Mohy began teaching at the Ecole des Beaux-Arts at Bourges. He created models for the Virebent porcelain factory and was the first to obtain the Vallauris grand prix in 1966; this prize-winning piece is exhibited in the museum of Vallauris which contains some of the world's finest works.

209 LANDWEER, Sonja (Netherlands–Ireland, 1933–). *Vase,* 1977. Earthenware. H. 17.8 cm.

Sonja Landweer was born in Amsterdam and studied at the School of Industrial Design there before opening a studio in 1954. In 1956, with the aid of a grant, she undertook a study tour of Spain, France, Denmark and England. In 1963 she perfected a ceramic technique inspired by batik. During the winter of 1964–5 she was invited by the Arabia Company of Helsinki to work at their factory and in 1965–6 was employed at the Kilkenny Design Workshops in Ireland. She has participated in many individual or group exhibitions and was awarded a prize at Vallauris in 1974.

210 NASH, Grete Helland-Hansen (Norway, 1939–). *Vase,* 1978. Porcelain. H. 14 cm.

After studying in Oslo, Grete Nash became a designer for the Royal Copenhagen Factory in 1962–3, before leaving for the University of Minnesota in Minneapolis (1970–2) and eventually opening her own studio in 1974. Since then she has taken part in many exhibitions in her own country and abroad, lectured at Bergen and Oslo, and made several study tours. She works in tin-glazed earthenware as well as in porcelain, practices the *raku* technique, and decorates her pieces with the brush.

206

211 GREENAWAY, Vic (Australia, 1947–). *Plate,* 1980. Stoneware. W. 30 cm.

Following his art school training, Vic Greenaway opened his first studio in Victoria in 1968, before joining the Mungeribar Pottery in 1969, where he acted as director in 1972 in the absence of Jan Sprague. In 1974, with the aid of a grant, he went on a study tour to Japan, where he worked for two months with a potter, then to Scandinavia and the United Kingdom. On his return to Australia he opened the Broomhill Pottery, where he worked with local materials and took on apprentices. His plates, formed from slabs of clay, are fired at a temperature of 1300° and decorated with magnesium and cobalt glazes.

206 DEBLANDER, Robert (France, 1924–). *Vase,* 1975. Stoneware. H. 56 cm. J. Piffaut Collection.

Deblander studied from 1940 to 1944 at the Ecole nationale des Arts décoratifs in Paris and in 1960 established a workshop at Saint-Amand-en-Puisaye where traditional stoneware techniques were employed. In 1969 he made his first experimental trials in a kiln fired by propane gas. In 1965 he received the Marseilles grand prix and in 1968 was awarded a gold medal in Munich. He resided in Quebec in 1974 and in 1976 was sent by the United Nations to help found a pottery studio in Chad. His works are exhibited in numerous museums in Tokyo, New York and Paris.

212 SMAIL, Ian (England–New Zealand, 1949–). *Bottle,* 1980. Stoneware. H. 25 cm.

Born in England, Ian Smail emigrated to New Zealand in 1953. He took his first steps into the world of ceramics in 1974. He is self-taught, claiming to have learnt 'about pots from other potters'. He has constructed several oil-fired kilns, including a small one for salt-glazed stonewares; the kiln in current use, which has three chambers and is wood-fired, was built with the help of Warren Tippett. In 1978 Smail travelled to Japan and from 1979 to 1981 shared his studio with Nicolas Stather, a potter who studied in England and works with slips. He uses felspathic glazes or those derived from local rocks and wood ash, firing his pots at 1280°.

207

208

209

210

211

212

213

213 **BENZ,** Sophie (Switzerland, 1948–). *Vase,* before 1979. Earthenware. H. 26 cm. Musée Ariana, Geneva; AR 6064.
Born in Berne in a region where traditional potteries still survive, Sophie Benz established herself along with her husband, the potter Fredy Benz, in the market town of Laupen where they produce useful wares while continuing their experimental work.

214 **CAIGER-SMITH,** Alan (England, 1930–). *Bowl,* 1979. Earthenware. D. 34 cm.
After studying painting (1948–9) and pottery (1954–5) in London as well as history at Cambridge (1949–52), Alan Caiger-Smith opened the Aldermaston Pottery in 1955, where he initially worked alone and then took on assistants with whom he shares all the various tasks. In particular he produces tin-glazed earthenware with painted decoration and metallic lustres over wood-fired stanniferous glazes, which he calls 'smoked lustre'. He is particularly fond of large goblets and bowls, mostly thrown. Moulded elements are sometimes combined with coils or slabs.

214

215 **SIESBYE,** Alev Ebüzziya (Turkey, 1938–). *Bowl,* 1980. Stoneware. D. 14 cm. 'Kunst Foreningen', Copenhagen.
After taking a sculpture course in her native Istanbul from 1956 to 1958, at which time she also frequented the Füreya pottery studio, Alev Siesbye worked at various factories: Höhr-Grenzhausen (1958–64), Istanbul (1960–2), and then in Denmark, where she now lives when she is not in Paris. She began by working in association with the Royal Copenhagen Factory (1963–6) before opening a studio in the same city. Since 1975 she has been a designer for the Rosenthal Company at Selb, while continuing her own production. She has participated in very many exhibitions, both on an individual and group basis, throughout the world and her work is featured in several museums and collections.

216 **BRITTON,** Alison (England, 1949–). *Three Coffee-pots.* Max. h. 35 cm. Princessehof Museum, Leeuwarden and Crafts Council, London; left: GMP 1978/144.
Alison Britton first studied fine art at Leeds, then learnt traditional pottery techniques in London. From 1973 to 1975 she worked with Carol McNicoll in a co-operative studio where she mainly produced tiles commissioned for bathrooms and swimming-pools. From 1975 she was associated with Jacqueline Poncelet. Her first exhibition was in 1976. Her work consists above all of receptacles (bowls, jugs, pitchers, cups) assembled by hand from slabs. The decoration, of animals, plants, figures or geometric motifs, is executed by the most varied techniques; sometimes, for example, coloured pastes are applied to the slabs before their assembly or else they are painted with a brush.

215

216

216

216

217 **LINDH-MASCITTI,** Francesca (Italy, 1931–   ). *Bowls,* 1979. Mixture of various ceramic materials. H. approx. 20 cm.
After studying in Rome and Helsinki, Francesca Lindh-Mascitti went on to work with the firm Oy Arabia Ab of Helsinki from 1955; she works with chamotte, stoneware and porcelain, often combining these different materials. She is especially well known for her bowls, vases and murals and likes to use naturalistic figurative decoration.

219 **VAN LOON,** Johan (Netherlands, 1934–   ). *Vase,* 1975 (?). Stoneware. H. 17.5 cm. Stedelijk Museum, Amsterdam; KNA 5416.
After studying textiles in Amsterdam and Copenhagen, Van Loon turned to ceramics in 1958, working with Jos Eppens van Veen, Thera Hofstede Crull and Jan van der Vaart. In 1960 he worked in the research studio of the Arabia company in Helsinki. In 1961 he studied in England with Lucie Rie and made his first porcelain trials, meanwhile designing tapestries and continuing to make ceramics. He has worked on several occasions for the Royal Copenhagen Factory.

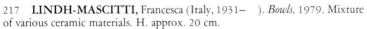

220 **PETERSEN,** Gerd Hiort (Denmark, 1937–   ). *Dish,* 1977. Stoneware. L. 87 cm.
After her apprenticeship with Michael Andersen from 1954 to 1956, Gerd Petersen studied in Vienna in 1957–8 and then at the School of Applied Arts in Copenhagen from 1962 to 1965. She worked on a free-lance basis at the Royal Copenhagen Factory from 1965 to 1973, and then opened her own studio on Bornholm in 1973. She produces chamotte stoneware plaques and reliefs, adding texture to the surfaces to be decorated by putting one or more unevenly spread layers of slip under scattered areas of glaze. She sometimes adds a pattern in gilt or gold-leaf.

221 **ANDERSEN,** Hans Munck (Denmark, 1943–   ). *Vase* and *Bowl,* 1977. Porcelain. H. 16.5, 11.5 cm.
Andersen gained his diploma in 1968 at the School of Applied Arts in Copenhagen, where he worked in association with the Royal Factory before opening a studio on Bornholm in 1973. He makes moulded porcelain pieces, applying coils of coloured pastes on to the object while still in the mould, then reworking it to give a smooth finish after removing the plaster, and applying a clear or coloured glaze.

218 **COSIJN,** Lies (Netherlands, 1931–   ). *Pot with Lid,* 1975. Grogged stoneware. H. 34 cm. Princessehof Museum, Leeuwarden; OKS 1975/38.
Lies Cosijn worked from 1956 to 1962 in the experimental section of the De Porceleyne Fles factory at Delft. Since then she has been working at Petten. She has exhibited at Faenza in 1958, in Paris in 1959, at Düsseldorf in 1960 and at Darmstadt in 1967.

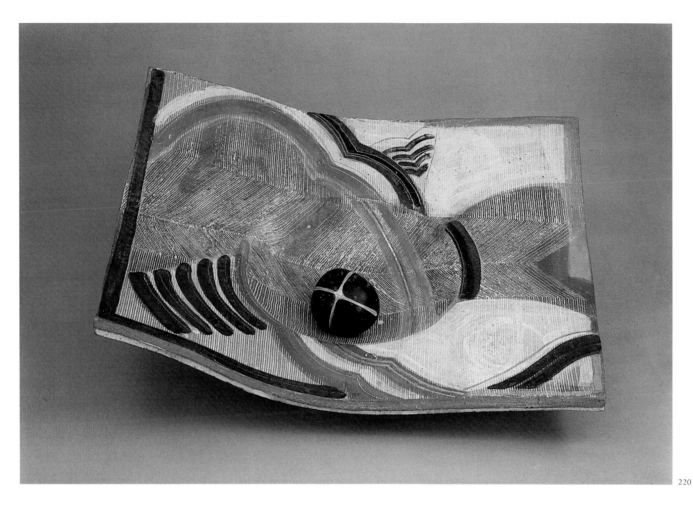

222

222　**TSOLAKOS,** Panos (Greece, 1934–). *Vases,* 1968. Stoneware. Max. h. 65 cm.

It was in Greece that Panos Tsolakos was taught the rudiments of his craft by local potters. When he had completed his elementary studies he attended the Académie des Beaux-Arts in Paris and was given a grant to study in Italy. He settled at Faenza where he took courses at the Istituto Statale d'Arte per la Ceramica, specializing in technology. After winning gold medals at Faenza in 1966 and 1967 and a special prize at Vallauris in 1970, he was awarded the Prix Faenza in 1971. These stoneware vases are fired at 1280° in a reducing atmosphere in a gas-fired kiln, using ash glazes.

223　**COPENHAGEN** (Denmark, Royal Factory). *Round Covered Pots,* 1981. Porcelain. Max. h. 15 cm.

Anne-Marie Trolle is one of the outstanding free-lance artists working for this factory. In 1970 she created the 'Domino' service, which won many awards, and in 1975 made the 'Indigo' service and a planisphere in porcelain to celebrate the factory's bicentenary. On these pieces she updates the traditional underglaze blue.

224　**CHRISTENSEN,** Kari (Norway, 1938–). *Winter Landscape,* 1976. Porcelain. L. 27 cm.

After graduating from the National School of Arts and Crafts in Oslo in 1961, Kari Christensen studied at the Royal Danish Academy for three years and designed for the Royal Copenhagen Factory over a five-year period. She then taught at the Istanbul School of Arts and Crafts in 1965, before setting up her own studio in Oslo in 1966. In 1971 she won a gold medal at the Florence International Biennale. This piece, fired in a reduction atmosphere at 1300°, is decorated with metallic oxides and underglaze colours, and is left unglazed.

223

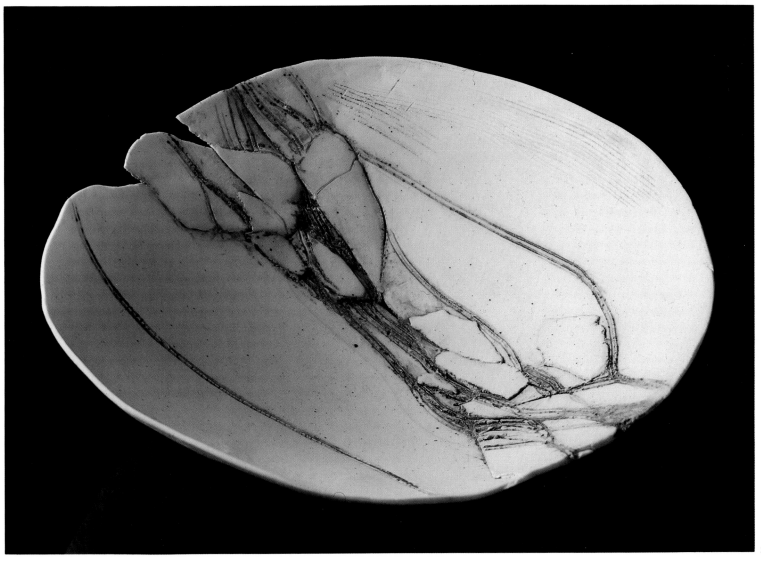

224

through Bernard Leach's teaching that potters in the West began to understand that Japanese ceramics must be considered as an expression of a way of thinking, of an understanding of the world and of the artist's role that differed totally from its Western counterpart. The earliest converts to Japonism generally tried to reproduce the restrained forms of Japanese pots, with their sophisticated glazes or discreet geometric patterns incised under the glaze.

In the early 1880s Auguste Delaherche made his first experiments with salt-glazed stonewares at the factory known as 'L'Italienne' in the Beauvais region, where this technique had been continued since the Middle Ages. In 1886 he took over Chaplet's Paris studio in the rue Blomet, and in 1889 won a gold medal for his *flambé*-glazed stoneware and his brown stonewares decorated with copper-red flow-glazes. From 1894 he was established at Armentières, where he regularly exhibited his monochrome-glazed stoneware before devoting himself entirely to porcelain after 1900.

The most profound influence of all was exercised by Jean-Joseph-Marie Carriès, the real leader of this school of stoneware potters. He was trained as a sculptor, working on wax and plaster models for casting in bronze. Captivated by the Japanese pottery he had seen in Paris, he turned to stoneware in 1888, settling first at Cosne and then at Saint Amand-en-Puisaye. He produced vases of simple form, which were sometimes asymmetrical or deliberately deformed, and were decorated with highly sophisticated glazes. These featured a 'curdled' white glaze highlighted with pink or brown spots, and occasional traces of gold. He also produced glazed sculpture, sentimental busts and portraits of historic personages. In addition he modelled monsters and grimacing masks, intended for a monumental door commissioned by the Princess of Scey-Montbéliard for the library housing the manuscript of Wagner's *Parsifal*. His death in 1894 unfortunately prevented the completion of this monumental work.

The Puisaye region was rich in traditional potteries where craftsmen continued to make salt-glazed domestic stonewares with modest incised decoration. Carriès attracted a group of followers that included both potters and local collectors of art pottery, such as Jean Pointu or the Abbé Pacton, as well as art potters working in a similar way to Carriès. Paul Jeanneney was already established at Saint Amand and was the owner of a collection of Far Eastern ceramics which had influenced Carriès. Georges Hoentschel was an avid collector of French art of the seventeenth and eighteenth centuries. An architect and decorator and friend of Carriès, his collection was eventually presented to the City of Paris. Emile Grittel completed a bas-relief stoneware portrait of Carriès in 1894. William Lee and Henri de Vallombreuse also formed part of the group.

In Germany several potters were working in much the same spirit. The Japanese stoneware collection in the Hamburg museum had an enormous influence on the work of Richard and Hermann Mutz at Altona, and then on Richard Mutz's work in his Berlin studio from 1903. Here he produced faïence and stoneware decorated with flow, matt or iridescent glazes. Similarly Johann Julius Scharvogel made some very beautiful pieces of stoneware with simple shapes, decorated either with incised motifs or with *flambé* glazes. He worked in Munich and Darmstadt, collaborating for a while with designers such as Theodor Schmuz-Baudiss around 1899–1900, as well as working with the painter Walter Magnussen and the graphic artist Paul Haustein.

In Denmark, as we have seen, Patrick Nordstöm introduced stoneware at the Royal Copenhagen factory in 1912, although Hans Hjorth was already working in this medium from 1902.

We have left until the last consideration of stoneware which has links with the Art Nouveau movement, either because of its naturalistic modelled decoration or because of its painted floral decoration.

Pierre-Adrien Dalpayrat belongs to the first group. In 1889 he opened a factory at Bourg-la-Reine with the sculptor Alphonse Voisin-Delacroix. He produced stoneware with original glazes, including his 'rouge Dalpayrat', as well as marbled effects, brown or buff glazes with spots of green or blue. Besides pieces with simple forms he also created some zoomorphic shapes and naturalistically sculpted ornamentation. At the same time he was producing figures and objects modelled by the sculptors Constantin Meunier and Ferdinand Faivre and by the interior designer Maurice Dufrêne. Edmond Lachenal, who from 1887 onwards was established at Châtillon-sous-Bagneux, worked only in stoneware after 1890. He produced pieces modelled by such sculptors as Prosper d'Epinay, Sarah Bernhardt, Pierre-Félix Fix-Masseau and Auguste Rodin. Lachenal also designed pieces with lizards, leaves or flowers, or even a bevy of ducks, in relief. Lastly, Emile Decœur, who subsequently disowned his 'youthful mistakes', at the beginning of his career produced some pieces in plant form decorated with lustrous or matt glazes.

In the field of decorated stoneware, Max, Hans, Fritz and Rudolf von Heider produced, at their establishment at Schongau-am-Lech, calcined stoneware with lustre glazes and painted or modelled decoration. In England Owen Carter developed the art pottery section of his family firm after 1880, creating vases with floral or geometric motifs or metallic lustres. In 1905 Bernard Moore set up a studio at Stoke-on-Trent; although he himself was particularly interested in research into glazes, he employed a number of artists to decorate pieces at his workshop. William Moorcroft, who was designer for the James McIntyre Company in Burslem from 1897 to 1913, perfected Florian ware, which was decorated with trailed white slip outlines enclosing each coloured area. Later he continued on his own, employing the same processes and motifs, which were usually floral or botanical, but from 1919 onward concentrated on *flambé* glazes.

Chinese porcelain influenced Western ceramics as much as Japanese stonewares did, but in a quite novel manner. At first blue-and-white porcelain and the rather later coloured wares were admired and copied; then Europeans went on discover the splendour of archaic porcelain with its simple and graceful forms, emphasized by incised underglaze decoration or the most subtle touches of colour. At the same time Western collectors began to appreciate the richness of copper-red *flambé* glazes, deep turquoise glazes, and the infinite nuances of the so-called 'hare's fur', 'oil-spot', 'aubergine' and brown-ware glazes. It was as though all these glazes had already been invented but had to be rediscovered by later generations. Ernest Chaplet was the first to throw himself into this dizzy adventure. He started out by studying the craft of painting on porcelain with Emile Lessore, before going to work at the Laurin faïence works at Bourg-la-Reine, where in 1871 he mastered the *barbotine* process. In 1875 he joined the Haviland brothers' workshop at Auteuil; this was directed by the print-maker Félix Bracquemond, who was a collector of Oriental art and introduced Chaplet to Chinese *flambé* porcelains. When he became director of the Auteuil *atelier* in 1882, before its move to the rue Blomet, Chaplet made stoneware and also conducted his first experiments into copper-red glazes, which he tried out first on unglazed Limoges 'blanks'. In 1887 he won a medal of honour at the exhibition held by the Union centrale des arts décoratifs and left Auteuil to set up on his own account at Choisy-le-Roi.

Taxile Doat's introduction to porcelain was somewhat different. He opened an *atelier* in Paris in 1892, then moved to Sèvres in 1898. He produced both naturalistically-conceived works with *flambé* glazes and wares decorated by the earlier *pâte-sur-pâte* process, limiting his figurative designs strictly to logically positioned medallions. He taught ceramics at the University of St. Louis from 1904 to 1930 and contributed much to the development of art porcelain in the United States.

51 Adelaide Alsop Robineau edited the journal *Keramik Studio* from 1899. She published Doat's treatise *Grand-feu Ceramics,* and herself worked with porcelain from 1903, actually potting instead of merely decorating the wares as had been the established practice till then. Another American, Mary Louise McLaughlin, concentrated increasingly on designs on porcelain.

47 We have seen that after becoming well known for his stone-wares, Auguste Delaherche worked only in porcelain from 1900, throwing his own 'one-off' pieces and finishing them with coloured, *flambé,* flow or crystalline glazes. Later he produced deli-36 cate vases with incised and pierced decoration. Pierre-Adrien Dalpayrat also progressed from stoneware to porcelain in or about 1902.

This return to traditional materials, which had led to a revival of stoneware, also brought about renewed enthusiasm for lead-glazed pottery and faïence as well as for the use of *sgraffiato* decoration, incised through a layer of slip. One of the pioneers of the 62 revival of glazed folk pottery was the Belgian painter Alfred William Finch. He made his first rustic pieces in Belgium from 1895 onwards. In 1897 he was invited to direct the Iris studios opened at Porvoo, Finland by the painter Akseli Gallén-Kallela and his friends. Here he produced some very sober wares decorated with incised slip and touches of colour. His teaching at the Central School of Industrial Art in Helsinki from 1902 to 1930 was considered so valuable that he earned the title of 'father of modern Finnish ceramics'.

In Holland several potters became involved with the simple materials just mentioned. Lambertus (Bert) Nienhuis first made decorated tiles and designed vases for various factories, one of which concerns was his own and named 'Lotus'. In 1911 he joined the von Osthaus colony at Hagen as an independent artist and, while teaching there, began to make 'one-off' pieces with coloured glazes. To Willem Coenrad Brouwer, who worked at Leiderdorp 63 from 1901, we owe monumental vases glazed in white or crackled grey and powerful thrown glazed earthenwares, soberly decorated with geometric motifs incised through a layer of slip. Chris Lanooy, working in Gouda and then in Epe, made some elegant pieces and researched indefatigably into colour and glazes, experimenting with lead, pewter, chemical salts and lustre.

The leading potter in this field in Germany was Max Laeuger, 32 who was also a graphic artist, architect, landscape gardener and designer. In 1895 Ernst Kammüller's 'Kanderner Tonwaren-fabrik' opened an art department to produce pieces Laeuger had designed. The factory made vases, tiles and other objects decorated in relief in slip under clear or monochrome glazes or in strongly-coloured slips. Although these processes had been employed elsewhere, Laeuger's work is distinguished by its rich palette and the vigour of his stylized motifs. In 1913 he became director of the grand-ducal factory at Karlsruhe.

Meanwhile, in Denmark, Thorvald Bindesbøll was working in 33 faïence in a strongly personal style. He decorated his wares with balanced, powerful, geometric designs in bright colours.

In the United States another potter who used faïence was 91 George E. Ohr. Until 1909 he had a studio at Biloxi in Mississippi, where he produced pieces of striking originality. Their technical virtuosity was extraordinary. The humour he displayed in the choice of subject matter and of titles put him greatly in advance of his time.

Among those who revived a local tradition was Francesco Randone, who in or about 1910 took up the early technique of *terra sigillata*. His work marked the beginning of a return by Italian craftsmen and other artists to their glorious pre-Renaissance past. Until then only Renaissance art had been admired, to the exclusion of that of other periods.

In contrast, there were few potters who practised traditional overglaze decorative techniques. The most famous of these, André 114 Metthey, was self-taught, and turned to ceramics after receiving a book by Garnier as a prize in a sculpture competition. He set up a pottery workshop at Asnières in or about 1901 and immediately started to produce decorated faïence. We have mentioned his short-lived but most important collaboration with a number of young painters. Afterwards he worked alone on faïence, and then used lead-glazed earthenware which permitted a livelier palette of stronger colours. His patterns, which were geometric at first, gradually began to include plant forms, animals and the human figure.

However, a number of first-generation potters chose to pursue an eclectic path rather than concentrate on one material only.

(continued on p. 158)

225

225   **LINCK-DAEPP,** Margrit (Switzerland, 1897–   ). *Vase,* 1979. Terracotta. H. 30 cm.
Born in the canton of Berne, Margrit Linck-Daepp took courses in ceramics there and in Munich before going to learn the craft with a potter. In 1933 she opened her own studio and worked on slips. Around 1946 she completed a series of Surrealist ceramic works which were exhibited in many museums. Since 1957 she has concentrated on unglazed earthenware and carried out research into shapes.

226

227

226   **LEACH,** David (England, 1911–   ). *Bowl,* 1959. Porcelain. H. 7 cm.
Dr. H. Thiemann Collection, Hamburg.
David is the eldest son of Bernard Leach and studied pottery first with his father and then in Devon and Stoke-on-Trent. For a long time he worked in association with his father at St. Ives and played an important role as a teacher and adviser. In 1956 he opened the Lowerdown Pottery in Devon. Apart from his creative work, he markets several types of bodies and glazes.

227   **ANTIBO,** Attilio (Italy, 1930–   ). *Plate Covered with Sections of Clay,* 1980. Terracotta. D. 35 cm.
Attilio Antibo lives and works in Savona. He has taken part in numerous one-man and group exhibitions in his own country and abroad. In his research into the possibilities of terracotta, he professes to be passionately engrossed in the changes that take place in the clay during the different stages of its fashioning, as well as in the drying and the firing and in the inter-relation of the various states of the material with everyday objects. He says that he is trying to discover the ritual gestures which would reveal the intrinsic value of the basic material and is preoccupied by the relationships between domestic objects and their raw material, and the processes which give them life.

228   **SCHEID,** Ursula (Germany, 1932–   ). *Vase,* 1974. Porcelain. H. 10.7 cm. Dr. H. Thiemann Collection, Hamburg.
Ursula Scheid studied ceramics at Darmstadt from 1952 to 1954 and in 1958 started to work with her husband. She prefers to use stoneware and especially porcelain for thrown and hand-built objects, giving particular emphasis to their profile and decorating them with the brush. With her husband, she is also engaged in methodical research into glazes and firing methods.

228

229

229 **PEARSON,** Colin (England, 1923–). *Vase,* 1975. Stoneware. H. 58.7 cm. Oxford Gallery, Oxford.
Colin Pearson studied painting at Goldsmiths' College, London, and worked at the Winchcomb Pottery with Ray Finch, at Royal Doulton in Lambeth and then with David Leach at the Aylesford Pottery. In 1961 he opened his own studio where he began by making reduction-fired domestic stonewares. Since 1971 he has been producing individually-modelled pieces in stoneware and porcelain while teaching at Camberwell and at the Medway College of Design. He has taken part in numerous exhibitions and in 1975 was awarded the 33rd Prix Faenza. He paid a long visit to Japan in 1980.

230 **LILJEFORS,** Anders Bruno (Sweden, 1923–70). *Plaque,* 1970. Porcelain. H. 22 cm. Janus Pannonius Múzeum, Pécs; 52.K.81.4.
Born in the United States, Liljefors studied in Sweden and in Denmark, first sculpture then painting. Having settled in Sweden, he collaborated from time to time with the Gustavsberg factory. He perfected his own special technique of sand-casting which enabled him to cast large blocks or fragile parts in one stroke, since the dried sand allows removal from the mould to take place without danger while also improving the final glazed surface texture. Liljefors made a great number of murals and decorative panels and died suddenly during a symposium at Siklos in 1970, during which he modelled this piece, which remains unfinished.

230

231 **SUAREZ,** Jaime (Puerto Rico, 1946–). *Winged Vase,* 1975. Terra-cotta. H. 40 cm.
Jaime Suarez was trained in the United States, first studying architecture at the Catholic University of Washington, D.C., then design at the Columbia University of New York. Since 1975 he has taken part in individual and group exhibitions, especially in his own country and the United States. He has also exhibited regularly at Faenza where he received a *prix d'honneur* in 1981.

232 **CSEKOVSZKY,** Árpád (Hungary, 1931–). *Oblique Crosses,* 1974. Chamotte. H. 50 cm. Artist's collection.
From 1951 to 1956 Árpád Csekovszky studied at the School of Decorative Arts in Budapest, where he was taught by István Gador and Miklós Borsos, and became a teacher at the school in 1957. In 1962 he received the Munkacsky prize, in 1975 the first prize at the Pécs Biennale and in 1977 the prize given by the Ministry of Culture for a work shown on an outdoor site. He concentrates especially on architectural ceramics, and has completed numerous works in Hungary.

231

232

233

234

233 **JOULIA,** Elisabeth (France, 1925–). *The Large Petal,* 1975. Stoneware. H. 29 cm. Musée des Arts décoratifs, Paris; 11,776.
After studying at art schools in Clermont-Ferrand, Paris and Bourges, Elisabeth Joulia settled at La Borne in 1949, following in the footsteps of the Lerat family, who had a considerable influence on her. The 'Dame de la Borne' puts her heart and soul into each work, marrying form and material with an uncanny instinct.

234 **DUCKWORTH,** Ruth (Germany, England, U.S.A., 1919–). *Form,* 1978. Porcelain. H. 10.2 cm. Helen Drutt Collection, Philadelphia, Pa.
Born in Hamburg, Ruth Duckworth came to England in 1936 to continue her studies of drawing, painting and sculpture. She lived there for twenty-eight years before emigrating to the United States. She was originally a sculptor, sometimes using terracotta, before taking up ceramics in 1956. Working in many different materials and in various scales, she made small sensitively-conceived fine porcelain pieces as well as robust stonewares with innovative shapes. From 1968 she began to produce monumental panels and murals. She helped to change English potters' outlook by making them aware of the sculptural possibilities of ceramics.

235

236

235 **LEWENSTEIN,** Eileen (England, 1925–). *Bouquet,* 1977. Stoneware. L. 30 cm.
Eileen Lewenstein studied painting before attending the University of London. In 1946–7 she worked at the Donald Mills Pottery in London and in 1948 at the Briglin Pottery with Brigitta Appleby, where whe produced objects in limited series. In 1959 she opened her own workshop in London and in 1976 went to live in Sussex. There she produces individually-created pieces in stoneware and porcelain. In addition she plays an important role through her teaching (from 1960 to 1969), her co-editorship of the influential *Ceramic Review,* and as a member of the Craftsman Potters' Association.

236 **VIOTTI,** Ulla (Sweden, 1933–). *'Bowl-sculpture, Traces of Life',* 1979. Stoneware and chamotte. H. 20 cm. Artist's collection.
After studying sculpture in Blackpool, England (1950–1) and then ceramics in Stockholm (1952–6), Ulla Viotti worked with various ceramic factories before opening her own studio in 1960. During a trip to Israel (1967) she first tackled sculpture and mural reliefs, mostly representing seemingly disembodied human silhouettes. She is particularly interested in the structure and texture of surfaces, and shapes the borders of her bowls so that they bear no relation to traditional vessels.

237

238

237 **RADY**, Elsa (U.S.A., 1943–). *Untitled Object,* 1979. Porcelain. H. 14 cm. National Museum of American Art, Smithsonian Institution, Washington, D.C. (gift of Jill I. Cole); 1981.21.
After studying at the Chouinard Art Institute in Los Angeles, Elsa Rady first worked form 1966 to 1968 as a designer of services and tiles for the Inter-Pace Franciscan China Corporation at Glendale, California and was commissioned to do several murals. Today she produces works with elegant outlines and sharply jagged edges.

238 **RIE**, Lucie (Austria–England, 1902–). *Bowl,* 1975. Porcelain. D. 20 cm.
Born in Vienna, Lucie Rie studied ceramics there with Michael Powolny and had her own studio from 1926 to 1938. In 1939 she went to London where she opened a workshop and had to produce tea and coffee services. It was only after the first exhibition of her original works in 1949 that she started to become known in England. Today she produces individually-created pieces in stoneware or porcelain, often combining several separately thrown elements. As well as using monochrome glazes, she also frequently uses incised slip.

239

239 **BARRY**, Val (England, 1937–). *Three Vases,* 1977. Max. h. 34 cm. Fina Gomez Collection, Paris.
From 1967 to 1970 Val Barry studied at the Sir John Cass School of Art in London, where she has had a studio since 1970. She produces porcelain and stoneware pieces which are thrown or else built up from rather thick slabs, for she prefers bold forms. In order to preserve these angular shapes she colours the unfired pot or impresses already coloured plaques of porcelain on to the outside of her pots, so that they are not totally immersed in glaze.

240 **ROGERS**, Mary (England, 1929–). *Double Flower Head,* 1980. Porcelain. H. *c.* 9 cm. Artist's collection.
After studying calligraphy and illustration, Mary Rogers went over to ceramics in 1960, and initially produced stonewares inspired by natural forms. In 1968 she began to work with porcelain because she felt that its translucence enabled her to understand better the internal and external structure of the object. She was one of the first to reject the myth that porcelain was a difficult body to work with and her latest pieces are formed directly by pinching and modelling, the outlines being tidied up by scraping once the piece has dried. She prefers matt or semi-matt glazes and fires her work in an oxidizing atmosphere at 1300°.

240

241

241 **PONCELET,** Jacqueline (Belgium–England, 1947–). *Vessel,* 1974. Bone china. H. 10.5 cm. Oxford Gallery, Oxford.
After studying at Wolverhampton College of Art and the Royal College of Art, Jacqueline Poncelet worked in London while doing part-time teaching at the West Surrey College of Art and Design. She received grants to travel to the U.S.A. in 1977 and 1978. She first chose to work in bone china, used in the English ceramic industry, casting vessels in which she included coloured zones of geometric motifs. The surfaces were then incised or perforated. Since 1976 she has also produced slab-built stonewares.

242 **FRITSCH,** Elizabeth (England, 1940–). *Tall Optical Bottle,* 1975. Stoneware. H. 26 cm.
After attending the Royal Academy of Music and the Royal College of Art in London, Elizabeth Fritsch spent a year at Bing and Grøndhal. She produces individually-created stoneware pieces assembled by hand or vessels cast in porcelain. Their hollow forms lack even a foot-rim that might disturb their contour line. She attaches particular importance to the outline of the mouth of each piece. Her abstract geometric decoration, usually matt or semi-matt, are based essentially on rhythmic motifs which demonstrate her love of music.

242

243 **ROGERS,** Mary (England, 1929–). *Striped Flower Head,* 1981. Porcelain. H. approx. 13 cm. Cf. Pl. 240.

244 **FAVRE,** Aline (Switzerland, 1932–) and **ZELLER,** Florent (Switzerland, 1945–). *Bowl,* 1979. Porcelain. H. 12 cm.
At the Juriens pottery Favre and Zeller work in co-operation with other Swiss potters; for several months in 1980 they played host to Mireille Gafagno, Danièle Pestalozzi, Lani Weber, Philippe Barde and Jacques Kaufmann. They both studied at the School of Applied Arts in Geneva, where Aline Favre became an instructor. They have participated in many exhibitions and won medals at Faenza in 1978 and at Sopot the next year.

243

244

245

246

247

245 **LEVKIV,** Taras (U.S.S.R., 1940–). *Large Family,* 1981. Terracotta. Max. h. 15 cm.
Taras Levkiv graduated from the L'vov National Institute of Decorative and Applied Arts in 1971, has been a member of the Union of Artists of the U.S.S.R. since 1971 and has participated in international competitions at Faenza, Sopot and Vallauris.

246 **FEKETE,** László (Hungary, 1949–). *Sculpture,* 1979. H. 50 cm. Studio de céramique, Kecskemét; 79/7.
Born in Budapest, László Fekete studied there under Imre Schrammel at the School of Applied Arts. He graduated in 1974 and since then has exhibited, alone or as part of a group, in his own country and abroad. He spent three months in France in 1977. Fekete 'folds' the clay and uses a coil-building technique.

247 **SCHLICHENMAIER,** Hildegund (Germany–France, 1941–). *Vase,* 1980. Stoneware. H. 35 cm. Musée Cantini, Marseilles; C 81.09.
Hildegund Schlichenmaier was a pupil of the Lerats at Bourges from 1965 to 1968; she runs a workshop at La Borne and exhibits at Vallauris and at the Noella Gest gallery. She colours her pieces using natural earthenware slips; chamotte, sand and crushed stone give body and structure to the surface.

248 **RIE,** Lucie (Austria–England, 1902–). *Vase,* 1976. Ceramic. H. 26 cm. Fina Gomez Collection, Paris. Cf. Pl. 238.

248

249 **HÄUSERMANN,** Ernst (Switzerland, 1947–). *Sandwich Object,*
1978. Stoneware. H. 12 cm.
After studying in Basle and Zurich, Ernst Häusermann learned to pot with
Arnold Zahner, and worked for a while with him and with Jean-Claude de Crousaz before opening his own studio in Oberkulm in 1972. He very soon started
exhibiting, in Tokyo (from 1970) and all over the world as well as in his native
Switzerland. He teaches at the School of Decorative Arts in Zurich.

250 **SALVARO-HANI,** Hanibal (Yugoslavia, 1935–). *Object 'P'* and
Object 'F', 1981. Stoneware. H. 23 and 27 cm.
Hanibal Salvaro-Hani has worked with ceramics since 1958 in his studio in
Zagreb. He has received numerous commissions, for example one for the swim-
ming pool of the Toplice Hotel at Krapinske Toplice in 1967 and for the head-
quarters of the Department of Social Security in Zagreb in 1972. He has taken
part in many one-man and group exhibitions and received numerous awards, the
most recent being a medal at Faenza in 1981 for the pieces reproduced here.

251 **MINTZBERG,** Yvette (Canada, 1941–). *Facets II,* 1981. Stoneware.
H. 43 cm.
After taking courses in mathematics and psychology, Yvette Mintzberg studied
ceramics at the University of Aix-Marseilles, and then worked with a number
of potters. She teaches ceramics, participates in symposiums and training workshops, gives lectures and also produces useful or sculptural pieces in stoneware,
decorated with metallic oxides and coloured clays. She uses an electric kiln, making high-fired as well as *raku* or smoked wares. She says of her work: 'I am fascinated by mineral and glacial forms, by the simplicity of lines which make up complex forms... Each body has its own characteristics... In my pieces I try to
respect the individual qualities of the clay.'

249

252

253

254

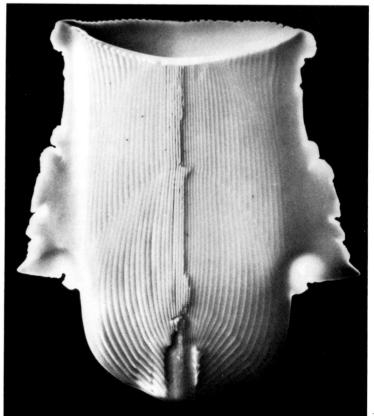

255

252 **SCHEID**, Karl (Germany, 1929–   ). *Vase,* 1979. Porcelain. H. 9 cm. Private collection.

From 1949 to 1952 Karl Scheid studied ceramics at Darmstadt and in 1952–3 took a practical course at Harry Davis's studio in England. From 1963 to 1975 he worked on a free-lance basis for several industrial firms. From 1953 to 1956 he shared a workshop with Beate Kuhn, before settling in 1956 in Düdelsheim where he has been working since 1958 with his wife Ursula (cf. Pl. 228). They are exploring glaze effects, concentrating on glazes derived from iron, and investigating the relationship between shape and decoration, using shallower and shallower reliefs.

253 **CASTLE**, Lew (New Zealand). *Suspended Form,* 1972. Stoneware. L. 32 cm.

Lew Castle studied science, then decided to teach himself ceramics, after reading Bernard Leach and Shoji Hamada. With the aid of a grant he studied in England in 1956 with Bernard Leach and went to Japan in 1966. In 1974 he undertook a study tour to China, South Korea and Japan as a member of a government cultural delegation. This piece was decorated in the biscuit state using a brush to apply pigment, before its final firing at 1300°.

254 **SIMPSON**, Peter (England, 1943–   ). *Vase,* 1975. Porcelain. H. 21 cm. Musée Cantini, Marseilles; 3946.

After studying at Bournemouth, Peter Simpson taught in several places. He is first and foremost a sculptor, who has chosen ceramics as his medium. He started by producing a series of pieces inspired by nature (poppy seeds, pomegranates, mushrooms) characterized by the refinement and delicacy of their numerous inner surfaces and their delicate enamel glazes. Today his pieces are larger and are decorated by means of the sgraffito technique and subsequently patinated.

255 **GEBHARDT**, Christa Helene (Germany, 1937–   ). *Vase,* 1979. Porcelain. H. 12 cm. Private collection.

After studying graphics from 1955 to 1960 at Kiel, Christa Helene Gebhardt worked in this field from 1960 to 1973. In 1973 she started to work in ceramics with her husband Johannes Gebhardt. This hand-built vase was reduction-fired at 1300 °C in a gas-fired kiln and has a celadon glaze.

256 **GEBHARDT**, Johannes (Germany, 1930–   ). *Plant-life Form,* 1978. Porcelain. H. 19 cm. Private collection.

Johannes Gebhardt studied drawing, sculpture and painting. He was taught ceramics by Hubert Griemert and others. His influence as a consultant in Pakistan and particularly as a teacher in Kiel has been considerable. Since 1963 he has participated in numerous exhibitions and was awarded a silver medal at Istanbul in 1967. In 1973 he set up a studio with his wife Christa Helene.

256

257 **BRESSON**, Alain (France, 1948–). *Flight*, 1980. Porcelain. H. 50 cm.
Bresson obtained his certificate of proficiency as a potter at the Cannes lycée. In 1976 and 1978 he won prizes at the Vallauris Biennale; he participates in the exhibitions at Faenza, where in 1980 he received a purchase award. At the Vallauris Biennale he was awarded the grand prix 'without the jury meeting'. Nearly all Bresson's pieces could be entitled *'Flight'*, as he has 'given wings to porcelain', but in 1982 he appears to want to bring it down to earth.

258 **GOSSELIN**, Louis (Canada, 1934–). *Coquille-Ange IV*, 1974. Stoneware. H. 73.5 cm. Fondation Maeght, Saint-Paul-de-Vence.
After practising a host of different trades, Louis Gosselin took evening courses in ceramics and sculpture and joined Claude Théberge's studio. At that time he worked on the decoration of public and religious buildings and then joined Marc Dumas's studio; Dumas had been a pupil of Bernard Leach. After a spell in the theatre he returned to ceramics and at the Maeght Foundation studio created his series of *Coquilles-Anges, Livres* and *Oraisons solaires,* before making the large *Disques.* At present he is working in association with the Sèvres factory for whom he has perfected a 'ripple-marks' decorative pattern which he has used on a bowl and a series of boxes and vases.

259 **MARTEINSDOTTIR**, Steinunn (Iceland, 1936–). *Vase*, 1980. Stoneware. H. 81 cm.
Steinunn Marteinsdottir studied at the Icelandic Arts and Crafts school in 1955–6 before going to the Hochschule für Bildende Künste in West Berlin (1956–60). At Hulduholum she opened a studio which also served as a gallery. Since 1975 she has participated regularly in one-man and group exhibitions throughout Scandinavia.

257

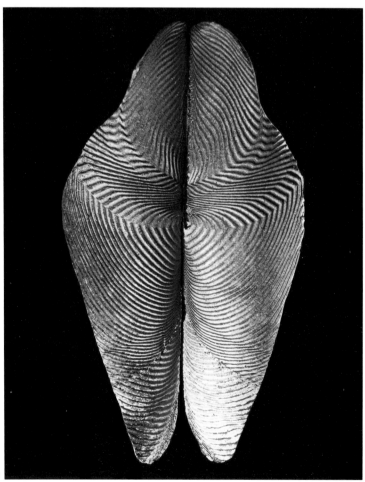

258

259

146

260 **COPER,** Hans (Germany–England, 1920–81). *Vase,* 1968. H. 17 cm. Fina Gomez Collection, Paris.

Hans Coper began by studying engineering at Dresden and Mittweida while experimenting with painting and sculpture. He emigrated to England in 1939 and worked with Lucie Rie form 1946 before opening his own studio. From 1963 to 1973 he taught at the Camberwell School of Arts and Crafts in London and from 1966 to 1974 in the ceramics department of the Royal College of Art. He purposely limited his range of forms and glazes in order to concentrate on exploring the relationship between form, texture and colour. The interiors of his incomparable works are always glazed.

261 **COPER,** Hans (Germany–England, 1920–81). *Pot,* 1975. Stoneware. H. 28 cm.

It is sometimes said in criticism of certain ceramic objects that they could be produced just as well, if not better, in metal. The present piece seems to justify such a reproach. However, one should not forget that photography is a misleading art which does not do justice to the surface texture of the material and indeed distorts its true qualities out of all recognition.

260

261

262

262 **VALENTINI,** Giovan Battista (Italy, 1932–). *'Pima del polipo' Vase,* 1980. Terracotta with stoneware additions. H. 50 cm.
After studying ceramics at Pesaro and Faenza and painting in Bologna and Paris, Valentini practised pottery at Pesaro until 1957 and in his Milan studio from 1957 to 1962. He has received many awards and taken part in exhibitions in Italy as well as abroad. After a period devoted to painting and graphic arts, in 1968 he returned to ceramics, opening a workshop at Arcore near Milan.

263 **DUTCH,** Doris (England—New Zealand). *'Winged' Hanging Form,* 1980. Porcelain. H. 14 cm. Artist's collection.
Doris Dutch emigrated to New Zealand in 1951 after studying in England. Although she began to exhibit her pots from 1964, she has only devoted herself to them entirely since 1971. She works in stoneware and porcelain, producing useful wares as well as individually-created pieces. She mixes her body from various ingredients to produce a heterogeneous texture and prefers light touches of glaze that allow the body to show rather than extensive glazed areas. This piece is modelled by hand and decorated with slip.

264 **SCHRAMMEL,** Imre (Hungary, 1933–). *Sea-gull,* 1980. Earthenware and calcined bone. D. 40 cm. Artist's collection.
Schrammel studied sculpture, ceramics and jewellery from 1952 to 1957 in Budapest with Miklós Borsos and István Gador. Since 1958 he has been teaching porcelain manufacture, specializing in ceramic sculpture. He also works for industrial concerns and has created a great many stoneware murals decorated in relief.

265 **SWINDELL,** Geoffrey (England, 1945–). *Pots,* 1981. Porcelain. Max. h. 12.2 cm.
After studying painting, Swindell learnt ceramics at Stoke-on-Trent, his native town, and then went to the Royal College of Art in London where he was taught by Hans Coper (1967–70). Since 1970 he has had a studio in York and then in Cardiff where he now teaches. Initially he produced small works inspired in turn by shells and lead soldiers, but has now graduated to large thrown pots which flare out like flowers from narrow bases; they are often left unglazed and have wavy rims.

263

264

265

266

267 **LUKANDER**, Minni (Finland, 1930–). *Urn,* 1979. Stoneware. H. 40.5 cm. Museum of Applied Arts, Helsinki.
After studying at the Institute of Craft and Design in Helsinki, Minni Lukander made ceramic sculpture and domestic wares, while continuing to teach. She opened her own studio in 1961 and joined the 'Pot Viapori' co-operative workshop. She has participated in many group exhibitions both at home and abroad and has won a number of awards, including one at Faenza in 1966. This example was hand-modelled.

268 **PIT**, Nicolas (Luxemburg, 1939–). *Sculpture,* 1981. Chamotte. H. 26 cm. Galerie Intérieurs, Paris.
Pit is a talented mason, sherwd and constructive, with clear-sightedness and self-discipline. He studied at the Schools of Fine Art in Nancy, Paris and Vienna. Since 1965 he has been teaching art education in Luxemburg, and has taken part in numerous exhibitions since 1972 in France, Luxemburg, Belgium and Germany. In 1980 he was responsible for the chancel of the church at Steinsel in Luxemburg, a work which combined wood, stone and ceramics. His ceramics are slab-built, biscuit-fired in an electric kiln at 950°, sprinkled with manganese, iron and cobalt oxides, glazed with zinc-based glazes, and then fired in an oxidizing atmosphere at 1050°.

266 **HENDERSON,** Ewen (England, 1934–). *Vase,* 1979. Porcelain and stoneware. D. 25 cm. Victoria and Albert Museum, London; C. 139–1979.
Following his initial interest in painting and sculpture, Ewen Henderson studied ceramics at the Camberwell School of Art, London, with Lucie Rie and Hans Coper. He now teaches at Goldsmiths' College and the North London Collegiate School, while continuing his own work and exhibiting frequently. He is fond of combining stoneware and porcelain so that their juxtaposed textures form both the decoration and the structure of his spontaneously-modelled pieces. This pot was fired in an oxidizing atmosphere at 1260°, after applying a thin coating of feldspathic glaze.

269 **CHILLIDA,** Eduardo (Spain, 1924–). *Earthenware XI,* 1977. Chamotte. H. 16 cm. Galerie Maeght, Zurich.
After working mainly as a smith, the Catalan Chillida became interested in natural materials such as wood and various types of stone—alabaster, marble and granite—as well as in the potential of concrete for large-scale works. During a stay at the Fondation Maeght at Saint-Paul-de-Vence in 1973, he began to work with ceramic materials, in collaboration with Joan Gardy Artigas and later with Hans Spinner. He first made a series of powerful sculptural works in chamotte, accentuated by incised, carved or gouged marks. From 1977 he also worked with porcelain, while producing a new series of chamotte works painted with copper oxide and fired in an oxidizing atmosphere.

267

268

269

270 **SOLDNER**, Paul (U.S.A., 1921–   ). *Bottle,* 1964. *Raku.* H. 22.9 cm. Everson Museum of Art, Syracuse, N.Y.; P.C. 64.86.
In 1954 Paul Soldner joined a group of students working with Peter Voulkos, who had recently been appointed to teach ceramics at the University of California at Los Angeles. During a public demonstration in 1960 Soldner tried his hand at the *raku* technique which he then adopted, introducing this Japanese procedure to Westerners in a new spirit. *Raku* is particularly suited to spontaneous expression. He has also made a considerable contribution through his teaching at Scripps College, Claremont and has given many lectures.

271 **MASON**, John (U.S.A., 1927–   ). *Vase,* 1958. Stoneware. H. 60.6 cm. Scripps College, Claremont, California (gift of Mr. and Mrs. Marer); 78.1.218. After studying ceramics with Susan Peterson and Peter Voulkos, John Mason became a traditional potter who occasionally designed for industry. Later, from 1957, he turned to more sculptural and monumental work, creating modular murals and abstract totems before turning mainly to firebricks.

270

272 **AUTIO,** Rudy (U.S.A., 1926–). *Vase.* 1958–9. Stoneware. H. 25.5 cm. Scripps College, Claremont, California (gift of Mr. and Mrs. Marer); 78.1.418.
Rudy Autio was one of the leaders of the American Abstract–Expressionist ceramic revolution of the 1950s. After having served in the navy he became resident artist at the Archie Bray Foundation at Helena, Montana, where he carried out several architectural commissions. He then became professor of ceramics and sculpture at the University of Montana from 1957 to 1971, and today works almost exclusively with metal.

273 **VOULKOS,** Peter (U.S.A., 1924–). *Plaque.* 1963. Stoneware. L. 37.7 cm. Scripps College, Claremont, California (gift of Mr. and Mrs. Marer). This piece demonstrates above all the spontaneity of the creative act, but Voulkos has also made some profoundly revolutionary works, which some even find shocking, and has helped to bring about a virtual renaissance in ceramics.

272

274

274 **VOULKOS,** Peter (U.S.A., 1924–). *Vase,* 1958. Stoneware. H. 52.8 cm. Scripps College, Claremont, California (gift of Mr. and Mrs. Marer). Through his work and his teaching, Voulkos is among those who have made the greatest contribution to revolutionizing the fundamentals of ceramics. After working in a foundry and studying painting, he turned to ceramics and was soon successful, carrying off the Cannes gold medal as early as 1958. He taught at the Otis Art Institute in Los Angeles (1954–8) and then at Berkeley before devoting his talents principally to working in metal. His ceramics, which consist of assembled elements, demonstrate that his chief concern has been with mass rather than volume.

275 **NAGLE,** Ron (U.S.A., 1939–). *Bottle with Stopper,* 1960. Low-fire clay, glaze and china paint. H. 60.6. cm. Scripps College, Claremont, California (gift of Mr. and Mrs. Marer); 78.1.220.
After studying in California, Ron Nagle taught at several universities while simultaneously producing some pieces which at first were influenced by Peter Voulkos and Abstract–Expressionism. He then concentrated more and more on form, systematically exploring the possibilities of painted colour and photographic transfer.

They worked simultaneously or alternately with faïence, stoneware and porcelain. This was the case with Albert-Louis Dammouse and Fernand Rumèbe. Dammouse studied ceramics, and in particular the *pâte-sur-pâte* technique, with Marc-Louis Solon before opening a studio at Sèvres in 1871. He is most famous for his stonewares. These had simple shapes and were decorated with floral patterns in matt, dull colours. He also worked in faïence, porcelain and *pâte-de-verre*.

After spending some time with Decœur around 1903 and undertaking several study tours, Rumèbe made some thrown pots that were strongly influenced by the rich palette of Islamic ceramics that he admired. The painted decoration demonstrated his wide knowledge of glazes. Rumèbe's output was varied: porcelains with *flambé* glazes or with black decoration over an ivory glaze; stoneware with coloured enamels in patterns inspired by the East, in white or brown glazes; and porcelain or stoneware with monochrome glazes of grey, ivory, creamy-white and blue.

The inter-war period was for ceramics, as for other arts, a period of intense international co-operation, partly as a result of publications—illustrated reviews, treatises and conference papers—and partly because artists travelled more. Maija Grotell arrived from her native Finland in the United States in 1927, followed in 1929 by the Austrian Valerie (Vally) Wieselthier, a former pupil of Michael Powolny, whose work aroused such admiration that several American ceramists, for example Victor Schreckengost, left America to study in Vienna in the early 1930s. The tide of emigration from Europe became still more pronounced with the rise of Nazism. Susi Singer came to the United States at the end of this decade, as did Thomas Samuel (Sam) Haile and Gertrud and Otto Natzler, while Ruth Duckworth settled in London in 1936 and Lucie Rie moved there from Vienna three years later.

The great international exhibitions were also an important locale for the exchange of ideas. Apart from the 'Exposition Internationale des arts décoratifs et industriels' of 1925 in Paris and the 'Exposition Internationale des arts et techniques dans la vie moderne' of 1937, the most notable were the Trienniales held in Milan-Monza. European ideas were transmitted to the United States by way of the International Exhibition of Ceramic Art held in 1928 at the Metropolitan Museum in New York, which then toured several American cities. Specialized exhibitions on a national level started at the same time, among them the Ceramic National Exhibition in Syracuse, N.Y., which began in 1928, or those held in Faenza from 1938, which were initially on a national basis.

The most important influence in the ceramic world before the Second World War was that of Bernard Leach. Brought up in the Far East, he completed his art training in England before settling in Tokyo in 1909. Here, instead of teaching etching as had been his first intention, he became apprenticed to Ogata Kenzan VI, a traditional potter, and travelled extensively throughout the Far East. He returned to England in 1920 with Shoji Hamada and opened his own pottery at St. Ives in Cornwall. It was constructed according to a Japanese model, and only local materials were used.

One of Leach's main contributions was to foster a better understanding of Japanese civilization and its view of the potter and his craft. Unlike the 'gentlemen potters' who let others do the rough work of preparing and fashioning the clay and kept for themselves the 'noble' task of decoration, Leach maintained that the potter, like every other artist, should be totally responsible for his work. Each pot which was thrown according to craft principles, even if it were part of a series, seemed to him the result of an almost living process that was always unique and involved the potter completely. The distinction between artist and craftsman thus became absolutely meaningless.

Further, Leach emphasized the need for beauty in every day objects. His teaching led to the appearance of a school of potters, among them Harry and May Davis, who were anxious to produce high-quality domestic wares of artistic and technical merit.

Although Bernard Leach stressed the virtues of wares produced in this manner, he always regarded himself as a craftsman. In this he was the direct opposite of someone like William Staite Murray, who created purely decorative works to which he gave names. These were exhibited for the first time in England in art galleries and were sold at prices befitting works of art.

Bernard Leach combined Oriental influences with a desire to return to his own roots. He studied traditional English pottery such as medieval pitchers and jugs and slip-decorated wares. It was precisely this aspect of his work that most interested Leach's first pupil, Michael Cardew. In 1926 the latter acquired an old pottery at Winchcombe in Gloucestershire, and then moved to Wenford Bridge in Cornwall in 1939. Since then he has concentrated entirely on slip decoration. His love of folk pottery undoubtedly explains his several periods of teaching in Africa.

Bernard Leach's contribution to ceramics reached a wide audience since he was an impassioned theorist as well as an active creator. At St. Ives he welcomed and trained a number of young potters, and during his numerous journeys in Europe and the United States he exhibited his work, gave lectures and published some monographs of fundamental importance, such as *The Potter's Book,* which appeared in 1940.

An examination of ceramics in the inter-war period does not reveal any deep rupture with the preceding era. In many ways the work of the potters active at this time scarcely differs from that of their forerunners, whose research and experiments they seem merely to have continued. This is true of the work of the 'French group', who preferred simple balanced forms perfectly suited to subtle geometric decoration. This was either incised, modelled or painted, and was intended to enhance the glazes, produced as a

(continued on p. 160)

276 **MIRÓ**, Joan (Spain, 1893–   ). *Mural* (detail), 1968. Ceramic (cf. Frontispiece). Fondation Maeght, Saint-Paul-de-Vence.

result of skilful calculations. These pots suddenly seemed to be in perfect harmony with the decorative arts of the period, which were characterized by simplicity and a taste for geometry. But this trend was already evident in ceramics long before the French became aware of the necessity to adapt to the modern world by simplifying their conception of the decorative arts.

We are concerned here more with tradition than with fashion. This was a period when some talented potters, who were perfectly aware of the need to harmonize forms, decoration and glazes, produced work with a purely decorative aim. The best known is with108out doubt Emile Decœur, who as we have seen began his career by modelling naturalistic pieces. He experimented with a wide variety of materials, producing stoneware with *flambé* and flow glazes, then with incised and even painted decoration under the glaze as well as porcelain decorated in the same way. Finally he adopted a stoneware body mixed with kaolin and experimented with an unlimited range of glaze effects, while remaining constantly mindful of form.

In 1903 Emile Lenoble went to work in the studio of Chaplet, his wife's grandfather. Influenced by Chinese and Korean ceramics, he initially made pieces with incised decoration under monochrome glazes, and created some decorative schemes that were painted or obtained by inlaying coloured clays, before devoting himself to the study of glazes. He perfected a range of blues and celadons in which the incised decoration gradually became111secondary to the glazes. Lenoble was the first to throw pots which imitated the appearance of some Song wares, in places allowing the body to show through the layer of applied slip.

112Georges Serré served his apprenticeship at the Sèvres factory. Drafted to Saigon during the First World War, he studied Far Eastern ceramics there while also teaching at local art schools. On his return in 1922, he opened an *atelier* at Sèvres, where he issued the works of many sculptors such as Marcel Gimond, Louis Dejean and Gaston Contesse. He also created 'one-off' pieces which were hand-thrown and wood-fired. At first he worked in thick stoneware, which he ornamented only with glazes. Later he employed geometric or figurative patterns incised under the glaze.110Henri Simmen, who had been attracted by regional pottery, studied stoneware and faïence with Edmond Lachenal before acquiring his own kiln where he fired salt-glazed stoneware. After the First World War he left to study ceramics in the Far East and on his return to France set out to work only with natural materials.

109Folk pottery from the Savoy and Greece, as well as Islamic and African countries, exercised considerable influence on Jean Besnard. His wares are sometimes fanciful, with masks and humorous figures, and he made a reputation for himself with his particular finishes, such as imitation lace or 'wrinkled' white glazes. The influence of early Mediterranean ceramics was the inspiration behind Félix Massoul's work. He experimented in turn with the techniques of Hispano-Moresque lustres, Gallo-Roman terracottas and Greek vases, as well as the startling blues of Islamic ceramics; above all he sought to imitate the brilliant turquoise achieved by the Egyptians using their sandy clay.

It was in the same spirit that in Switzerland and the United States Paul Bonifas made his powerfully-formed pieces, with169painted or incised underglaze decoration. Maija Grotell, who as183we know left Finland for the United States in 1927, exercised a profound influence there, both through her teaching and through her oviform and cylindrical pots, patterned with geometric designs painted in pure colours. From the 1940s onward she gained a reputation for exciting experiments with glazes.

In Germany Paul Dresler, who studied medicine as well as painting, was drawn to ceramics through his admiration for works from the Middle East shown in the important exhibition of Islamic art held in Munich in 1910. He began by decorating, over the glaze, jugs and pitchers which were thrown for him. Then he learned to pot and opened a studio at Krefeld in 1913. He decorated his wares with lustre or incised decoration and then, after 1928, influenced by Chinese stoneware, he became chiefly concerned with experiments with glazes.

Some of the main trends of the preceding period continued. Hence the importance given to glazes and the research which they inspired. We have just noted the importance attached to them by French potters. The same preoccupations can be seen in Germany, where Gusso Reuss conducted systematic investigations into glazes fired in a reducing atmosphere and where Jan Bontjes van168Beek, who was more influenced than Reuss by Chinese ceramics, worked on glazes in the Chinese idiom. The importance of their research was all the greater in that both men were to teach from the 1940s onwards.

In England in 1925 Katherine Pleydell-Bouverie, after work-76ing for a year with Bernard Leach, opened a pottery at Coleshill in Wiltshire in partnership with a Japanese potter. From 1928 to 1936 she was joined by another of his pupils, Norah Braden.75Together they experimented with a great variety of glazes made from wood and plant ash.

In Denmark Nathalie Krebs started out by working at the Bing171and Grøndhal factory. In 1930 she opened her studio at Saxbo, so inaugurating the great era in the history of Danish art stoneware. Krebs experimented with glazes, firing techniques and surface structures. Her influence was felt throughout Scandinavia, particularly in Sweden, where from 1931 Gunnar Nylund, cofounder of the Saxbo studio, chose to work. Many potters either trained at the Saxbo studio or worked briefly there.

(continued on p. 162)

277 **LAMBERCY,** Philippe (Switzerland, 1919–). *Mural* (detail), 1968–9. Stoneware. City of Geneva Observatory, Sauverny.
After studying at the Swiss School of Ceramics at Chavannes-Renens, where he qualified as a ceramic decorator and designer, Philippe Lambercy worked for the ceramic industry while taking evening courses and participating in seminars on throwing. Hes has played a most important role through his teaching at the School of Decorative Arts in Geneva (since 1953), and has completed a large number of architectural works. He has produced slab-built and thrown stonewares, and has also experimented with glazes. His iron-red glazes are exceptional.

The traditional painted figurative motif tended to take on at this time, for what turned out to be a rather brief period, a slightly more important role. In France André Metthey's mantle was
84 assumed by René Buthaud, who opened his studio in 1919. He produced wares made of siliceous clays, then turned to faïence, which he decorated with stylized and almost monumental human
93 figures. In some of Jean Mayodon's vividly-coloured work similar stylized figures occur, but on a decorative scale better suited to the pots they embellish.

In Germany Max Laeuger, after making faïence and slip-decorated pottery, became influenced by the Islamic exhibition in Munich in 1910 and by the Middle Eastern ceramics which he studied in Berlin in 1916. He went on to make plaques, vases and other austere pots, occasionally embellished with sculptural additions, decorated with patterns which often included the human figure.

In Italy, the cradle of maiolica, a return to old values and new interest in the country's past contributed much to the re-use of
152 the human figure as an element of decoration. Pietro Melandri, after completing his studies in Milan where, in order to make ends meet, he painted pictures and theatre sets, established himself at Faenza in 1918. Until 1921 he worked with Paolo Zoli, and then
95 with Francesco Nonni. In 1922 he began to concentrate on lustres; these were soon replaced by acid-based finishes for wares with decoration featuring faces or human forms, animals and flowers or religious subjects. He also made *bas-reliefs* and worked with such architects as Gio Ponti. Among other artists who
175 worked in the same spirit were Guido Gambone, who was active
94 from 1925 at Vietri sul Mare and then in Florence, and Rodolfo Ceccaroni who, while teaching ceramics at Grottaglia and Sesto Fiorentino, adopted early craft methods, using a wood-fired kiln to produce hand-made pieces decorated with coloured slip applied to the body under a clear glaze. He consciously reinterpreted traditional themes, religious motifs, and scenes of everyday life.

A trend towards the revival of the use of figurative motifs was
113 also evident in England. It was led by William Staite Murray, who became head of the ceramics department at the Royal College of Art in 1926. As we have already seen, he considered ceramics to be one of the fine arts, and preferred to exhibit with painters and sculptors. He had a strong influence on his students, especially on
160 Henry Fauchon Hammond and Thomas Samuel (Sam) Haile. The former, working at Farnham, made stoneware, with decoration applied with a brush; after the war he adopted slip decoration, using local materials. Sam Haile, who also worked in slip-decorated stoneware, pursued his painting career at the same time. He decorated his pieces in a spirit that was very close to contemporary painting and exhibited them with works by the English Surrealists. In 1939 he emigrated with his wife Marianne de Trey, also a potter, to the United States. There he taught at Alfred University, then at Ann Arbor, finally returning to England where he died in an accident in 1948. The only other potter who was directly influenced by the Surrealist movement was Margrit Linck,
225 who created a whole series of Surrealist pieces.

162

Alongside these traditional trends, some original features marked the inter-war period. One of the most important was the appearance of a new school of sculptor–potters. The production of sculptural works in clay during the preceding period has already been mentioned, and we have stressed the fact that some of them had a liking for modelled decoration. Some potters, such as Josef Mendez da Costa, were even producing sculpture at this early date. In the chapter on factories we noted that production of this type was fairly important.

From now on ceramists became more and more involved with sculptural projects. Sometimes they continued to use the traditional techniques of the potter's caraft; at other times they produced purely decorative pieces.

The most typical case of a potter who employed craft methods is that of Paul Beyer. A former master glass-blower, he made use- 118 ful wares in salt-glazed stoneware, then progressed to figures and busts. Initially these were formed of thrown elements, which achieved a hieratic and monumental quality. About this time the 180 Belgian Pierre Caille and the German Richard Bampi were also 177 producing sculptural pieces.

The tendency towards decoration for its own sake is evident in some brightly-coloured figures made by various other potters, which reflect the teaching and work of Michael Powolny in Vienna. These comparatively lightweight works perhaps owe part of their success to the fact that their gaiety was welcome during the sombre years of this crisis period. In the United States in 1913 R. Guy Cowan opened a studio in Cleveland, making limited edi- 78 tions of moulded pieces; he also produced table services and sculptural works. A highly regarded teacher, he worked for the recognition in the United States of ceramic sculpture as a field in its own right. In 1928 he inaugurated an experimental laboratory at the Cleveland School of Art and continued to encourage the development of this new area of activity.

Having made a promising start as a painter, Carl Walters con- 56 centrated on ceramics, and following his research into Egyptian blue glazes, produced his first ceramic sculptures in 1922. Because

(continued on p. 192)

278 **LANGSH**, Elisabeth (Switzerland, 1933–). *Mural* (detail). 1980, Stoneware. Zurich.
After studying at the School of Ceramics in Berne, Elisabeth Langsh has successfully completed many pieces designed for architectural contexts in Zurich, Zug and Geneva. She has participated in many individual or group exhibitions in Switzerland, Washington, Frankfurt and elsewhere, and also in the Miniature Exhibition of the International Academy of Ceramics in Tokyo in 1980.

279 **BRYK**, Rut (Sweden, 1916–). *Tree*. 1970. Porcelain. H. 30 cm.
Since 1942, after studying graphics at the School of Industrial Art in Helsinki, Rut Bryk has been associated with the 'Arabia' factory in that city. In 1954 she married the designer Tapio Wirkkala, who has designed shapes for several factories, principally for Rosenthal, and she sometimes helps to decorate his forms; she has a particular fondness for murals decorated in relief with naturalistic subjects.

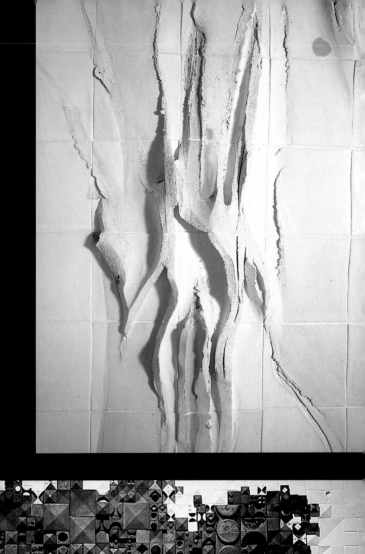

280 **GALATALI**, Attila (Turkey, 1936–). *Panel*, 1972. Terracotta. D.77 cm. Musée de la céramique, Vallauris.
After working on large mosaic wall panels until 1960, Attila Galatali joined a ceramics factory in order to learn all the techniques before opening his own workshop in 1974. He is passionately involved in the study of textures and colours and in the manner in which they interrelate.

280

281 **SPUREY**, Kurt (Austria, 1941–), and Gerda. *Form*, 1974. Porcelain. D.37 cm.
After working with earthenware, Kurt Spurey established and directed, from 1965 to 1968, a study workshop for the OSPAG factory, creating forms and decorations for industrial production. It was not until 1971 that he began to work independently. Since then, when he is not teaching, lecturing or acting as a consultant, he works particularly with porcelain. He uses very personal techniques to bring out the special qualities of this material by playing with light and its reflection.

281

282 **PIGNON,** Edouard (France, 1905–   ). *The Divers,* 1979. Terracotta with fire-clay centre and ceramic on lava. H. 8 m. La Londe – Les Maures.
After working as a miner and building labourer as well as in many other occupations while completing his studies, Pignon concentrated on painting. He also designed sets for the theatre. He learned to throw at Vallauris in or about 1949 with Picasso, and then created several monumental ceramic works, notably at Argenteuil, Lille, Le Creusot and for the Ecole des Beaux-Arts at Marseilles-Luminy. This scheme was realized with the help of the ceramist Michel Rivière at the Proceram factory at Aubagne and consists of 1250 tiles, fired at a temperature between 980° and 1000°.

283

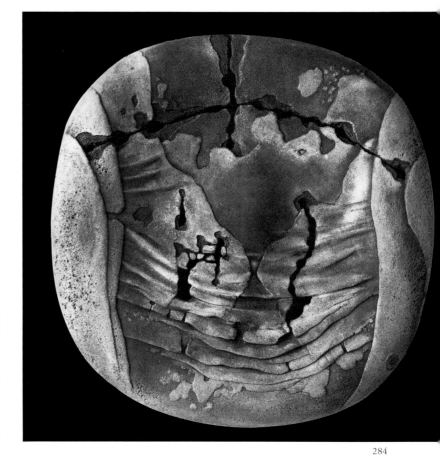

284

283 **BAEY**, Pierre (France, 1940–). *Open Town*, 1980. Terracotta.
H. 70 cm.
Baey treats ceramics as if he were an archaeologist suffering from hallucinations.
He is especially interested in portraying erosion and corrosion. He is attracted
by harbours and by the theatre. The feelings flowing from the heart of his works
are in harmony with his own, which are full of charm and unpredictability.

284 **KVĚTENSKÝ**, Vlastimil (Czechoslovakia, 1930–). *Perpetual Motion*,
1980. D. 80 cm.
After studying at the Industrial School of Ceramics at Teplice and at Béchyně,
Květenský continued his studies at the School of Decorative Arts in Prague
before teaching at the Industrial School of Ceramics at Karlovy Vary. Specializing in interior and exterior architectural ceramics, he has been awarded numerous
medals at Gualdo Tadino as well as a grand prix at Vallauris in 1978. This present
work won an award at Faenza in 1980.

285 **CUMELLA**, Antoni (Spain, 1913–). *Panel*, 1980. Stoneware.
H. 98 cm.
The 'three Catalan musketeers', Picasso, Miró and Artigas, might number four
if Cumella's considerable output were to gain the recognition it deserves.
Cumella has a profound knowledge of the potter's craft and is extraordinarily
versatile, producing vases as well as sculptural pieces. He completed important
murals at Bonn in 1961, Bilbao in 1962, the *Homage to Gaudí* in 1964, at
Nuremberg in 1967 and the grandiose Sandoz edifice in Barcelona in 1972.
Alberto Sartoris claims that Cumella, the master of Granollers, is the Morandi
of ceramic art.

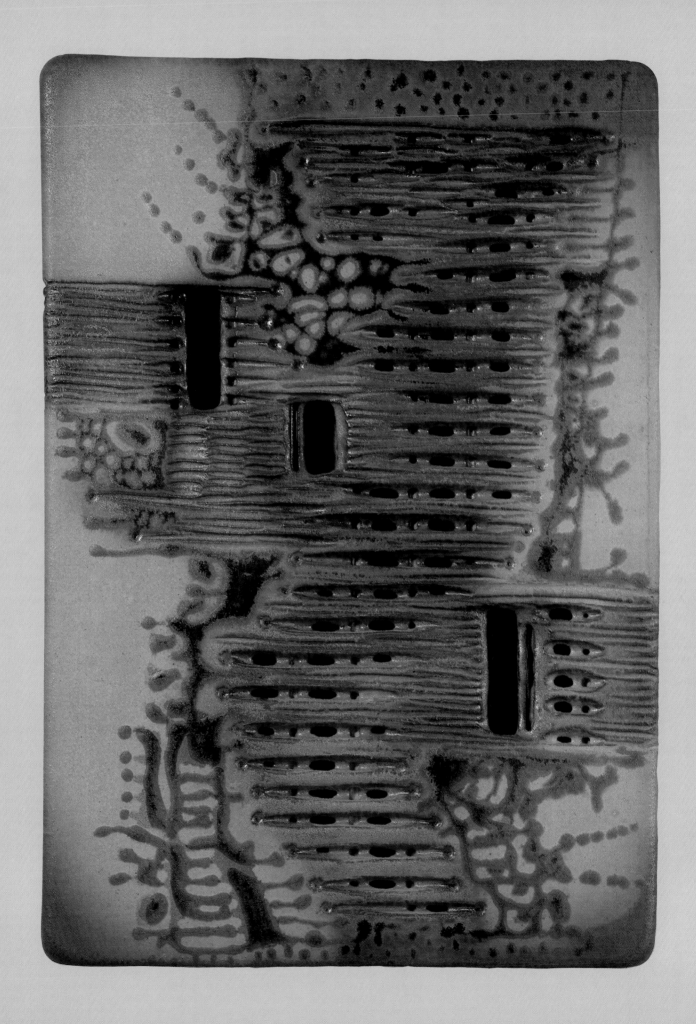

286 **DUCKWORTH**, Ruth (Germany–England–U.S.A., 1919–   ). *Mural Relief*, 1978. Stoneware. H. 81.5 cm. Private collection. Cf. Pl. 234.

287 **SASSI**, Ivo (Italy, 1937–   ). *'Vibrazione materica'*, 1973. Majolica. H. 63 cm. Museo internazionale delle Ceramiche, Faenza; 17,913.
After gaining his diploma at the Istituto Statale d'Arte per la Ceramica at Faenza, Ivo Sassi studied design and sculpture with Francesco Nonni at the Scuola de disegno Tommaso Minardi. He began as a painter in 1954, taking up ceramics in 1959. He progressed from relatively conventional pieces with figurative decoration to the use of abstract motifs. He has completed several panels with relief decoration, but lately his pieces have become more and more sculptural and comprise serial creations such as *Era tecnologica* or *E. T. Genesi*.

288 **ZAULI**, Carlo (Italy, 1926–   ). *Sphere*, 1978. Stoneware. H. 23.5 cm. Musée Ariana, Geneva; AR 5854.
Carlo Zauli studied in Faenza, where he has had his own studio since 1950. He very quickly devoted most of his activity to sculpture and architectural ceramics. He has received countless international awards and his works are to be found in a great number of museums. He is probably the most highly esteemed European sculptor-ceramist in Japan, where in 1980 a retrospective travelling exhibition of his work was held, coinciding with the Miniature Exhibition at the International Academy of Ceramics in Kyoto. This piece, fired in an oxidizing atmosphere at 1200°C, is decorated with feldspathic wood-ash glazes.

286

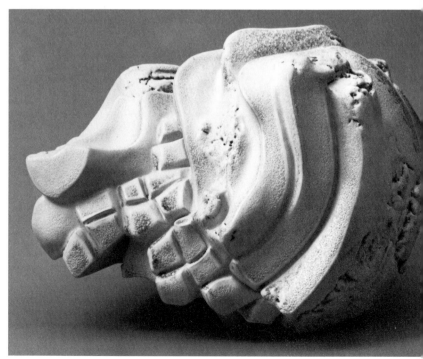

287   288

289 **MESTRE,** Enrique (Spain, 1936–). *Landscape,* 1979. Refractory earthenware with fire-clay. H. 55 cm.
Mestre studied ceramic technique at the San Carlos school in Valencia, his native town, and then at Manises technical school. In 1972 he participated in the international exhibition at the Victoria and Albert Museum, London, and also won the Spanish national prize for ceramics. Mestre's entries for the exhibition of miniatures organized by the International Academy of Ceramics in 1980 were highly acclaimed. His highly disciplined style is related to the dramatic quality of the Spanish landscape. This piece is covered with a glaze composed of felspar, fluorite and iron chromate; it was reduction-fired at 1280°.

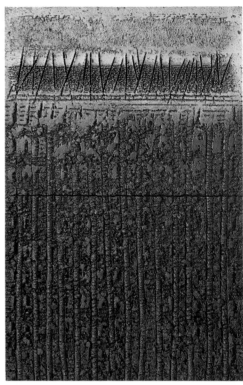

290 **WEBER,** Anne-Marie (Switzerland, 1953–). *Traces of Tiles, Tricks and Distortions,* 1980. *Raku.* 1 m². Musée Ariana, Geneva; AR 6145.
Anne-Marie Weber handles her materials with delicacy and sensitivity, mixing faïence, porcelain, fire-clay, kaolin and talc. She studied under Philippe Lambercy and Sylvie Defraoui and since 1975 has contributed to many group exhibitions. In 1981 she held an individual exhibition, *Les motifs du décor,* at the Galerie Dioptre in Geneva.

289

290

291 **SVOBODA,** Petr (Czechoslovakia, 1942–). *Vases,* 1978. Earthenware. Max. h. 39 cm.
After studying at the Industrial School of Ceramics at Béchyně, Petr Svoboda continued his studies at the School of Decorative Arts in Prague with Otto Eckert. The shapes of his vases, dishes and jardinières are pure and original, and his work is distinguished by its technical perfection. He also produces interesting monumental pieces. He takes part regularly in the biennales at Faenza and Vallauris as well as in the international exhibitions at Sopot and Gdańsk and received the Union of Czech Artists' award in 1979.

292 **SZEKERES,** Károly (Hungary, 1940–). *Sculpture,* 1979. Terracotta and red stone. H. 37 cm. Artist's collection.
Szekeres, who was taught by Imre Schrammel at the School of Decorative Arts in Budapest, has taken part since 1968 in numerous one-man and collective exhibitions at home and abroad, receiving the Vallauris gold medal in 1980. He has also produced several mural panels.

291

293 **BAGLIETTO,** Mireya (Argentina, 1936–). *Man Striding,* 1978.
H.35 cm.
In 1954 Mireya Baglietto studied ceramics in the studio of Ana Mercedes Burni-
chon and exhibited for the first time in Mendoza in 1958. She now exhibits regularly throughout South America and in 1962 received a gold medal at the International Ceramics Exhibition in Prague. This sensitive sculptress, skilled in
manipulating space, who enjoys a high reputation in Argentina, is not influenced
by passing fashions. Lately she has also taken up drawing and painting. Her exhibition in Bogotá in 1976 was outstanding.

293

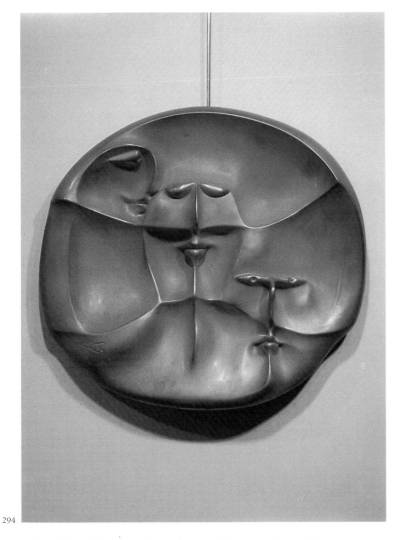

294

294 **TAVELLA,** Leo (Argentina, 1920–). *Figures,* 1978. Ceramic. H. 55 cm.

Tavella, with his dismembered bodies, must surely be *the* Surrealist ceramist in South America. He delights in entwining these disjointed white figures around chairs. He directs a ceramic studio, lectures and teaches, and was awarded a first prize at Faenza in 1971. He has exhibited at the Victoria and Albert Museum, London, as well as in Prague, Canada, the United States (at the University of Colorado) and Belgium. He won the first prize in the sculpture class at the National Salon in Rosario in 1979, and a grand prix at the Rosa Salon at the Rodriguez gallery in Santa Fé in 1980.

295 **BENKO,** Ilona (Hungary, 1937–). *Object,* 1979. Chamotte. H. 36 cm.
Ilona Benko was trained in sculpture at the School of Decorative Arts in Budapest under Miklós Borsos. Since winning a silver medal at the Pécs Biennale in 1968 she has exhibited and gained awards in many countries, and received a purchase award at Faenza in 1980. Her materials are almost unique.

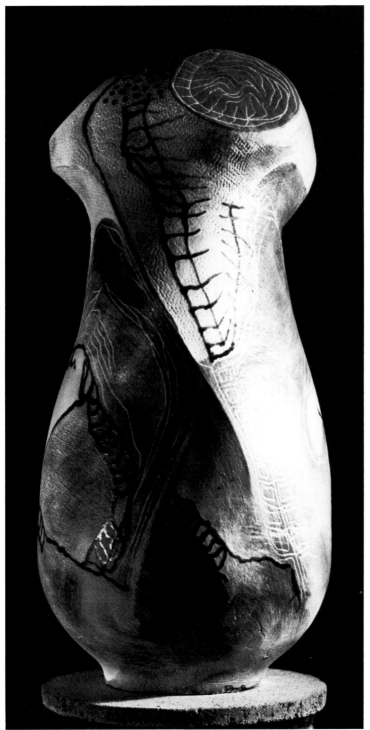

296 **CUMELLA,** Antoni (Spain, 1913–). *Torso,* 1972. Stoneware. H. 80 cm. J. Fernandez Collection, Madrid. Cf. Pl. 285.

297 **BLASCO,** Arcadio (Spain, 1928–). *Form,* 1979. Refractory earthenware. H. 23 cm.
After studying at the San Fernando School in Madrid, Blasco took part in the Biennale Internationale de Punta del Este at Montevideo in 1966 and in the Sao Paulo Biennale the following year. In 1969 he exhibited at Munich and in 1980 participated in the Miniature Exhibition organized by the International Academy of Ceramics in Kyoto.

298

299

298 **LINARD,** Jean (France, 1931–). *Boat Carrying Roses,* 1975. Stoneware. H. 65 cm. Dr. Jean Weber Collection.
Linard studied engraving at the Estienne school and worked in ceramics, mixing clay from the Borne region with sand from the Loire. Linard and E. Joulia are the only artists from the Borne region illustrated here. This is still an important centre where many potters are active, including Jean Girel, Jeanne Grandpierre, Kepp, Michel Lévêque, Michel Pastore, Evelyne Porret, Bernard Thimonnier and Anne Kjaersgaard who worked there from 1958 to 1979.

299 **JORN,** Asger (Denmark, 1914–73). *Mural* (detail), 1959. Ceramic. University of Aarhus.
After studying painting, first in Denmark and then in Paris with F. Léger, Asger Jorn joined Christian Dotremont's *Groupe Surréaliste Révolutionnaire* in Paris in 1947 and the next year helped to found the Cobra movement, which owes its name to the three cities, Copenhagen, Brussels, Amsterdam, whence its initiators came from. As a believer in spontaneous creation and the primacy of the material used, Jorn expressed himself mainly in painting, but also in the graphic arts, tapestry, stone and ceramics. He once stated: 'I do not work with colours, but with coloured materials.' This panel was made at Albissola in Italy and fired at 1000°.

300

301

300 BADEA, Costel (Rumania, 1940–). *'Stindardele Victoriei'*. Earthenware. H. 94 cm.
Costel Badea studied at the Nicolae Grigorescu Institute of Sculptural Arts, graduating in 1964. He now lectures there and since 1973 has been secretary of the Rumanian Union of Sculptural Arts. His works have been included in many exhibitions in his own country and abroad and he has taken part in a number of creative symposia, receiving a number of international awards, including several at Vallauris. Other noted Rumanian ceramists are Dimitru Radulescu and Ion Berendea.

301 MALOLETKOV, Valeriy A. (U.S.S.R., 1945–). *Fire of Olympus* (fragment), 1979. Chamotte. H. 120 cm.
A graduate of the Moscow School of Industrial Arts in 1969, Maloletkov was nominated as a member of the Union of Artists of the U.S.S.R. in 1973.

302 CARLÉ, Carlos (Argentina, 1928–). *Totems,* 1978. Refractory stoneware. H. 250, 220 cm. Private collections.
Carlos Carlé masters spheres as others endeavour to master the world. He pulverizes and slices them in search of a reality rooted in the depths of the pre-Columbian world. He has made many plaques, one of which won the grand prix at Vallauris in 1976. Since 1966 he has lived at Albissola. This work was made in refractory stoneware, reduction-fired at 1300°. Iron, copper and cobalt oxide have been used to patinate the piece.

303

303 **KARCZEWSKA**, Janina (Poland). *Eternity*, 1979. Clay and chamotte. H. 30 cm.
After her studies at Gdańsk under the direction of Piotr Potworowski, Janina Karczewska became a potter, painter and engraver. Since 1957 she has been based at Gmunden and has taken part in very many national and international exhibitions. She exhibits regularly at Vallauris and has received awards on several occasions; her works are displayed in numerous museums.

304 **HAUSNER**, Jan (Czechoslovakia, 1922–). *The Soldiers*, 1976. Grogged earthenware. H. 75 cm.
Hausner studied at the Prague School of Graphic Arts from 1938 to 1942. After a few years spent in a design studio for animated films, in 1947 he took up ceramics and specialized in the creation of pieces for outdoor sites and in monumental compositions for integration into buildings. He received a prize at Faenza in 1976 and subsequently participated in the Vallauris Biennale (1977) and the International Exhibition of Ceramics in Japan (1980); he won an award at the Sopot International Exhibition in 1979.

304

305 **KUCZYŃSKA**, Maria Teresa (Poland, 1948–). *Figures*, 1979. Porcelain.
After training at the National Institute of Plastic Arts in Gdańsk from 1965 to 1971, Maria Teresa Kuczyńska has been working since 1976 in Gdańsk, Sopot and Warsaw. She received the gold medal at Faenza in 1978, and won it again the following year as well as gaining a sculpture prize in Craców. The jury called these pieces 'forms which evoke the monumental quality of classical art, that breathe freely, and have warmth and clarity, movement and lightness'; adding 'unglazed porcelain is a hard but sensitive material.'

306 **ORLANDINI,** Mirko (Italy, 1928–   ). *Stelae and Busts,* 1978. H. of stelae 105 cm. Private collection.
Orlandini studied at the Academies of Fine Arts at Ravenna and Charleroi and lives in Belgium. He has taken part in countless group exhibitions in over twenty countries. In 1975 he won the prize awarded by the Ministry of Foreign Trade at Faenza and in 1978 received the grand prix. In 1979 a retrospective exhibition of his works was organized by the municipality of Faenza. These stelae are built from slabs, coloured with slips derived from calcined oxides and fired at 1280°. The busts have either an ash-based or gritty glaze.

306

307 **DIONYSE**, Carmen (Belgium, 1921–   ). *Purple Helmet.* Porcellanous stoneware. H. 47 cm. Musées royaux d'Art et d'Histoire, Brussels; CR. 248.
After studying drawing, painting, engraving and the decorative arts at the Ghent Royal Academy of Fine Art, Carmen Dionyse qualified as a potter. Since then, apart from her many study tours, she has divided her energies between her own research, teaching posts at Hasselt and Ghent, and contributions to various symposia and conferences. She has participated in a great many individual and group exhibitions and her work is displayed in many museums.

308 **CROWLEY**, Jill (England, 1946–   ). *Three Cats,* 1979. *Raku.* Max. h. 40 cm.
Jill Crowley studied pottery at Bristol with Gillian Lowndes, then at the Royal College of Art in London with Hans Coper and John Dickerson. In 1972 she opened a studio in London and also teaches from time to time. After creating heads in pottery whose modelling rendered them unsuitable for their primary function as vases, she moved on to true portraits, modelling cats and fish as well as human beings.

309 **BLACKMAN**, Audrey (England, 1907–   ). *La Bayadère,* 1980. Porcelain. H. 17 cm. Académie internationale de la Céramique, Geneva.
Audrey Blackman trained at Goldsmiths' College, London, Reading University and Oxford Technical College. She specializes in making coil-built figures and has recently completed a work using this technique. In this example, which was shown at the Miniature Exhibition in Tokyo in 1980, the paste is first coloured, then covered with a transparent glaze, and finally lustred so as to accentuate the oriental charm of this graceful dancer.

307

308

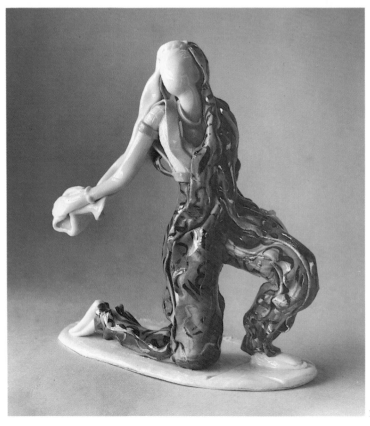

309

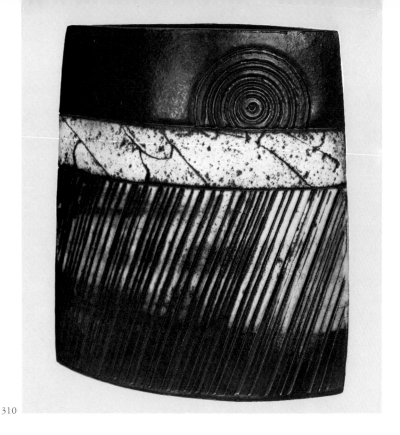

310

310 DE VINCK, Antoine (Belgium, 1924–). *Vase,* 1979. Stoneware. H. 52 cm. Musées royaux d'Art et d'Histoire, Brussels; CR 351.
De Vinck studied with Pierre Caille and took courses at Ratilly. He met Bernard Leach on several occasions and recently translated his fundamental work *A Potter's Book* into French. He works mainly in stoneware to create Japanese-influenced pieces whose elements are frequently inspired by nature or by sculptural works. He has received many international awards, from a medal at the Brussels World Fair in 1958 to an award at Faenza in 1966.

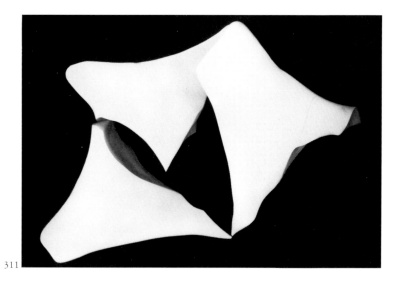

311

311 PANELLI, Tereza (Rumania, 1944–). *Evolution,* 1981. Earthenware. H. 170 cm.
After studying at the Nicolae Grigorescu Institute of Sculptural Arts in Bucharest, from which she graduated in 1970, Tereza Panelli has mainly produced panels or elements of interior mural decoration, often composed of interchangeable modular units. She has participated on her own or collectively in numerous exhibitions in her own country and abroad as well as attending many working symposia. She has been granted many national and international awards, among them prizes at Faenza in 1974 and at Vallauris in 1974 and 1976.

312

312 ALEXANDRE, Patrice (France, 1951–). *L'usine à cheveux,* 1980. Earthenware. H. 82 cm. Jean-Yves Legoff Collection.
By the year 2000 Alexandre will probably enjoy the reputation that Giacometti has today. He creates standing figures who people moving landscapes. *L'usine à cheveux* is somewhat reminiscent of *Black Country,* which announced its form, but is also a dreadful alley between houses, one of those black trenches which are to be found in Belleville where people touch each other but never meet' (Jean-Paul Guibert). Alexandre exhibited at the Paris Biennale in 1980, at the FIAC in 1980 and at the Noella Gest gallery in 1981. He has been resident at the Villa Medicis since 1981. The present piece is in white earthenware coloured with manganese oxide and fired at 960°.

313 MARTINSON, Peteris (U.S.S.R., 1931–). *Notes of Our Times,* 1979. Chamotte stoneware. H. 34 cm. Museo internazionale delle Ceramiche, Faenza.
Martinson qualified at the faculty of architecture of the Latvian State University in 1957, took up pottery and in 1968 became a member of the Artists' Union of the U.S.S.R. He contributes regularly to major international competitions and has won several awards, including one at Faenza in 1980 for this work, which integrates nature and architecture, the countryside and man-made constructions, marrying folklore with art.

314 TSIVIN, Vladimir (U.S.S.R., 1949–). *Greek Chorus,* 1980. Refractory clay. Museo internazionale delle Ceramiche, Faenza.
Tsivin graduated from the faculty of ceramics at the School of Industrial Arts in Leningrad in 1972 and has been a member of the Artists' Union of the U.S.S.R. since 1975. He received a purchase prize form the museum at Faenza in 1980 for his *Greek Chorus.* Made in refractory clay with a salt glaze, it is a combination of architecture and sculpture, part construction and part human figure. The columns seem to be in a garment with a peplum and the cylinders to be transfigured into female figures, so creating a new version of the Temple of the Vestal Virgins.

313

314

315

316

315 **RONTINI,** Aldo (Italy, 1948–). *Matrix of Man,* 1976. Terracotta and maiolica. H. 58 cm. L. Savioli Collection.
Aldo Rontini studied at the Istituto Statale d'Arte G. Ballardini in Faenza and attended courses in sculpture at the Academy of Fine Arts in Bologna. Since 1969 he has been teaching sculpture and modelling at Faenza. He has taken part in many exhibitions of ceramics and sculpture and has received numerous awards, including a gold medal at Faenza in 1980.

316 **ANDERBERG,** Astrid (Sweden, 1927–). *At the Bottom of the Sea, c.* 1979. Porcelain. H. 2.50 cm. Fröhunda Kulturhus, Gothenburg.
Astrid Anderberg studied at the Gothenburg School of Arts and Crafts (1946–50) and opened a studio in 1950. She has lived in Denmark since 1972 and is the author of numerous murals in public buildings. This sculpture, composed of seventeen pieces, was fired at 1300° in a strongly reducing atmosphere. The interior has a celadon glaze and the unglazed exterior is coloured with oxides of cobalt and manganese.

317 **LORRAINE,** Judy (Australia, 1928–). *Double Horn,* 1980. Stoneware. H. 35 cm. Artist's collection.
Judy Lorraine studied architecture and has travelled a great deal in order to study,

visiting Europe, Asia and South America. She is interested in the sound-giving possibilities of ceramics and with this in mind produces little bells or horns in various forms, derived from the ocarina. All the elements are ceramic, modelled in various pieces and assembled before firing.

318 **ZAMORSKA,** Anna Malicka (Poland, 1942–). *'The Cloud',* 1975. Biscuit porcelain, wood, string. H. 100 cm. Museum of Art, Gdańsk.
Anna Zamorska studied ceramics from 1959 to 1965 at the Academy of Arts in Wrocław, where she still works, principally using porcelain. Since 1970 she has taken part in symposia in her own country and abroad as well as in numerous collective national and international exhibitions, receiving many prizes, notably at Faenza in 1973 and 1980.

319 **BASSING,** Carolyn (U.S.A. 1937–). *Ocarinas,* 1978–9. Porcelain. Max. l. 7 cm. National Museum of American Art, Smithsonian Institution, Washington, D.C. (on loan from the artist).
Carolyn Bassing studied at the University of California and obtained her degree in 1959. Her twin interests in music and ceramics have led her to search for totally new ways of utilizing a material which since its origins in China has always been appreciated for, among other things, its clear sonorous quality.

184

317

318

319

185

320 **SALA,** Elisenda (Spain, 1938–). *The Door…and what lies behind it,* 1978. Refractory earthenware. H. 2.20 cm. Museum of Contemporary Art, Villafames.

An admirer of Artigas, Elisenda Sala studied in Barcelona, Stockholm and Japan. She is a poet, gifted with a sense of humanity and irony, who deals in the absurd. She has made numerous pieces which demonstrate her interest in absurdity. In 1966 she gained the prize given by the municipality of Barcelona and in 1969 and 1980 won several gold medals at Faenza. She has taken part in the symposia at Béchyně and has lectured in Vienna; she travels widely.

321 **KOPYLKOV,** Mikhail (U.S.S.R., 1946–). *'The Pink Dress and the Autumn Coat',* 1976. Glazed grogged earthenware. H. 110 cm.

Kopylkov studied at the Institute of Art and Industry at Mukhino until 1969, specializing in glass-making and ceramics. He became a member of the Union of Artists of the U.S.S.R. in 1975. Since 1968 he has participated in various exhibitions in his country and taken part in international competitions since 1976.

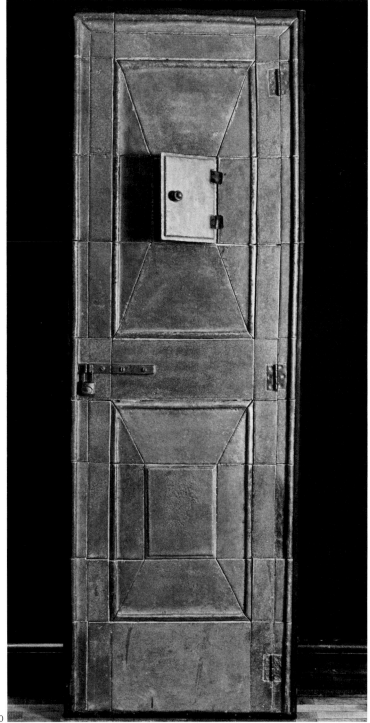

320

321

322 **FAFARD,** Joe (Canada, 1942–). *The Bull,* 1979. Earthenware. H. 29 cm. R. Campbell Collection, Edmonton.

Born at Sainte-Marthe in Saskatchewan, Joe Fafard studied at the University of Manitoba in Canada, then at the University of Pennsylvania in the United States. Since 1970 he has taken part at home in numerous one-man or group exhibitions, been interviewed for radio and television and belongs to several official organizations concerned with the fine arts. He has received several awards, among them the Queen's Jubilee silver medal in 1977, which perhaps explains his extraordinary, almost life-size terracotta portrait of the seated Sovereign (1978), decorated with glazes and acrylic colours.

323 **CROUSAZ,** Jean-Claude de (Switzerland, 1931–). *Rhinoceros,* 1981. Stoneware. H. 35 cm.

Born in Paris of Swiss parents, Jean-Claude de Crousaz studied graphic arts at the School of Decorative Arts in Geneva and then attended the Swiss School of Ceramics at Chavannes-Renens. He opened a studio at Bernex near Geneva and now teaches ceramic decoration at the Geneva School of Decorative Arts and at the Arts and Crafts School at Vevey, while continuing his studio work. He exhibited in Japan in 1970 and 1980 and won many awards, from a gold medal at Prague in 1962 to a prize at Vallauris in 1978. His decoration and sculpture are figurative and often inspired by fauna.

322

323

324 KUHN, Beate (Germany, 1927–). *Form,* 1977. Stoneware. H. 42 cm.
Private collection.
After studying history of art, Beate Kuhn went on to learn ceramics at Wiesbaden and Darmstadt. She shared a studio with Karl Scheid from 1953 to 1956 and established her own studio in 1957. From 1953 to 1957 she worked on a free-lance basis for the Rosenthal Company at Selb. She originally preferred figurative decoration, but now uses a combination of thrown elements to produce complex three-dimensional structures. She has also completed a number of relief murals.

325 ORBAN, Katalina (Hungary, 1950). *Twentieth-Century Icon,* 1979. Porcelain. H. 24 cm. Studio de céramique, Kecskemét.
After studying at the Hungarian High School of Decorative Arts, where she was taught by Csekovszky, Orban worked from 1974 to 1977 at the Budapest porcelain manufactory of the Fine Ceramics Industry Trust. She has done silk-screen mural decorations (Cultural Centre István Petakay, 1975; Hotel Hilton, Budapest, 1976). Since 1974 she has exhibited her oeuvre at home and abroad, and has been awarded a number of prizes. In 1981 she participated at the 'Linea' exhibition involving ten artists, among them two excellent Hungarian potters, Gyözö Lörincz and Maria Gesler.

324

326 HARARI, Shelly (Bulgaria–Israel, 1921–). *Tobacco Leaves* (detail), 1979. Ceramic. H. approx. 2 m.
Shelly Harari exhibits regularly in Tel-Aviv and showed her work in Munich in 1962 and in New York in 1968. She consistently focuses her contributions to exhibitions on a particular theme. Her pieces are solid in structure and predominantly decorated in natural colours.

325

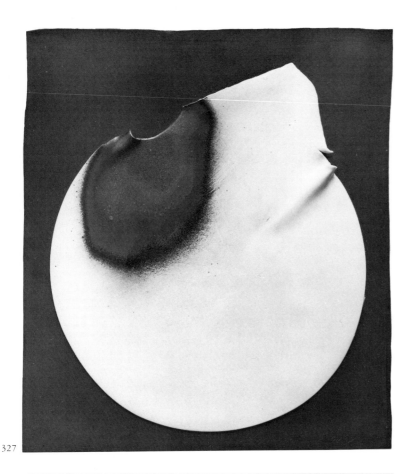

327

327 **LUCIETTI,** Giuseppe (Italy, 1936–). *Lastra quadrata con frammento.* 1981. Porcelain. H. 38 cm. Musée Ariana, Geneva.
Born at Nove, Lucietti attended the Istituto d'Arte per la ceramica at Faenza and worked at Bassano del Grappa. Since 1956 he has taken part in various painting and graphic arts competitions in Italy and abroad. His ceramic works have also been shown in many individual and collective exhibitions. He has received numerous international awards, the most recent being the International Ceramic Academy's purchase prize, conferred on the present work at Faenza in 1981.

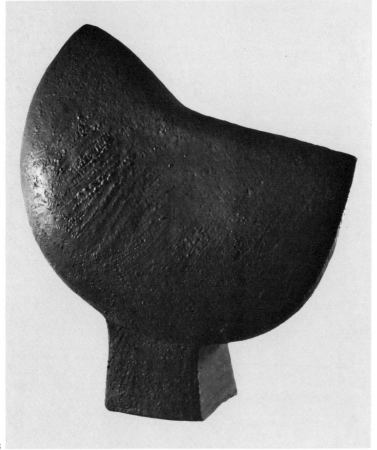

328

328 **MADOURA,** known as Suzanne Ramié (France, 1905–74). *The Bird,* 1971. Grogged earthenware. H. 60 cm. Private collection.
A former pupil of the School of Fine Arts in Lyons, who came to Vallauris in 1938, Suzanne Ramié showed a natural sobriety and a well-defined talent in her works, as the retrospective exhibiton held in 1975 at the Musée des Beaux-Arts in Lyons showed. The importance of her work is somewhat obscured by Picasso and other artists such as Matisse, Chagall, Lurçat as well as Reverdy, Eluard, Cocteau and André Verdet, who worked with her, providing designs for her studio.

329 WATT, Alan (Australia). *Cylinders.* Porcelain. H. 42 cm.
Alan Watt is the director of the department of ceramics at the Canberra fine arts school. He has frequently exhibited in one-man and group shows in his own country, where he has been awarded the highest prizes. He has also taken part in exhibitions abroad, notably at Faenza in 1979 and in New Delhi in 1980. These pieces are unglazed and coloured with a cobalt wash over a decorated coating and fired at 1300°.

329

330 FALK, Cathie (Canada, 1928–). *One hundred and fifty Suspended Cabbages,* 1978. Ceramic, rope, sand and dressing table. H. 131 cm.
Born at Alexander, Manitoba, Cathie Falk, who has lived in Vancouver since 1947, was trained at the University of British Columbia and, as she herself says, 'here and there'. She has exhibited in Vancouver and Calgary, as well as in Paris in 1974, and has taken part in countless group exhibitions. She also paints and sculpts, and is interested in environments made up of objects not normally associated with each other, and in artistic 'happenings'.

330

191

of their ornamentation of rosettes, bands and lines, these pieces remained purely decorative, although inspired by nature, especially by animals. Valerie (Vally) Wieselthier, an Austrian pupil of Powolny who emigrated in 1929, created large sculpted figures in her New York studio.

In the 1930s the development of ceramic sculpture in the United States expanded as a result of the Welfare Art Program set up by the Roosevelt administration to help artists fight the Depression. Potters received many private and public commissions, for example to do characters from children's stories for libraries, mural panels for public buildings, and garden ornaments. This ambitious programme led ceramists to rival even monument-builders by tackling works of huge size, such as the Fountain of Atoms made by W. DeSantis Gregory for the New York World Fair in 1939–40, with its twelve colossal faïence figures, each weighing more than a ton.

The contemporary period is too close to us and too abundant to be analysed according to the criteria of the past. We lack the necessary perspective to judge the production of recent years. We will therefore attempt only to outline the most striking features of its development, or should one say of its explosion.

Recent ceramics, which have been produced on a large scale, must be seen against the background of a rapidly changing world. The economic expansion of the post-war period, with the intense industrialization that accompanied it, quickly provoked a reaction, as had happened in the nineteenth century. Faced with mechanization and automation, the younger generation preached a return to the earth and to craft work, creating a kind of mythology around the hand-made object and placing a high value on individual creativity. Soon some people began to question even more radically the very need to produce, since in their eyes it implied an acceptance of the values of the consumer society that they rejected wholly.

Nevertheless, economic development is also beneficial to potters. It allows more and more collectors to act as patrons and to buy their wares. The attention, curiosity and even infatuation of the public with regard to potters is also evident in the increase in specialist galleries, in the concern shown by museums, and in the number of national and, particularly, international exhibitions. The annual events at Faenza should be mentioned. Initially, when they started in 1938, they were national but later became international. The biennial exhibitions at Vallauris began in 1966. It is symptomatic that the museum at Syracuse, in the United States, had to give up the Ceramic National Exhibitions, as it was swamped by the number of works and participants.

At the same time, the growing number of potters and the increasing interest shown in craft work by all kinds of official bodies and government agencies in many countries have contributed to shape the potter's career to a greater or lesser degree. In addition, the increased number of people engaged in ceramics has led to a development of training schemes, all the more important as teaching others is often the best and sometimes the only way the potter can finance his own experiments.

In the years immediately after the Second World War there was a remarkable increase in the production of hand-made domestic wares, due both to the necessity of replacing goods destroyed as a result of the war and to the rapid recovery of the economy. Although this phenomenon sometimes led to the mass production of objects that were made too hastily, it was important in so far as it encouraged good potters who were already making domestic wares of high aesthetic quality, and subsidized their experimental, and consequently unprofitable, research.

The years from the 1950s to the present are marked by a dual movement. On one hand the trends noted in the preceding period have persisted: some figurative painted decoration was still done, especially in France and Italy, but it soon disappeared almost totally. After the war the traditionalist influence of Bernard Leach, whose *The Potter's Book* was published as recently as 1940, began to make itself felt strongly in almost every country. It led to the production of pieces in which forms, glazes, and sometimes even decoration harmonized with and balanced each other. The work of his friend Francine del Pierre illustrates Leach's ideas particularly well. Potters captivated by the poetry of glazes also worked along these traditional lines, and the more intellectual potters, who are interested in incised or modelled ornamentation on traditional forms, can be included in this group.

However, since the early 1950s there have been signs of liberation from tradition. The ceramic structures of Axel Salto in 178 Denmark, of Richard Bampi in Germany, of Guido Gambone in 177, 175 Italy and of Georges Jouve in France exemplify this.

(continued on p. 194)

331 **LICHTENSTEIN,** Roy (United States, 1923–   ). *Ceramic Sculpture 12,* 1965. Earthenware. H. 22.9 cm. Mr. and Mrs. John Powers Collection, New York.
After studying in New York and in Ohio, Lichtenstein taught until 1964 before devoting himself to painting. Throughout 1965 he worked with the ceramist Ka-Kwong-Hui; the exhibition of his pieces–piles of everyday objects and moulded heads–had a great influence on the development of ceramics. Playing on the relationship between reality and illusion, he sought to de-bunk the functional object and to ridicule the qualities of craftsmanship necessary for its fabrication and decoration.

332 **MARIANI,** Guido (Italy, 1950–   ). *Perché un titolo? Parla da sé,* 1980. Refractory clay and maiolica. H. 60 cm.
Born at Faenza, Guido Mariani studied there at the Istituto Statale d'Arte G. Ballardini and then obtained his sculpture diploma from the Academy of Fine Arts of Naples. Since 1969 he has been teaching ceramic design while continuing to produce work in his studio. He belongs to the school of practitioners of *trompe-l'oeil* which chooses ceramic materials to achieve the illusion of commonplace objects or scenes of everyday life in order to ridicule them.

333 **SHAW,** Richard (U.S.A., 1941–   ). *Couch and Armchair with landscape and cows,* 1967. Earthenware. H. 24.1 cm (couch), 22.9 cm (armchair). Museum of Contemporary Crafts, New York.
Shaw played the most influential part in the formation of the school of makers of 'super-realist objects', which originated in California and then spread throughout the United States. Influenced by Surrealist art, in particular by Magritte's work, his later pieces, which are built up from disparate elements, often simulate commonplace objects. They explore the relationships between image and reality in its actual and created form.

331

332

333

193

The true revolution that occurred in the middle of the decade originated in the United States. Several factors may have played a part in this: on one hand, the intervention of artists untrained in this field showed that ceramics offered a means of expression that was as direct as it was original. Picasso worked with marvellous freedom, but still made useful objects: vases, pots, plates, dishes, while Lucio Fontana and the Futurists working at Albissola, and Joan Miró, liberated their creations from any pretence of mere usefulness.

Constructivist sculptors working with heterogeneous materials could not but fertilize potters' imagination. They were conscious of the provocative nature of the Dada and Surrealist movements. Marcel Duchamp's 'ready-mades' and Meret Oppenheim's fur tea-cup challenged the very idea of a 'work of art' and questioned the 'usefulness' of everyday objects.

At the same time a cult of spontaneity was evident in other art forms such as jazz, where the act of doing is almost more important than the result, or in Abstract-Expressionist painting, triumphantly personified by Jackson Pollock. The importance of spontaneous expression and its risks were recognized by Japanese potters, whose work was being discovered at that very moment on the West Coast of the United States. Contact with Japan was now direct, and not through Bernard Leach as intermediary.

273, 274 Peter Voulkos was the catalyst who brutally transformed consideration of the creative act and the finished work where ceramics terms are concerned. Starting out as a traditional potter producing
272 functional wares, he worked with Rudy Autio at the Archie Bray Foundation until, in 1954, he accepted the task of founding the ceramics department of the Otis Institute in Los Angeles. He soon gathered around him a group of young enthusiasts. They cannot be said to have been taught, in the normal sense of the word, but instead they worked as a group and handled clay in a totally free manner, each individual expressing himself according to his own artistic sensibility. The major innovations introduced by Voulkos, who set an example with his astonishing appetite for work, were based on his research into the dynamic role of decoration, into the construction of objects from separately-worked elements, and into the role of mass rather than volume. This interest in volume seems of fundamental importance and distinguishes him quite radically
190 from the 'potter', however free his approach. Francine del Pierre expressed admirably this feeling for internal volume: 'Contours, forms and volumes are notions common to sculpture and pottery. But the contours of a pot have to relate absolutely to the dilation of the internal hollow of the object, this hollow that is its core... it could also be said of a pot that it depends on its internal space in order to breathe... to me, it is just because a pot is hollow and because it breathes that it differs essentially from abstract sculpture...' ('My Motives and Reasons for Modelling', text edited in 1967 for the catalogue of her exhibition in Hamburg).

The influence exerted by the creations of Peter Voulkos and his followers was enormous. Initially, some potters almost everywhere abandoned the manufacture of functional wares made according to norms of varying degrees of strictness in order to

express themselves freely through the ceramic medium. Sometimes they attributed more importance to the message transmitted and to spontaneous creativity than to the final result. This first period shows almost a lack of awareness of the starting point of the movement. This was spontaneous expression within the limits imposed by the medium. The important characteristic of most works by American ceramists is the contrast between their freedom of expression and their complete technical mastery. Happily, this aspect has gradually come to be better understood.

The continuation of experimental research of this type occasionally implies a rejection of some aspects of contemporary civilization. Evidence of this can be seen in paintings and sculpture which, in order to denounce the general mess in which we live, include bits of rubbish in the work or hold up to ridicule typical objects of daily life by using ambiguous *trompe-l'œil* devices or by reducing such objects to absurdity. The culmination of this trend is 'Funk art' which rejects all commonly accepted aesthetic values, and especially the idea of 'good taste'. This notion is put to severe trial by the provocative works of Robert Arneson and others. In the future, 'taste' alone will be able to distinguish between the affectations which clothe vulgarity, caricature, and the vitality of despair.

(continued on p. 200)

334 **CICANSKY**, Victor (Canada, 1935–). *Preserves,* 1979. Glazed earthenware. H. 23, 16 and 10 cm.
Victor Cicansky studied at Regina in Saskatchewan, where he was born, and then at Davis, California. He received several official commissions for mural panels and has taught at the University of Regina since 1970 while giving many lectures and seminars all over the country. He is fond of depicting the most everyday objects humorously, rendering them absurd by their scale and position, while his strong colours emphasize the aesthetic quality of the resulting ensembles.

335 **ARNESON**, Robert (U.S.A., 1930–). *Whistling in the Dark,* 1976. Terracotta. H. 92.4 cm. Whitney Museum of American Art, New York; 77.37. Robert Arneson has been teaching since he finished his studies and it was his students who encouraged him to give more attention to ceramics. From the 1960s onwards he created a series of sculptural works which were extremely disturbing because of their aggressive or ironic themes; he thus contributed to the major revolution that shook American ceramics. With his great technical ability and strong personality, he explores the possibilities of his materials while raising questions about the very nature of artistic activity.

336 **LEVINE**, Marilyn (Canada–U.S.A., 1935–). *Hanging Bag with Rope Handle,* 1975. Ceramics, wood, metal, rope. H. 81.5 cm. Hansen Fuller Gallery, San Francisco.
Born in Canada, Marilyn Levine studied chemistry and then sculpture in Canada and in California. Her work belongs rather to the so-called 'purely objective' movement than to hyper-realism. She likes to translate leather objects into ceramics as, through its suppleness, this material is particularly qualified to preserve traces of human history that are recorded involuntarily.

337 **WILHELMI**, William (U.S.A., 1939–). *Cowboy Boots,* 1980. Porcelain. Max. h. 35,9 cm. National Museum of American Art, Smithsonian Institution, Washington, D.C. (gift of the artist); 1981.07.
Wilhelmi studied at San Diego State College then at the University of California in Los Angeles. He has completed many tile murals, such as that in the Post Office at Laredo, Texas (1976), and is now teaching while continuing his creative work.

334

335

336

337

338 **VIOTTI,** Ulla (Sweden, 1933–   ). *Traces of Life* (detail of 'Drama Installation'), 1980. Stoneware and chamotte. H. 20 cm. Cf. Pl. 236.

338

339 **CARUSO,** Nino (Italy, 1928–   ). *Modular Sculpture,* 1974. Earthenware. H. 8 m.

Nino Caruso directs the International Centre of Ceramics in Rome and the ceramics department of the Istituto d'Arte Statale. He has worked in association with many industrial factories and taken part in numerous exhibitions at home and abroad. He is concerned with problems relating to creative activity in clay, and also organizes symposia and edits articles for specialist reviews. He has lectured on architectural sculpture at various American universities and has created several monuments and *bas-reliefs,* including those in the church of Savona and in a metro (subway) station in Marseilles.

339

340

341

340 **CYBIŃSKA,** Krystyna (Poland, 1931–   ). *Garden Composition,* 1977.
Chamotte. H. 2 m.
Krystyna Cybińska studied from 1949 to 1954 in the studio of Stanislas Dánski
and Julia Kotarbińska at the School of Fine Arts in Wrocław. She is at present
in charge of the ceramic studio at this school. Since 1960, when she took part
in a national exhibition of ceramics and glass and received second prize, she has
also participated in numerous exhibitions in her own country and abroad and
has gained many awards, including a prize at Faenza in 1977.

341 **PENNONE,** Giovanni (Italy, 1947–   ). *Siamo integri,* 1979–80.
Grogged earthenware. Max. h. 3 m.
Giovanni Pennone has participated in numerous one-man exhibitions and in
collective shows such as Documenta 5 at Kassel in 1972 and the Venice Biennales of 1978 and 1980. More a painter than a potter, his interest centres less
on single pieces than on elements, of ceramic or other materials, arranged so that
they inter-react in space. His works are featured in many museums, especially
those with contemporary art collections.

342 **FIOR,** Candido (Italy, 1942–   ). *Group of Objects,* 1981. Terracotta.
Until 1970 Fior was studying, principally in Venice and at Nove di Bassano;
today he owns a studio at San Martino di Lupari, where he works mainly on terracotta sculpture. He has taken part in the Venice Biennales as well as in many
craftsman potters' exhibitions.

343 **PONTOREAU,** Daniel (France, 1947–   ). *Landscape,* 1981. Terracotta, mirror and light. H. 80 cm. Artist's collection.
This self-taught sculptor won the Prix d'Architecture in 1972 at Vallauris, where
he received the grand prix in 1974. He also won the Prix de la Jeune for sculpture
in 1973 and a scholarship for monumental art from the town of Ivry in 1979.
He created a monument at Saint-Yrieix to mark the discovery of kaolin in 1768.

198

342

343

After some years of rather discordant, though often fascinating, experiments it seems that the present economic crisis is once again playing a moderating role. The necessity of finding a buying public, not just an interested one, has brought a new sobriety into the work of a number of potters. Today the two contradictory trends of the old and the new are seen to co-exist.

On occasion members of the old school reproach Picasso for his rakishness, his virtuosity and his authority; their criticisms remind one of those of certain sport-lovers who cast doubt on Borg's tennis-playing.

This book compares the work of artists, painters and sculptors who have taken up ceramics at one time or another and analyses the contribution made by professional potters. Each seems to be the instrument of a marvellous disparity, choosing the means to promote his or her talents and enthusiasms from the prodigious variety of processes. Technical possibilities are put to the service of their imagination and talent. All potters, when trying to master fire, must agree with Edouard Chapallaz who wrote: 'The result depends not on the type of kiln or fuel but on a choice. It depends on the potter's knowledge and mastery of the firing process, not on chance.'

Within the constraints of this book it is not possible to explore the relations between European potters and those of Japan, Korea, India, China or Taiwan. Just as members of juries commit injustices in good faith, the authors are painfully aware of having omitted some notable potters. We have deliberately left out of our discussion utilitarian ceramics, traditional pots, pitchers, jugs, and folk pottery in general. Their merit and charm are in no way impugned by their absence from these pages.

We have endeavoured, for the period 1970–80, to establish an almost equal balance between pieces of true sculpture and examples of pots in which coloured glazes almost acquire the value of paintings. Artigas co-operated enthusiastically with Miró as an equal when he created his masterpiece at the Barcelona museum.

Without our intending particularly to draw attention to the national characteristics of the works of any one country, this has sometimes happened unintentionally.

In France alone there are some forty public art institutions where instruction is given in ceramics. In the wake of Jacques Prolongeau in Limoges, Jean and Jacqueline Lerat in Bourges, in 1982 it is Jean Biagini of Aix-en-Provence who vigorously thrusts his students into their future careers. He introduces them to teachers, students from other schools, museum curators, art critics and gallery directors. The latter sometimes show a faith in the young that is not always backed up by commercial success.

Apart from official schools, there are a number of potters from Germany to Australia who open their studios to groups of pupils. In this way Ratilly Jeanne and Norbert Pierlot were originally assisted by Georges Jouve. Perhaps we shall see the disappearance of the individual apprentice working for a solitary master, who teaches him also the virtues of humility.

The proliferation of reviews (*Ceramic Review* in England, *Pottery in Australia*, *Form Function* in Finland, *Ceramica* in Spain, *Céra-*

mique moderne, l'Atelier des métiers d'art in France, etc.), monographs, exhibition catalogues and specialist works justifies Hamada's remark: 'The secret is that there is no secret.' Two potters, the German Hildegard Storr-Britz and the Englishman Peter Lane, have published two important works in which they charmingly give credit to many of their colleagues.

We have not dealt with the comparative virtues of throwing, modelling, moulding and casting. While we may feel dizzy watching a pot being thrown, it is just as intoxicating to watch Francine del Pierre assemble the parts that make up her work.

All over the world men and women are rejecting city life and dedicating themselves to the art of pottery. They give form to clay with the aid of fire, that indispensable element of civilization.

If there is one craft that has preserved its original virtues and its quality of poetry, it must be that of the potter. Its letters patent of nobility are written in the book of Isaiah: 'Surely your turning of things upside down shall be esteemed as the potter's clay, for shall the work say of him that made it: He made me not? Or shall the thing framed say of him that framed it: He had no understanding?'

(Isaiah, 29, 16.)

The sculptor fashioned all too well
The figure of the god so proud
That people said his Jupiter lacked nought
But the facility to speak aloud.

(La Fontaine, *Fables* IX, VI.)

344 **RIOPELLE,** Jean-Paul (Canada, 1923–). Plaque (detail of a wall), 1981. Stoneware and earthenware. H. 50 cm. Fondation Maeght, Saint-Paul-de-Vence.
After studying at the Montreal Polytechnic, and simultaneously taking a correspondence course in architecture, Riopelle gained his diploma at the Ecole de Meuble before settling in Paris in 1947. Although he is primarily a painter, he has also modelled sculpture. In 1979–80 he worked on the elements of a large ceramic wall, constructed in the studio of the Fondation Maeght. Fascinated and encouraged by this first attempt, he has made sculptural pieces and plaques and is planning to do a ceiling for a major Canadian bank.

345 **SPINNER,** Hans Ulrich (Germany, 1941–). *Totems,* 1975. H. 80, 60 cm. Artist's collection.
Hans Spinner studied at Kiel from 1962 to 1967 and operated a studio there from 1967 to 1970. He stayed in Vence from 1970 to 1972 and then returned to Kiel for three years before taking over from Michel Muraour the direction of the ceramic studio at the Fondation Maeght. Chillida, Buri and Riopelle found in him an invaluable partner, as did Meurice and d'Adami, in the production of their mural, measuring 160 m², for Cergy-Pontoise. Spinner exhibited at Faenza and in Munich in 1968 and in Granada in 1977. He allows his own oeuvre to take second place to his work in co-operation with great artists, in order to raise the prestige of ceramic art.

Techniques

From its very origins ceramic art has had a dual aspiration. The potter sought to provide suitable vessels for containing and conserving foodstuffs, liquids and all types of matter, while at the same time aiming to produce decorative objects. From the very first, forms were embellished with either painted or incised motifs in order to obtain a harmonious equilibrium between function and decoration.

During the course of their development ceramic techniques have undergone a double evolution. In the first period—the longest, since it extends from the origins to the nineteenth century—the bodies, as well as processes of fashioning, firing and decoration developed continually towards a much greater acceptability for those using the finished products, particularly by the transition from porous to vitrified bodies, and towards an increase in production resulting from the successive inventions of the wheel, the mould, and then of the casting and jollying processes. During this period there was also a transition from the primitive wood-fired kiln to two-chamber kilns fed by wood and then by coal; simultaneously painted decoration gradually gave way to processes of transfer-printing, lithography and finally chromolithography. A second period began in the second half of the nineteenth century, when the heyday of discoveries allowed production on an industrial scale of objects in great quantity and marketable at a relatively low cost. Automatic jollying by increasingly complex machines ensured uniform drying of the wares. This progress continued into the twentieth century with the building of tunnel kilns powered by gas or fuel oil, controlled by the newly-perfected Seger cones, luminous instrument panels and optical pyrometers which served to control firing temperatures and the atmosphere in the kiln.

But it was at the very moment when ceramic art seemed to have been developed to its highest point that its methods were questioned most strongly. On one side was an industrialized production which nevertheless sought to maintain the aesthetic qualities indispensable to its success, and which therefore increasingly had to resolve difficulties with designers. On the other side there arose, as a reaction, a preference for the work of the 'studio potter', as he was called in England, the ceramist who worked alone and was totally responsible for his creations.

The broadest possible range of bodies and processes is available to the contemporary potter. Methods of fashioning and decoration inherited from the traditions of Europe as well as of Asia and the Far East, Africa and America, are combined with industrial

346 **CHINESE SLOPING KILN,** 25 m³. La Borne, France, 19th century. Is it not fitting that this kiln should be named as if it were itself an artist? In 1978 it was still being used to fire an enormous load of 1,000 pieces which required 67 hours of firing, 5 cubic metres of rough wood, 3 cubic metres of charcoal, and 14 cubic metres of split wood, including hornbeam, oak and birch, at a temperature of 1350°. Twenty participants from La Borne, eleven from abroad including Van Lith, Evelyne Porret and Michel Pastore (who left his large pot there) celebrated changing times and the unchanging brotherhood of lovers of clay and fire.

347 **KUJUNDZIC,** Zeijko (Hungary–U.S.A., 1920–   ).
A graduate of the Budapest College of Art and a professor at the College of Art
and Architecture of the University of Pennsylvania, Kujundzic is determined to
perfect a solar kiln for the firing of ceramics. He has exhibited in Hungary in
1977, in Toronto in 1978, in Mexico in 1979 and at Kyoto in 1980.

methods or even completely new techniques, often resulting from
work in the ceramic medium by artists who are complete strangers
to its rules, and whose ignorance makes them innovators. It would
be impossible to give here a comprehensive description of all the
procedures now in use during the different phases of manufacture
of a ceramic object, but the captions to our plates provide a practical catalogue. They indicate the extreme diversity of materials and
methods from which each potter can make his choice in order to
express himself.

The present situation is very different from that at the beginning of this century. Several generations of impassioned craftsmen
have succeeded in gaining public attention, creating a market and
attracting to their number a growing band of young practitioners.
This 'return to the earth' has in its turn induced some establishments to specialize in potters' supplies. A young potter eager to
establish himself today will easily find in the trade a range of kilns
of different capacities, bodies which he can use in their present

state or fashion according to his own ideas, and ready-made glazes.
Technical training, supplemented by specialist journals and
works, will give him the necessary formulae. We are far removed
from the pioneers who had to construct their own kilns at the cost
of much trial and error, who slowly worked out formulae for their
ceramic bodies, often made from local clays, and who painstak-
ingly perfected glazes, the recipes of which they kept secret, prefer-
ring to destroy them rather than to share them. This situation does
not in the least prevent the more adventurous spirits from creating
their own personal recipes. There are many potters even today who
conduct systematic research into the possibilities offered by
different materials. Quite simply, this research is no longer a necessity, but their choice. Others prefer to devote all their energies to
investigations of a different nature.

From the middle of the nineteenth century the European countries gradually rediscovered their own traditional types of pottery:
tin-glazed earthenware (faïence), lead-glazed earthenware and
stoneware, which can be either salt-glazed or decorated with
painted or incised slip. Contact with foreign countries led to the
adoption of new processes and materials. These included Islamic
faïence with painted decoration highlighted with metallic lustres,
Japanese stoneware with sophisticated glazes, and primitive
ceramics and early porcelains from China with incised underglaze
patterns and inexhaustible variations of glazes. The 1920s and
1930s saw in addition the return to plain earthenware, in the
manner of antique *terra sigillata,* influenced by pieces from pre-
Columbian America or Africa.

The two materials most commonly used by present-day potters
are stoneware and porcelain. The first, which Carriès called *ce mâle
de la céramique* ('this most masculine of ceramics'), is massive,
robust and calls for powerful handling; furthermore, thanks to the
raku technique, it allows for highly spontaneous expression. The
second is beginning to lose its reputation as a difficult medium
and is at last forfeiting its legendary aura. A number of potters are
using porcelain for reasons that have nothing to do with those
qualities traditionally ascribed to this material. They appreciate
the way the brilliant white surface sets off the colours and patterns;
they take advantage of the extreme fineness which can be attained
in order to emphasize differing thicknesses and reliefs; and they
are fascinated by its unique manner of reflecting, absorbing or
diffusing light.

Contemporary potters employ very many different fashioning
methods. Some of them take advantage of industrial techniques,
such as casting or jollying, while producing only limited editions
of their work. Very early methods are being revived, such as the
technique of superimposed coils, or of throwing on the wheel—
the latter sometimes used unconventionally, for beside simply-
thrown shapes we find examples which, after throwing, have been
reworked directly by pinching and modelling; the swelling contours of some works have been created by superimposing separately thrown sections; and even completely experimental works of
sculpture, built up of thrown elements, are fashioned by methods
of the most traditional kind.

Another early method, that of moulding, can be used in quite novel ways, as with the sand-casting process perfected by Anders Liljefors, which is well suited to the construction of large-scale pieces or pierced forms; also certain substances may be deposited at the bottom of the mould to modify the surface texture of certain areas, and thus to alter the appearance of the object.

During our period quite novel methods of working clay, independent of tradition, have been introduced: slabs of clays are assembled or rolled by hand to form figures; direct modelling by pinching is practised; and the use of instruments totally foreign to the field of ceramics, such as the *moulinette* or herb-mill employed by Nicole Giroud to obtain shredded pieces of clay, is not uncommon.

There is a similar variety in the field of decoration. An interesting effect can be achieved by blending colouring oxides directly with the paste and by combining with it traces of various colours. This mixture can be left to chance, or else may be controlled by arranging coils of coloured paste in a pre-selected order to obtain effects similar to early *millefiori,* 'agate wares' or *marqueteries.*

Other decorative procedures are piercing, carving and incising. Besides true openwork decoration, practised especially on thin-walled porcelain, the potter can play with the different thicknesses, either by removing layers by carving or adding layers of *barbotine* (slip) to modulate the light. He can emulate the *niello* technique, by carving either into the body or on to a coating of slip hollow motifs that are subsequently filled in with coloured slips; and by incising in intaglio into a layer of slip he can allow a small area of a different colour to show through.

The craftsman can also modify the surface of the object by applying, while the body is still soft, some element of a plant or a piece of fabric whose form will become imprinted on the object.

He can, if he wishes, encrust the object with non-ceramic elements, often of natural origin, such as wood, horn, ivory, feathers and so on. Lace motifs are produced by two early methods still practised today: either by laying a piece of real lace on to the body before firing, which then burns during this process, leaving its imprint on the object, or by making a piece of porcelain lace by soaking the lace itself in slip before firing, the strands of lace burning slowly enough to leave behind their porcelain shadow.

Painted figurative decoration is nowadays fairly rare. Glazes or slips can be applied with the brush or ladle; and the potter can also either draw directly on to the piece with special lithographic crayons or apply the patterns by lithographic, silk-screen or photographic printing processes, or by stencil.

In addition, research into glazes continues. Investigations are carried out into metallic lustre or crystalline effects, or into the revival of Oriental glazes such as 'oil-spot' or 'hare's fur'. There are many craftsmen exploring the possibilities offered by the different kiln atmospheres and various vegetable ashes. Alongside those who pursue these traditional lines of inquiry, many others play with daring combinations or engage in trials on heterogeneous materials new to the ceramic world. One can only regret that some confuse the means with the end, in the words of Bernard Leach, and become so totally caught up with their constant experimentation that they run the risk of forgetting that glazes are for decoration only and are intended to emphasize forms whose importance must never be neglected.

Today, then, two schools co-exist: one which, while innovating, respects the ancient techniques of the craft, the other expressing itself freely, treating ceramics as a material like any other, refusing to restrict it by the norms, whether technological or craft-oriented, of its own past.

Select Bibliography

ALBIS, A. d', *La Porcelaine artisanale*, Paris, 1975

—, *Faïence et pâte tendre*, Paris, 1979

ALBIS, J. d' and ROMANET, C., *La Porcelaine de Limoges*, Paris, 1980

ANQUETIL, J. and VIVIEN, D., *La Poterie*, Paris, 1978

ARWAS, V., *Art Deco*, London–New York, 1976

BAIRATI, E., BOSSAGLIA, R. and ROSCI, M., *L'Italia Liberty. Arredamento e arti decorative*, Milan, 1973

BALL, F. C. and LOVOOS, J., *Making Pottery without a Wheel*, New York, 1965

BATTERSBY, M., *The Decorative Twenties*, London, 1969

—, *Art nouveau*, Feltham, 1969

BEAUCAMP-MARKOWSKI, B., *Musée des arts décoratifs, Cologne. Porcelaines européennes et porcelaines orientales d'exportation, pièces de service et objets d'art*, Cologne, 1980

BIRKS, T., *Potiers contemporains*, Paris, 1977

BLACKMAN, A., *Rolled Pottery Figures*, London, 1978

BLOCH, G., *Keramik und Graphik von Picasso*, Berne, 1972

BODELSEN, M., *Gauguin's Ceramics*, London, 1964

BODELSEN, M. and GRANDJEAN, B.L., *Dansk Keramik*, Stockholm–Copenhagen, 1960 (nos 5–6 of the review *Porslin*)

BONNET, G.-H., NEVEUX, M.-A. and ROEGIERS, M.-P., *Poterie au colombin*, Paris, 1978

BOSSAGLIA, R., *Il «Deco» italiano. Fisionomica dello Stile 1925*, Milan, 1975

BOTT, G., *Kunsthandwerk um 1900: Jugendstil/Art nouveau/ Modern Style* (Catalogue of the Hessisches Landesmuseum, Darmstadt), Darmstadt, 1965

BRÖHAN, K.H., *Kunst der Jahrhundertwende und der zwanziger Jahre, Sammlung Karl H. Bröhan, Berlin*, vol. II, pt. 1. *Kunsthandwerk: Jugendstil, Werkbund, Art Déco, Glas, Holz, Keramik*, Berlin, 1976

—, *Kunst der Jahrhundertwende und der zwanziger Jahre, Sammlung Karl H. Bröhan, Berlin*, vol. II, pt. 2. *Kunsthandwerk: Jugendstil, Werkbund, Art Déco, Metall, Porzellan*, Berlin, 1977

BRUANDET, P., *Décors et matières en céramique*, Paris, 1974

BRUNET, M. and PREAUD, T., *Sèvres, des origines à nos jours*, Fribourg, 1978

BRUNHAMMER, Y., *Le Style 1925*, Paris, 1975

—, *1925. Exposition internationale des arts décoratifs et industriels modernes 1925. Sources et conséquences*, Paris, 1976

BUFFET-CHALLIE, L., *Le Modern Style*, Paris, 1975

BURCKHARDT, L., *Le Werkbund, Allemagne, Autriche, Suisse*, Venice, 1977

CAMEIRANA, A., 'Stile 1925 nella ceramica albisolese', in *VIII convegno internazionale della ceramica: Atti*, 1975, pp. 209–24 (Centro Ligure per la storia delle ceramica, Albissola)

CARDEW, M., *Pioneer Pottery*, London, 1969

CASSON, M., *Pottery in Britain Today*, London, 1967

CASSOU, J., LANGUI, E. and PEVSNER, N., *Les Sources du XXᵉ siècle*, Paris, 1961

CEFARIELLO GROSSO, G., *La Manifattura Chini dall 'Arte della Ceramica' alle 'Fornacci San Lorenzo'*, Florence, 1979

CHARLESTON, R.J., *World Ceramics*, London, 1968

CHAUMEIL, P., *La Céramique, l'art et la matière*, Paris, 1971

CHAVANCE, R., *La Céramique et la verrerie*, Paris, 1928

CLARK, G., *Ceramic Art: Comment and Review, 1882–1977, An Anthology of Writings on Modern Ceramic Art*, New York, 1978

—, *A Century of Ceramics in the United States 1878–1978. A Study of its Development*, New York, 1979

CLARK, R.J. (ed.), *The Arts and Crafts Movement in America*, Princeton, 1972

COLBECK, J., *La Poterie: technique du tournage*, Paris, 1974

COOPER, E. and LEWENSTEIN, E. (ed.), *Potters: an Illustrated Directory of the Works of Full Members of the Craftsmen Potters Association of Great Britain. A Guide to Pottery Training in Britain*, 5th ed., London, 1980

COTTIER-ANGELI, F., *La Céramique*, Geneva, 1973

COYSH, A.W., *British Art Pottery, 1870–1940*, Rutland, 1976

DEMEL, E., *La Peinture sur porcelaine: comment la réaliser*, Fribourg–Paris, 1979

DESPRES, P., *L'Art du potier: la faïence*, Paris, 1976

DESY, L., *La Céramique*, Quebec, 1977

DICKENSON, J., *Raku Handbook. A Practical Approach to the Ceramic Art*, New York, 1972

DREXLER, A. and GRETA, D., *An Introduction to Twentieth Century Design, from the Collection of the Museum of Modern Art*, New York, 1959

DUPLAN, M., *Poterie au tour*, Paris, 1980

EVANS, P., *Art Pottery of the United States: an Encyclopedia of Producers and their Marks*, New York, 1974

FARÉ, M., *La Céramique contemporaine*, Paris, 1954

FOURMANOIR-GORIUS, A., *Comme l'argile dans la main du potier*, Paris, 1979

GYSLING-BILLETER, E., *Objekte des Jugendstils aus der Sammlung des Kunstgewerbemuseums Zürich ...*, Berne, 1975

HARTUNG, R., *L'Argile*, Paris, 1972 and 1979

HASLAM, M., *English Art Pottery 1865–1915*, Antique Collectors' Club, Woodbridge, 1975

HAUSSONNE, M., *Technologie céramique générale*, 2nd, ed., Paris, 1969

HEILIGENSTEIN, A. C., *Précis de décoration dans les arts du feu, céramique, porcelaine, faïence, verrerie*, 2nd ed., Paris, 1968

HERMAN, L. E., *American Porcelain: New Expressions in an Ancient Art*, Forest, Grove, 1981

HINDER, J. W. and REIMERS, L., *Moderne Keramik aus Deutschland*, Deidesheim, 1971

HOCZOGH, A., *Mai Magyar Iparmüvészet, Keramia, Porcelan, Üveg*, Budapest, 1975

HOFSTEDT, J., *Des Activités manuelles pour le temps des loisirs: poterie*, with the collaboration of W. and S. Sayles, Paris, 1974

KELLY, A., *The Story of Wedgwood*, London, 1975

KENNY, J. B., *The Complete Book of Pottery Making*, Philadelphia, 1962

—, *Ceramic Sculpture, Methods and Processes*, Philadelphia, 1974

KLESSE, B. and HEUSER, H. J. and M., *Französische Keramik zwischen 1850 und 1910. Sammlung Maria und Hans Jörgen Heuser*, Cologne, 1974

KLINGE, E., *Deutsche Keramik des 20. Jahrhunderts*, Düsseldorf, 1975 and 1978 (catalogue of the Hetjens-Museum)

KÖLLMANN, E., *Berliner Porzellan, 1763–1963*, 2 vols. Brunswick, 1966

LANE, P., *Studio Porcelain: Contemporary Design and Techniques*, London, 1980

LEACH, B., *Beyond East and West*, London, 1978

—, *Hamada*, Tokyo, 1975

—, *Kenzan and his Tradition*, London, 1966

—, *A Potter's Book*, London, 1939

—, *A Potter's Work*, London, 1967

LEISTIKOW-DUCHARDT, A., *Die Entwicklung eines neuen Stils im Porzellan*, Heidelberg, 1957

LESIEUTRE, A., *The Spirit and Splendour of Art Deco*, London–New York, 1974

LEWENSTEIN, E. and COOPER, E., *New Ceramics*, London, 1974

LOEWY, R., *Industrial Design*, London–Boston, 1979

LUCIE-SMITH, E., *The Story of Craft: the Craftsman's Role in Society*, Oxford, 1981

MAENZ, P., *Art Deco 1920–1940*, Cologne, 1974

MISEREZ-SCHIRA, G., *L'Art et la technique de la peinture sur porcelaine*, Paris, 1974

MONTMOLLOIN, D. de, *L'art de cendres, émaux de grès et cendres végétales*, Taizé, 1976

—, *Le Poème céramique, introduction à la poterie*, Taizé, 1974

MOSEL, C., *Kunsthandwerk im Umbruch: Jugendstil und zwanziger Jahre; Bildkataloge des Kestner-Museums Hannover XI*, Hanover, 1971

MUNDT, B., 'Vom Bidermeier bis zur neueren Zeit: 1830–1930', in Propyläen Kunstgeschichte, Berlin, 1980

NAYLOR, G., *The Arts and Crafts Movement*, London, 1971

NELSON, G. C., *Ceramics: a Potter's Handbook*, New York, 1971

NEUWIRTH, W., *Wiener Keramik: Historismus, Jugendstil, Art Deco*, Brunswick, 1974

—, *Österreichische Keramik des Jugendstils*, Munich, 1974

NOBLET, J. de and BRESSY, C. de, *Le Design*, Paris, 1974

PANSERE, A. K., *Soviet Porcelain: the Artistry of the Lomonosov Porcelain Factory, Leningrad*, Leningrad, 1974

PAQUETTE, J.-P., *Le Guide des artisans créateurs du Québec*, Montreal, 1974

PELICHET, E., *La Céramique Art nouveau*, Lausanne, 1976

PEVSNER, N., *Pioneers of Modern Design: from William Morris to Walter Gropius*, New York, 1949

PIERRE, J. and CORREDOR-MATHEOS, J., *Miró et Artigas: céramiques*, Paris, 1974

POLI, C., *La Poterie et ses techniques*, Paris, 1977

RAMIÉ, G., *Céramique de Picasso*, Paris, 1974

RHODES, D., *Clay and Glazes for the Potter*, Philadelphia, 1973

—, *Pottery Form*, Radnor, 1976

—, *Kilns: Design, Construction and Operation*, Philadelphia, 1968

RIEGGER, H., *Raku, Art and Technique*, New York, 1970

—, *Primitive Pottery*, New York, 1972

ROSE, M., *Artist–Potters in England*, 2nd ed., London, 1970

RUSCOE, W., *Sculpture for the Potter*, London, 1975

SAVE, C., *Le Livre de l'artisanat et de la création*, Paris, 1972

STERNER, G. and BANGERT, A., *Jugendstil. Art Deco*, Munich, 1979

STORR-BRITZ, H., *Internazionale Keramik der Gegenwart/Contemporary International Ceramics*, Cologne, 1980

The Royal Copenhagen Porcelain Manufactory 1775–1975, Copenhagen, 1975

TRESKOW, I. von, *Die Jugendstil Porzellane der KPM. Bestandskatalog der Königlichen Porzellan-Manufaktur Berlin 1896–1914*, Munich, 1971

TYLER, C. and HIRSCH, R., *Raku*, New York, 1975

VALOTAIRE, M., *La Céramique française*, Paris, 1930

VERONESI, G., *Stile 1925. Ascesa e caduta delle Arts deco*, Florence, 1966

VITTEL, C., *Pâtes et glaçures céramiques*, Preface by Rudolf Schnyder, Vevey, 1976

WILCOX, D. J., *New Design in Ceramics*, New York, 1970

Principal Journals

AUSTRALIA
Pottery in Australia

GERMANY
Keramos

ENGLAND
Ceramic Review

FINLAND
Form. Function

FRANCE
Cahiers de la céramique, du verre et des arts du feu
La Céramique moderne
La Revue de la céramique
L'Atelier des métiers d'art

ITALY
Bolletino del Museo internazionale delle Ceramiche, Faenza

SWITZERLAND
Mitteilungsblatt, Keramikfreunde der Schweiz

SPAIN
Ceramica

USA
Studio Ceramics

Recent Exhibitions

1962
Maître potiers contemporains. Musée des Arts décoratifs, Paris

1963
Angewandte Kunst in Europa nach 1945. Museum für Kunst und Gewerbe, Hamburg (catalogue by H. Spielmann)

1967
Neue Formen der Keramik aus den Niederlanden. Hessisches Landesmuseum, Darmstadt (catalogue by B.R.M. de Newe)

1968
Deutsche keramische Kunst der Gegenwart. Keramion, Frechen (catalogue by G. Cremer)
50 Years: Bauhaus. Royal Academy of Arts, London

1969
Céramiques de peintres. Musée de Peinture et de Sculpture, Grenoble (catalogue by H. Lassale)

1971
L'Art de la poterie en France de Rodin à Dufy. Musée national de céramique, Sèvres

1972
Jugendstil. Hessisches Landesmuseum, Darmstadt (catalogue by C.B. Heller)

1972/1973
Deutsche keramische Kunst der Gegenwart. Badisches Landesmuseum, Karlsruhe, and Kunstgewerbemuseum, Berlin

1974
Europäische Keramik des Jugendstils. Hetjens-Museum, Düsseldorf (catalogue by B. Hackenjos and E. Klinge)
Schweizer Keramik heute. Gewerbemuseum, Winterthur

1975
Sammlung Gertrud und Dr. Karl Funke-Kaiser; Keramik vom Historismus bis zur Gegenwart. Kunstgewerbemuseum, Cologne (catalogue by G. Reineking von Bock and C. W. Schürmann)

1976
Kunsthandwerk und Industrieform des 19. und 20. Jahrhunderts. Staatliche Kunstsammlungen, Dresden (catalogue by K. P. Arnold)
Europäische Keramik der Gegenwart. Keramion, Frechen (catalogue by G. Reineking von Bock and others)
Minton 1798–1910. Victoria and Albert Museum, London (catalogue by E. Aslin and P. Atterbury)

1977
Jugendstil. Palais des Beaux-Arts, Brussels
Céramique 'Liberty' de Faenza. Palazzo delle Esposizioni, Faenza
Französische Keramikkünstler um 1925: Sammlung M. und H. J. Heuser. Museum für Kunst und Gewerbe, Hamburg (catalogue by H. J. Heuser)
Cinquantenaire de l'exposition de 1925. Musée des Arts décoratifs, Paris
Zsolnay Keramia. Museum Janus Pannonius, Pécs (catalogue by E. Hars)

1978
Meister der deutschen Keramik 1900 bis 1950. Kunstgewerbemuseum, Cologne (catalogue by G. Reineking von Bock)
Keramik der Gegenwart aus Europa und Japan: Sammlung Frank Nievergelt. Zurich (catalogue by S. Barten)

1979
Albissola 1925, ceramica degli anni '20'. Villa Gavotti della Rovere/Villa Trucco, Albissola (introduction by R. Bossaglia)

1979/1980
Cristopher Dresser. Camden Arts Centre, London and Middlesborough

1980

Europäische Keramik seit 1950: Sammlung Dr. Hans Thiemann, ein Bestandskatalog. Museum für Kunst und Gewerbe, Hamburg (ed. H. Spielmann, compiled by H. Thiemann; with detailed bibliography and a list of permanent exhibitions)

Berlin Porcelaine, Wanderausstellung in den U.S.A. (catalogue by W. Baer)

The Thirties: British Art and Design before the War. Hayward Gallery, London

1981

Keramik aus Historismus und Jugendstil in Frankreich mit Beispielen aus anderen europäischen Ländern. Ausgewählte Objekte aus zwei Privatsammlungen. Staatl. Kunstsammlungen, Hessisches Landesmuseum, Kassel (catalogue by H. Makus)

Céramique française contemporaine. Sources et courants. Musée des Arts décoratifs, Paris (catalogue by Y. Brunhammer and M.-L. Perrin)

Acknowledgments

Our sincerest thanks are due to those who, especially in museums, have contributed in making known the work of the ceramists we have chosen, and with patience and kindness have given us all the essential information: M. Aav (Museum of Decorative Arts, Helsinki), Artex (Budapest), E. Aslin (Bethnal Green Museum, London), G. Blake-Roberts (Wedgwood Museum, Barlaston), H. Boisseau-Béharn (Paris), G.C. Bojani (Museo internazionale delle Ceramiche, Faenza), J. E. Broughton Perry (Bethnal Green Museum, London), Y. Brunhammer (Musée des Arts décoratifs, Paris), A. Cameirana (Savona), M.-Th. Coullery (Musée Ariana, Geneva), H. Dalbäck-Lütteman (Nationalmuseum, Stockholm), J. du Paquier (Musée des Arts décoratifs, Bordeaux), E. Ebbinge (Gemeentelijk Museum Het Princessehof, Leeuwarden), A.C. Funck (Karl Ernst Osthaus Museum, Hagen), L.B. Grandjean (Museum of the Royal Porcelain Factory, Copenhagen), A. Hallé (Musée national de Céramique, Sèvres), C. Join-Diéterle (Musée du Petit Palais, Paris), B. Klesse (Kunstgewerbemuseum, Cologne), M. Latour (Musée Cantini, Marseilles), S. Lecomte (Musée d'art moderne de la Ville de Paris), J. V. G. Mallet (Victoria and Albert Museum, London), A.-M. Mariën-Dugarden (Musées royaux d'Art et d'Histoire, Brussels), M. Richet (Musée Picasso, Paris), R. Riché (Porcelaines Bernardaud, Limoges), G. Sarrauste de Menthière (Musée national de Céramique, Sèvres), R. Schnyder (Académie internationale de Céramique, Geneva), D. Tucna (Uméleckoprùmyslové Muzeum, Prague), Uniunea Artistilor Plastici din R.S.R., Bucharest, C. Van Hasselt (Fondation Custodia, Paris), O. Watson (Victoria and Albert Museum, London), as well as all those collectors and galleries who have given permission for some of their treasures to be reproduced in this volume.

Index of Personal Names

Photo Credits

The publishers would like to thank the following photographers and also the potters and authorities in the museums and other institutions who kindly allowed their works to be reproduced.